Leasing in Canada: A Business Guide

Second Edition

R.F. Selby, FCA
Price Waterhouse

Butterworths
Toronto and Vancouver

Leasing in Canada: A Business Guide

© Butterworths Canada Ltd. 1992

The Butterworth Group of Companies

Canada	Butterworths Canada Ltd., 75 Clegg Road, MARKHAM, Ontario, L6G 1A1 and 409 Granville St., Ste. 1455, VANCOUVER, B.C. V6C 1T2
Australia	Butterworths Pty Ltd., SYDNEY, MELBOURNE, BRISBANE, ADELAIDE, PERTH, CANBERRA and HOBART
Ireland	Butterworths (Ireland) Ltd., DUBLIN
New Zealand	Butterworths of New Zealand Ltd., WELLINGTON and AUCKLAND
Puerto Rico	Butterworth of Puerto Rico, Inc., SAN JUAN
Singapore	Butterworths Asia, SINGAPORE
United Kingdom	Butterworth & Co. (Publishers) Ltd., LONDON and EDINBURGH
United States	Butterworth Legal Publishers, AUSTIN, Texas; CLEARWATER, Florida; ORFORD, New Hampshire; ST. PAUL, Minnesota; SALEM, New Hampshire

Canadian Cataloguing in Publication Data

Selby, R.F.
    Leasing in Canada : a business guide

2nd. ed.
Includes index.
ISBN 0-409-90904-1

1. Leases – Canada – Accounting.   2. Leases –
Taxation – Canada.   I. Title.

HF5686.L42S35 1992   657'.75   C92-093971-6

Sponsoring Editor — Morag MacLean
Editor — Agatha Cinader
Cover Design — Artplus
Production — Marlene Roopsingh

Printed and bound in Canada by
John Deyell Company Limited.

Preface

In the past thirty years, leasing in Canada has undergone a number of changes. Violent swings in interest and inflation rates, shifting tax policies, and rapid increases in technology in most industries have all been experienced. As well, the international leasing arena has seen a concerted effort to achieve, if not uniformity of accounting treatment, at least a marked similarity; the accounting professions in Canada, the United Kingdom and the United States have issued quite similar statements on the classification and treatment of leases. Now that the initial impact of these changes has been felt, it seems appropriate to summarize the current status of leasing today.

This book surveys a wide range of leasing issues and introduces a number of terms common in the leasing industry. The focus is on the application of the appropriate accounting and tax treatment, given the particular facts of the lease. The position of the lessee is explored with respect to the proper accounting treatment and then with respect to the required tax treatment. The lessor's position is then examined. There is, of course, a considerable amount of overlap between the lessee's and the lessor's position, since "symmetry" of treatment is strived for, both in accounting and in tax treatment. Finally, a few important topics of concern to both lessees and lessors are examined and a chapter on insolvency has been added to deal with this important subject. No attempt has been made to address the lease or buy decision itself, as this subject is covered in various financial texts.

Although the responsibility for the views in this book are mine, I want to express my appreciation to those who have assisted in this endeavour. Larry Ward kindly authored the chapter on insolvency. Harvey Graham and Gerry Wood have both provided invaluable assistance in reviewing the income tax aspects of this revision which were much more demanding due to the changes to the *Income Tax Act* resulting from the April 1989 budget and the introduction of the Goods and Services Tax.

Chris Drummond has reviewed all of the material and provided many helpful suggestions.

In addition, several members of the staff have reviewed individual sections or helped in updating. My thanks to all and, in particular, to my secretary for handling the technical chore of revising, which proved harder than writing the original!

Table of Contents

Preface . . . .　iii
Table of Exhibits . . . .　viii

1. Objectives of Leasing . . . .　1
   Why Lease? . . . .　1
   Determining Lease Rates . . . .　3

2. Accounting for Leases . . . .　5
   Lease Classification . . . .　5
   Some Technical Terms to Consider . . . .　8
   Sale and Leaseback Transactions . . . .　11

3. Income Tax Treatment of Lease Transactions — Lessee . . . .　13
   The Present Position of Revenue Canada . . . .　14
      Example of the New CCA Calculation . . . .　15

4. Controlling the Financial Impact of Long-Term Leases . . . .　19
   Criteria for a Capital Lease . . . .　20
   Application of the Guidelines . . . .　21
   Structuring the Lease Agreement . . . .　21
   Controlling the Impact of the Lease Agreement . . . .　22
      Some Problem Areas . . . .　24
      Non-cancellable Term and Contingent Rentals . . . .　24
      Residual Value . . . .　25
      "Tax-trade" Sale/Leaseback . . . .　25
      CICA Research Report on Leasing Issues (September 1989)　26
      EIC-19 October 1990 . . . .　28
      EIC-21 December 17, 1990 . . . .　28
      EIC-25 April 22, 1991 . . . .　30
      EIC-30 October 16, 1991 . . . .　32
   The Best of Both Worlds . . . .　33

5. Certain Real Estate Leases: How Do You Measure the Useful
   Life of a Shopping Centre? . . . .　35
   The Problem . . . .　35
   The Useful Life and Cost Recovery Tests . . . .　36

	Who Has the Risks and Benefits of Ownership?	37
	What is Happening in the "Real World"?	39
6.	Accounting for Leases — Lessor	43
	Accounting for an Operating Lease	44
	Direct Financing Leases	45
	Sales-type Lease	47
	Sale of Lease Property or Assignment to a Third Party	48
	Tax-oriented Leasing	49
7.	Tax Implications of Leases for the Lessor	53
	Investment Tax Credit	54
	Capital Cost Allowance	54
	"Stretch" Leases	56
	What if the Lease is a Sale?	57
	Rental Credits	58
	Sale of Options	58
	Revised Leasing Regulations — April 26, 1989	58
	Specified Leasing Property — CCA Calculation	60
	Specified Leasing Property	63
	What's Exempt Property?	63
	Leasing and the Goods and Services Tax	65
	Introduction	65
	Input Tax Credit	65
	Compliance Requirements	65
	Operating vs. Capital Lease	66
	Real Property Leases	66
	De-minimus Test for a Financial Institution	66
	Transitional Rules	67
8.	What You Should Know About Your Lease	69
	Length of Term/Renewal	69
	Payment Frequency	69
	Contingent Rents, Insurance, and Other Costs Payable by the Lessee	70
	Purchase Option/Residual Value	70
	Early Termination/Buyout	71
	Upgrade Privilege	71
	Ownership/CCA Rights	71
	Assignment	72
9.	Measuring Return to the Lessor	87
	Cash Flow-related Risks	87
	Investment Amount — Before or After Debt (Leverage)	90

Tax Benefits In or Out of the Calculation? 92
Pay-back Period 94
Net Present Value Method 95
Internal Rate of Return(IRR)........................... 96
After-tax Rate of Return............................... 98
    After-tax Equals Pre-tax Times (1 - Tax Rate) 99
    After-tax Rate Divided By (1 - Tax Rate)............... 99
Net-tax Payments Over the Life of a Contract............. 99
Dealing with a Negative Investment Balance............... 105
Contractual Versus Estimated Cash Flows 110

10. The Lessor and the Insolvent Lessee 115
    Introduction... 115
    Validity of a Lease..................................... 115
    Classification of Leases................................ 116
        Disguised Sales 116
        Disguised Loans 116
        True Lease 117
        Other Factors 117
    Personal Property Security Acts 117
    When to Register Under the PPSA....................... 118
    The Insolvent Lessee 119
    Obligations of the Receiver or Trustee................... 119
    Considerations for the Prudent Lessor................... 120
        Steps to Consider Prior to a Formal Insolvency 120
        Steps to Consider After a Formal Insolvency............ 120
    Lessor Beware 122

11. Odds and Ends of Business Issues 123
    International Leasing 123
    Summary of Taxes to be Paid by Domestic Lessors
    and Lessees in Cross-Border Leases 126
        Withholding taxes...................................... 127
        Carrying on Business in Canada or a Foreign Jurisdiction . 128
        Operating Lease, Conditional Sale or Immediate Sale? 129
        Double Dip Transactions 130
    A "Hodgepodge" of Tax Caveats 136
    Business Issues to Reduce Risk or Imprive Return 138
    Conclusion 140

Appendix: Lease Examples 143

Glossary.. 191

Index 201

Table of Exhibits

Exhibit 3-1	New CCA Calculation	16
Exhibit 4-1	Criteria That Indicate a Capital Lease	20
Exhibit 4-2	Desired Treatment of a Lease	23
Exhibit 4-3	Research Report on Leasing Issues	27
Exhibit 4-4	Accounting for Lease Inducements	29
Exhibit 4-5	Accounting for Sales with Leasebacks	31
Exhibit 5-1	Selected Public Company Retail Chains Lease Data	41
Exhibit 7-1	The New Rules – Example – Showing CCA Restriction and Terminal Loss	60
Exhibit 7-2	Taxable Income (Loss)	62
Exhibit 8-1	Standard Lease Examples	73
Exhibit 9-1	Example Loan #1	100
Exhibit 9-2	Lease With 50% CCA – No Residual	101
Exhibit 9-3	Example Loan #2	103
Exhibit 9-4	Lease With 20% CCA – 30% Residual	104
Exhibit 9-5	Lease With 50% CCA – 30% Residual	105
Exhibit 9-6	Leveraged Lease With 100% CCA – 30% Residual	107
Exhibit 11-1	Canadian Lessor – Foreign Lessee (Assuming Canadian Lessor has no Permanent Establishment in the Foreign Jurisdiction)	126
Exhibit 11-2	Foreign Lessor – Canadian Lessee	127
Exhibit 11-3	Penetration of Leasing in Capital Formation, 1978-1982, 1989	132
Exhibit 11-4	Growth of Leasing in Europe, 1972-1989	133
Exhibit 11-5	Equipment Investment Incentives of Selected Countries	134
Exhibit 11-6	Recipient of Tax Depreciation Allowances	135
Exhibit 11-7	Offset Leasing Losses Against Other Income in Same Company	136

Chapter 1

Objectives of Leasing

In this book the business rationale for leasing and sufficient accounting and tax commentary is reviewed to indicate that it is essential to consider both the accounting and income tax results of a proposed, significant lease prior to completing negotiations. In this way the transaction can be designed so that the accounting and income tax results conform to the expected business result. In addition, a degree of assurance can be provided that the accounting and income tax results of the transaction will be known in advance of the documentation, rather than some months, or even years, later, when the tax man cometh!

One of the difficulties with leasing is the confusing terminology. The terms as defined by the Canadian Institute of Chartered Accountants (CICA) in their *Handbook*, section 3065 will be used herein. There are two primary types of leases: operating leases and capital leases. In general, the definition of an operating lease does not cause difficulty since common business usage conforms to the CICA usage. There are a variety of alternatives to the CICA's capital lease terminology. Ordinarily, the leasing industry's terminology for a capital lease would include a full-payout lease or full-term lease. Similarly, in the auto industry the "open-end lease" would be a capital lease for accounting purposes. (In that industry the open-end lease refers to the situation where the lessee guarantees the residual or "end value" of the equipment at the termination of the lease. The lessor receives the periodic rentals plus the end value to provide the return on capital invested in the automobile.) Finally, in real estate transactions there are particular terms (for example, net lease, net net) which are beyond the scope of material to be covered here.

WHY LEASE?

A lessee normally wishes to acquire an asset by lease, rather than acquisition, for the following reasons:

1. The asset is required for only a short period of time and is readily available on an operating lease basis.

2. The asset is available on an operating lease basis negotiated with the lessor in a manner that provides the lessor with an acceptable return on a reasonably assured basis, and the lessee wishes to have an operating lease.

3. The lessee perceives that the cost of leasing is less than, or at least not significantly greater than, the cost of owning.

4. The lessee perceives that the after-tax cost of leasing is less than that of owning, and the asset is not likely to appreciate in value.

5. The cost of leasing is not much greater than the cost of owning, and the lessee has an option to acquire the asset at the end of the lease; accordingly, appreciation can be retained.

6. The use of the leased asset is required, and the lessee perceives that the cash flow from leasing can be less onerous than the cash flow from owning. For example, in many leasing situations the lessee can obtain financing for the cost of the asset plus installation and delivery, perhaps including "tune-up time." If the lessee were to buy the asset outright, he or she would likely pay the full cost on delivery and also bear the costs of installation, delivery, and tune-up as incurred. Accordingly, leasing permits more spreading of the cash flow, which may not be available if the asset is acquired directly.

7. Over a medium- to long-term period, leasing can be a hedge against inflation in that the lease payments are made by reference to the cost of the asset unadjusted for inflation and the payments are in "current" rather than "constant" dollars. Of course, in a deflationary period the opposite would prevail. Also, if a leased asset is bought outright with borrowed money repayable on a long-term, fixed-rate basis, the inflationary effect on the cash flow could be roughly the same.

8. Lease payments can frequently be organized to meet the seasonal or cyclical cash flow of the lessee. This is a convenience that often makes leasing more attractive to seasonal businesses.

9. In some cases leasing, even on a capital lease basis, can be done without affecting existing credit lines.

10. In some industries, particularly the computer industry, the lessor will provide equipment "up grades" which might be more difficult to obtain otherwise. In addition, the lessor will remove the necessity to dispose of the equipment that has been replaced and may well have better marketing facilities for this than does the lessee.

11. In some cases, lessors will offer their product only on a lease basis.

12. Some lessees can negotiate lease credit on more favourable terms than they can negotiate debt credit. For example, they avoid the cost of a formal borrowing agreement and the multitude of constraints from restrictive covenants, compensating loan balances, and "rest" period common in some short-term agreements in the United States, and they

2

avoid definitions for covenants that may conflict with existing borrowings or may be more restrictive than existing debt.

DETERMINING LEASE RATES

With all these reasons for leasing, it might reasonably be wondered why everyone doesn't lease. If all the lessees receive such benefits, in a perfect world the lessors must be losing. How can this be? One might contemplate how a lessor could price a product to achieve an acceptable return while not withdrawing all of the lessee's apparent benefits.

A typical pricing algorithm for the lease might be as follows:

(a) The normal selling price is used as the starting point for the determination of the leasing payments.
(b) Interest is computed at the lessor's borrowing cost plus a margin of ½ of 1% or more.
(c) A lease administration charge is calculated either as a percentage of funds in use or as a fixed monthly payment. This charge is proportionately higher for smaller amounts (leases less than $25,000, typically referred to as "small ticket" leases).

Accordingly, lessors who are also manufacturers realize their normal retail mark-up, a small financing margin, and an administration fee.

If income tax, accounting, and other business factors could be ignored, the question of lease pricing and lease benefits would stop at this pricing calculation. For many products, however, at least the following factors should be considered from either a pricing perspective, a financial statement disclosure perspective, or an income tax perspective.

1. If the credit rating of the lessee is relatively poor, the interest margin and the security deposit can be expected to increase.
2. The lessee's use of the asset, the type of asset, or the location where it is to be used, may permit the lessor or lessee to receive tax incentives or grants. In some cases only the lessee will be eligible for the grants, and in other cases only the lessor will be eligible. Clearly, these cases have to be reviewed carefully to see that overall cost is minimized.
3. The *Income Tax Act*, S.C. 1970-71-72, c. 63, presently permits the deduction of the cost of a fixed asset, in the form of annual capital cost allowances (CCA), at a variety of rates. In some cases the user would be unable to take advantage of maximum deductions. This could happen, for example, if the user was in a tax loss position or if the income was not taxable in any event, as in the case of a non-profit organization, a Crown corporation, or a pension fund. In this circumstance a lessor may be able to use the capital cost allowance more effectively, and the user becomes a lessee. The lessee and lessor would negotiate the various income tax benefits, and the lessee would have to recognize

3

that not all benefits could be passed on in the form of lower rents. This is due to the variety of factors that can affect the ability to benefit from capital cost allowance in the future, including changes in tax rates or CCA rates, changing interest rates, and potential changes in the lessor's tax position or ability to deduct capital cost allowance in excess of rents from other income.

4. A lessee may receive a favourable rental rate if the term of the lease can be adjusted to suit the lessor and if the lessee can guarantee the lessor that a "residual value" will be received which, together with the rent, will provide an adequate return. In general, the lease will not be cancellable without the payment of a significant penalty by the lessee.

5. Some lessors will require a deposit and/or prepaid rents as additional security for the due observance of the lease terms by the lessee.

This chapter has introduced some reasons for leasing, the method lessors will use to arrive at their monthly rent, and some areas in which the lessor and lessee can carry out negotiations to ensure that the lease agreement is satisfactory to both sides. The following chapters will review: accounting and tax issues, some methods of appraising the return on a lease, techniques of controlling the financial impact of long-term leases, and, in a final chapter, a variety of points to consider before entering into a long-term lease.

Chapter 2

Accounting for Leases

LEASE CLASSIFICATION

Before lessees negotiate all of the terms and conditions of the lease, they are advised to consider how the lease will be reflected in their annual financial statements. If lessees wish to sign an operating lease and have only the rental payments reflected in their income statement, with no indication of "ownership" of the leased asset in their financial statements, they can do so. But to achieve this end they must ensure that the lease is an operating lease for accounting purposes and not a "capital lease." In most cases the distinction is unimportant. However, if the lessee has a piece of equipment which is very expensive and represents a large dollar value compared to total assets, the lessee may wish to be certain of the accounting treatment, as it may well affect his or her borrowing power.

In the early 1970s, many agreements were signed which were treated for accounting purposes as operating leases, although in effect they were outright purchases. This distorted the financial position of the lessee and made financial statement comparisons from one company to the next more difficult. In addition, the cost reflected in the income statement of the lessee for an operating lease could be dramatically different from the cost reflected had the asset been acquired and depreciated in accordance with the company's normal practices. In many cases, where the lessee treated the transaction as an operating lease, the lessor treated the transaction as an effective sale and as financing to the lessee. As a result, various accounting bodies felt a need to codify accounting practices to ensure consistency, comparability, and some conformity of lease accounting as between the lessor and the lessee. Accordingly, accounting standards for leasing have been developed in many countries to clarify when an individual has effectively acquired an asset and when an individual has acquired only the use of an asset.

In Canada leasing was codified by the CICA in Section 3065 of the *CICA Handbook* (the "Handbook"). Leases were divided into two categories for the lessee:

5

- operating lease;
- capital lease.

For the lessor three categories of leases were recognized:

- operating lease;
- sales-type lease;
- direct financing lease.

This section will concentrate on accounting for the lessee. The main criteria for classification of leases are as follows:

1. Leases should be accounted for according to their substance rather than their legal form.
2. "A lease that transfers substantially all of the benefits and risks of ownership related to the leased property from the lessor to the lessee should be accounted for as a capital lease by the lessee and as a sales type or direct financing lease by the lessor" (*CICA Handbook*, Section 3065.09).
3. "A lease where the benefits and risks of ownership related to the leased property are substantially retained by the lessor should be accounted for as an operating lease by the lessee and lessor" (*CICA Handbook*, Section 3065.10).

The *CICA Handbook* contains several pages of discussion summarizing the rationale and certain other issues relating to lease classification. Accordingly, in matters where classification is important, lessees should consult their accounting advisors.

In determining whether benefits and risks of ownership have been transferred to the lessee, the *CICA Handbook* has outlined a number of guidelines to indicate whether or not the lease is in substance a purchase:

1. There should be reasonable assurance that the lessee will obtain ownership of the leased property by the end of the lease term. This could be by an automatic transfer of title contained in the lease agreement or by the provision for the lessee to have a purchase option at an amount significantly less than the expected fair market value of the property at the end of the lease (a "bargain purchase" option).
2. The non-cancellable portion of the lease term should represent a significant amount of the useful life (usually 75% or more) of the leased asset. In effect, the lessee is deemed to have received substantially all of the economic benefits from the utility of the leased asset if it has been leased for more than 75% of its useful life.
3. If the lease provides terms by which the lessor recovers his or her investment and is earning a return on the investment as a result of the lease agreement, then it is to be assumed that the lessor has no further economic interest in the asset and the lessee has "de facto" acquired it. (For this purpose the lessor is assumed to recover substantially all of its investment if the present value of the lease payments calculated in

6

accordance with the *Handbook* exceeds 90% of the fair value of the leased asset at the inception of the lease.)

An exception is made for the lease of land. It is assumed that land has an indefinite useful life, so all leases of land that do not transfer ownership by the end of the lease term are treated as operating leases.

These criteria do not overrule the use of judgement, however, and the judgement factors centre around the transfer of benefits and risks of ownership, not discrete criteria.

The following two examples will distinguish an operating lease from a capital lease:

(a) Lessee wishes to rent a computer for a special project for three years. He could buy the computer for $1,000,000 today, and it is expected to have a fair market value in three years of 30% or $300,000. The lease is non-cancellable without the payment of a large penalty during the 36-month term, but at the end of the 36 months the equipment is returned to the supplier. Under these circumstances the lessee would have an operating lease, assuming that:

   (i) there are no side agreements indicating that he will have a bargain purchase option;

  (ii) title to the equipment is not transferred to the lessee by any terms of the lease;

 (iii) the equipment is assumed to have several more years of useful life; and

 (iv) the present value of the monthly rent does not equal 90% of the initial $1,000,000 fair value.

Under these circumstances the lease would be reflected as an operating lease, with rentals charged to income on a monthly basis. This conclusion results from the lessor's retention of the benefit of ownership (right to lease again and to realize on the residual) and of the risk of ownership (that the lessor may lose on sale of the asset or may not find a lessee at termination of the lease).

(b) Suppose, however, in the above example that the lessee was required to guarantee the residual value of $300,000, or the lessor has arranged the lease payments at such a high rate that the present value of the minimum rent was sufficient to recover 90% or more of the investment. Under these circumstances, even though there is no transfer of title to the equipment at termination of the lease, the lessee is usually required to treat the computer as purchased, reflected in the books of the lessee and depreciated in accordance with the company's usual method for depreciating similar assets. A liability would be recorded for "obligation under capital lease" which would be split between current and long-term in accordance with usual accounting practices. In this example, the lessor is indifferent as to the future use of the asset, and the lessee

would often have a purchase option which removes the benefit of ownership from the lessor.

An example of the recording of this transaction is included in the Appendix as Example 1(a) for the operating lease and as Example 1(b) for the capital lease.

SOME TECHNICAL TERMS TO CONSIDER

There are a number of technical issues to be dealt with in the mathematical
determination of whether a lease is capital or operating. For example, the
definition of "lease term" includes both the initial term, plus all "bargain
renewal option" periods. The reason for this definition is to include in the
initial term of the lease, periods during which the rent is sharply reduced
to a bargain amount. In addition, if the lessee is required to renew the lease
or pay a substantial penalty for failure to renew, the period covered by such
penalty would also be included in the fixed, non-cancellable period of the
lease. If there is a bargain purchase option, any renewals prior to the bargain purchase option would be included in the basic lease term, since it would
be presumed that the lessee would renew a lease up to the point where the
asset could be obtained at a "bargain." And finally, if the lessor can require
the lessee to renew, such renewal periods are included in the lease term for
purposes of the 75% test referred to above. All of these are designed simply
to ensure that the economic substance of the transaction is considered in addition to its legal form.

Moreover, the "minimum lease payments" required for the purposes
of the calculation to determine whether or not 90% of the lessor's investment has been recovered, as referred to above, are intended to ensure that
the same economic substance test is continued. For example, minimum lease
payments would include any partial or full guarantee, by the lessee, or a third
party related to the lessee, of the residual value of the leased property. In
addition, any penalty required to be paid by the lessee for failure to renew
or extend the lease at the end of the lease term is included in minimum lease
payments.

There are a number of specific items included in the *CICA Handbook*,
Section 3065 which attempt to deal with the myriad of actual lease terms
included in many leases. Since the type and complexity of leases has been
changing over the years, and is likely to continue to do so, it is necessary
to fall back on the basic tests (transfer of benefits and risks of ownership)
rather than to rely on specific provisions which may or may not exist in the
CICA Handbook. For example, a number of leases of real property, whether
for shopping centres, food stores, or offices, could be treated as capital leases
if the mere clerical tests relating to useful life and recovery of investment
are adhered to slavishly. This subject is explored in Chapter 5. The main
difficulty in this area is that the present value of the rent for many commer-

cial leases in shopping centre transactions would appear to equal at least 90% of the fair market value of the leased property. This is due to the difficulty in removing from the basic rent the amount which is applicable to services and premises outside the leased property ("common areas" — entrance area, security service area, elevator area, parking, etc.). In addition, it seems unrealistic to treat any rental of commercial property or of relatively small portions of a shopping centre as though the lessee had acquired ownership interest therein. In most cases, the owner/lessor certainly intends to retain title to the leased property, and the recovery of the investment of the lessor is rather academic. In any event, in determining the "minimum rent" under the lease agreement, it is important to ensure that such items as contingent rent (which is based on something other than the passage of time), common area costs and executory costs (those costs related to the operation of the leased property, such as insurance, maintenance, and property taxes) are excluded from minimum rents.

A peculiarity associated with lease accounting is that the definitions of a capital lease and an operating lease are not mutually exclusive. For example, there is a difficulty with a lease in which the lessor retains substantially all of the benefits of ownership while substantially all of the risks of ownership are transferred to the lessee. This is a common transaction in automobile leasing where the lease provides for the recovery of substantially all of the lessor's investment — thus meeting the 90% test referred to above, and indicating a capital lease — but retains the *benefit* of ownership which is implicit in the ability of the lessor to realize a margin on sale of the automobile at termination of the lease. If one reviews the wording of the *Handbook*, one might treat these transactions as capital leases by the lessee since they meet the 90% test, and as operating leases by the lessor since they do not transfer the benefits of ownership to the lessee. These and similar transactions should be treated as operating leases, as should most transactions where ownership is not transferred at the end of the lease term and the useful life extends for several years beyond the primary lease term. The technical rationale for this treatment is that the *Handbook* deals with transfers of risks *and* benefits of ownership, not just risks *or* benefits. The 90% calculation is merely a guideline in assessing risk transfer.

In circumstances, however, where the lease transaction is clearly a purchase, particularly where there is a bargain purchase option, the financial statement presentation and calculation of the lease amount are technical problems which are well dealt with in the *CICA Handbook*. In this transaction, the lessee is treated as though he or she had acquired an asset and obtained a loan of approximately the same amount at the inception of the lease. An example of this financial statement presentation and the calculations relating thereto is shown in the Appendix in Example 2 wherein Example 2(a) is an operating lease and Example 2(b) is changed to show the treatment as a capital lease. The amount to be recorded as an asset is the present value

9

of the minimum lease payments after removing therefrom any amount relating to "executory costs" such as insurance, maintenance, taxes, etc. To compute the present value, the lessee must use an interest rate. For purposes of the accounting calculation, the interest rate used to compute the present value is the lower of the interest rate implicit in the lease and the lessee's incremental borrowing rate. If either of these results in a value for the asset in excess of fair value at inception of the lease, only the fair value may be recorded. It should be noted that the interest rate implicit in the lease is arrived at as that rate which discounts the net minimum lease payments and the unguaranteed residual value of the leased asset to an amount equal to the fair value at inception of the lease.

The calculation of the present value for the lessee is made somewhat theoretical as a result of the following:

1. Executory costs in the lease payments are not known to the lessee.
2. The lessee's incremental borrowing rate for similar assets, with similar security and repayment terms, is not a common rate known to the lessee, since most debt is incurred on lenders' normal terms, not on those terms found in a specific lease.
3. The interest rate implicit in the lease requires knowledge of the estimated residual value to accrue to the lessor and the lessor's tax position. These are rarely known to the lessee.

Assuming that the interest rate implicit in the lease and the lessee's incremental borrowing rate are not far apart, one would ordinarily expect the present value of the minimum rents to be less than the fair value of the asset at the inception of the lease. This is due to the exclusion of the unguaranteed residual value from the calculation.

The amortization of the capitalized asset value would be the same as for any similar asset owned by the lessee. Accordingly, depreciation would be recorded in the financial statements, and the interest element of the payment would be recorded on the diminishing balance of the lease obligation as interest expense. This contrasts with the allocation of operating lease payments over the term of the lease, since they are usually allocated on a straight-line basis. It should be noted, however, that under an operating lease it is possible to charge the rental on a basis other than straight-line if the contract is negotiated on that basis, or if the alternative basis is appropriate under the circumstances. In some circumstances, it could be appropriate to allocate rental costs over machine-hour usage, on a mileage basis for trucks and similar equipment, or perhaps, based on sales in a retail establishment. In addition, there could be circumstances where it is expected that the asset will earn far more revenue in the early years. It may be appropriate, therefore, to charge extra rental expense in the early years even though the lease payments are equal throughout the lease term.

SALE AND LEASEBACK TRANSACTIONS

In periods of downturn in the economy when companies experience cash shortages, it has been common for some companies to increase their liquidity by selling major assets to an investor and leasing the asset back. If the lease is on a basis which permits the owner/lessee to reacquire the asset or to use up substantially all its useful life (the same tests as for a capital lease), then the sale and leaseback is treated as a financing. If the lease qualifies as an operating lease, then it is treated by the lessee as an operating lease. However, in either circumstance, if the fair value at the time the sale leaseback transaction occurs is less than the book value at that time, the loss must be recorded by the seller immediately. If the sale-leaseback transaction gives rise to a gain on sale, the gain is amortized in accordance with the amortization of the leased asset, for a capital lease, and in proportion to rental payments, for an operating lease. Accordingly, the sale-leaseback transaction will improve the cash flow or liquidity of the selling company, but any expected gain on sale will only be reflected over the term of the lease.

This has been altered by CICA Emerging Issues Committee (EIC) opinion 25 which permits immediate recognition of a gain where only a minor portion of the property is leased back and a portion of the gain in other circumstances. In these cases, the excess of the gain over the present value of the rents is recognized immediately, with the balance amortized over the lease term.

This chapter has dealt with the main issues in accounting for leasing transactions from the perspective of the lessee, including the differences in treatment of operating leases, capital leases, and sale and leaseback transactions. The important set of concepts affecting the income tax treatment of lease transactions will be reviewed in the next chapter.

Chapter 3

Income Tax Treatment of Lease Transactions — Lessee

Ordinarily, a lessee would claim the rental payments under an operating lease as an expense for income tax purposes in the taxation year in which the rental is due for payment. By contrast, the owner of a similar piece of equipment can claim capital cost allowance, usually on a diminishing balance basis, at specified maximum rates which vary depending upon the class of asset. Over the years, a number of incentives have been included in the *Income Tax Act*, S.C. 1970-71-72, c. 63, or the "ITA" as we shall call this Act, to assist with the purchase of new equipment. These include faster write-offs (accelerated capital cost allowance) that allow all of the cost of certain assets to be written off in as short a period as one or two years. These incentives vary from year to year, but have generally not been altered retroactively. In addition, a further incentive has been provided through investment tax credits, which are deductions from income tax otherwise payable in amounts that reflect the type of asset on which the credit is allowed and the region in which the asset is to be used.

Why is the write-off method for ownership of assets relevant to a lease? This becomes quite evident if the income tax department's view of one's lease transaction is that it is in substance a purchase. Under these circumstances, Revenue Canada may assess the lease as though it were a purchase. In that event, the investment tax credit (ITC) is available to the lessee; however, the lessee may claim only capital cost allowance (CCA) rather than the amount of rent the lease calls for as a deduction in calculating taxable income. In some circumstances, this can be a benefit (where ITC is an important part of the cost and where CCA is quite high), but in many cases this will be a disadvantage, particularly for short-term leases. For example, by the time of its conclusion, a three-year lease of an asset now eligible for 20% CCA could have 57.6% of the asset cost not claimed for tax purposes. This unclaimed capital cost (UCC) can be deducted for income tax purposes at the same annual rates (20% in this case) on a diminishing balance basis until

13

there are no more assets of that class remaining in the company's asset pool. At this point in time, the remainder can be deducted. As can be imagined, this results in claiming ever-decreasing amounts of CCA over a long time period. If the leased asset had been used to earn a large amount of income in the early years, with the income quickly tailing off, the taxpayer would be taxable on the income in the year received, but would be allowed a deduction only for the cost of the asset over a large number of years, even if the asset no longer existed. This can result in a payment of income tax on income which will be recovered by deducting CCA in the future. This advance payment can, of course, cause a serious strain on a company's cash flow and requires careful asset management if it is to be avoided.

THE PRESENT POSITION OF REVENUE CANADA

Clearly it is incumbent on a prospective lessee to know how his or her lease will be treated for income tax purposes. Fortunately, the Department of National Revenue has provided guidance as to the treatment of leases under IT-233R, an Interpretation Bulletin issued February 11, 1983, outlining the department's position and its rationale. Revenue Canada has the following major concerns with transactions that are recorded as leases but which, in its view, are in substance purchases:

- The lessee is likely to claim rent as an expense for tax purposes, and this rent is likely to be higher than capital cost allowance otherwise deductible.
- If the lessee has an option to purchase the leased asset for a nominal value at the termination of a lease and can subsequently sell the asset for more than the option price, thereby realizing a capital gain (only 75% of which is subject to income tax), then there is a risk that Revenue Canada would lose tax that would otherwise be recoverable through the recapture of CCA.

The issue of IT-233R and the addition of s. 13(5.2) of the *ITA* were designed to set out Revenue Canada's position and to ensure that gains on sale of property acquired through a lease-option agreement are taxable to the lessee.

Although Interpretation Bulletins do not have the force of law, they do indicate Revenue Canada's general position with respect to specific transactions. In addition Revenue Canada affirmed that IT-233R still reflects their position at the 1991 "Revenue Canada Round Table" of the Canadian Tax Foundation. Accordingly, Interpretation Bulletins will be reviewed to establish how a transaction is likely to be dealt with for income tax purposes.

The tax department has a number of guidelines to determine whether a transaction is in effect a purchase. These are similar to the CICA guidelines in some respects, but do not copy them with respect to the "useful life," the "90%" test, or with respect to third party guarantees. The department will treat a lease as a purchase if:

1. ownership to the asset is transferred to the lessee by the end of the lease term;
2. the lessee is required to purchase the asset;
3. the lessee is required to guarantee that the lessor will receive the full option price;
4. the lessee has the right during or at the expiration of the lease to acquire the property at a price which, at inception of the lease, is substantially less than the probable fair market value at the time permitted for acquisition by the lessee;
5. the lessee has the right during or at the expiry of the lease to acquire the property at a price or under terms or conditions which at the inception of the lease are such that no reasonable person would fail to exercise the option.

Under any of these circumstances, the lease transaction is treated as a purchase, and the lessee is permitted to claim capital cost allowance, interest expense, and is eligible to claim investment tax credits.

In the budget proposals of April 1989 which were subsequently enacted in December 1990 a new section of the *ITA*, s. 16.1 was inserted relating to leasing properties. This permits a lessee meeting certain criteria to treat an asset which has been leased as though it had been purchased. The cost for income tax purposes is the fair market value at the time the lease comes into effect, and the lessee is deemed to have borrowed funds at the "prescribed rate" set out in s. 4302 of the Regulations. Accordingly, the lessee may deduct capital cost allowance and interest by splitting the lease payments into principal and interest components at the prescribed rates and deducting the interest in the same manner as if the lessee had purchased the asset and borrowed the funds. It should be noted that a lessee has the option of making the election under s. 16.1, but not the obligation to do so. Therefore, the lessee can do a calculation to see which provides the better tax benefit — making the election or claiming the rents. In general this is a mechanical calculation to see which provides the higher write-off in the early years of the lease. However, it may be particularly important in years when the lessee is operating at a loss or has a loss carry forward which might expire. Treating these payments as acquisition of an asset means that the lessee can defer the claiming of CCA until the later year, thereby increasing taxable income for the particular year and perhaps permitting loss carry forwards to be used up faster. The following example shows the effect on the lessee for an asset with a 25% CCA rate.

Example of the New CCA Calculation

Taxpayer A leases an asset having a fair market value of $10,000 from another person for a period of five years. The prescribed rate in effect at the time of the commencement of the lease is 10%. The annual rent is $1,314 and the CCA rate that is applicable in respect of the property is 25%, on a diminishing balance basis, subject to the half year convention. Taxpayer A jointly elects with the lessor to treat the lease as a loan and purchase for the lease term and deducts interest expense and CCA as follows:

Exhibit 3-1

New CCA Calculation

Year	Lease Payment	Principal Element	Deductible Interest	CCA Deductible	UCC
					$ 10,000
1	$ 1,314	$ 314	$ 1,000	$ 1,250	8,750
2	1,314	345	969	2,188	6,562
3	1,314	380	934	1,641	4,921
4	1,314	418	896	1,230	3,691
5	1,314	460	854	923	2,768
Total	**$ 6,570**	**$ 1,917**	**$ 4,653**	**$ 7,232**	

There are a number of conditions relating to use of s. 16.1, including the following:

(a) the lease is for tangible property other than "prescribed property" that would, had it been acquired by the lessee, have been depreciable property;
(b) the lease must be from a person resident in Canada or, if from a non-resident, the lessor must be leasing the asset in the course of carrying on a business through a permanent establishment in Canada;
(c) the lessor and lessee must be at arm's length;
(d) the lease term must be for more than a year; and
(e) the lessor and lessee must file an election which sets out the fair market value of the leased asset at the time.

At the end of the lease the lessee is deemed to have disposed of the asset at an amount equal to the unpaid principal in the assumed loan adjusted for any amount received or paid by the lessee whether on expiry, assignment or sub-lease. This will also occur where the owner of the property ceases to be a resident in Canada (except if the person holds the lease in the course of carrying on a business through a permanent establishment in Canada).

At the end of the five-year lease described in the above example, Taxpayer A will be deemed to have disposed of the property for the remaining principal amount of the deemed loan — $8,083 ($10,000 original principal less $1,917 repayments of principal). If the property were the only property in that Class, A would be subject to the recapture of CCA of $5,315 ($8,083 deemed proceeds of disposition less $2,768 undepreciated capital cost). The total deductions allowed to A with respect to the property over the term of the lease would be $6,570 (interest of $4,653 and CCA of $7,232 less recapture of $5,315).

There are a number of other provisions in s. 16.1 to which reference should be made if it appears that the election might be beneficial to the lessee. For the purposes of this election, the lessee may not elect on "prescribed property" set out in Regulation 8200 and comprising essentially "exempt property" and assets of a fair market value of $25,000 or less per lease. There are additional special exemptions for certain trucks, trailers and railway cars; accordingly reference should be made to the Regulation. It should be noted that the lessor's tax position is not affected by the joint election. The main purpose for having a joint election is to ensure that the lessor and the lessee both agree on the fair market value applicable to the leased assets on which the lessee wishes to make the election.

Lessees should note that the election is only available for tangible property (other than prescribed property) that would have been depreciable property if it had been acquired by the lessee. Accordingly property which is not depreciable (such as land) and intangible property are not eligible for the s. 16.1 election.

As far as the lessee is concerned, there is little else of interest in the tax treatment of leases. However, it is important to consider how to use the tax treatment for one's benefit, and this will be shown in Chapter 4.

Chapter 4

Controlling the Financial Impact
of Long-term Leases

The release of *CICA Handbook*, Section 3065 focused attention on the importance of planning and carefully constructing lease agreements. The principles set out in the *Handbook* section make it apparent that the details of the lease contract and any correspondence related to it can significantly affect accounting and income tax positions. Both must be considered if the result is to reflect accurately the economic agreement between the lessor and the lessee.

For accounting purposes, the pertinent principle centres on the risks and benefits of ownership of the leased asset. If the lessor retains these, then the transaction is accounted for as an operating lease. If they are transferred to the lessee, then the lessee treats the transaction as a capital lease and, consequently, reflects the acquisition of an asset and the incurrence of a lease obligation in the financial statement.

The income tax position is outlined in Interpretation Bulletin IT-233R, para. 3. The stated intent of this bulletin is "to ensure that significant sums paid for the purchase of property are not charged against income as rent but are accounted for in such a manner that they may, if applicable, be subject to capital cost allowance and its recapture."

As they apply to long-term leases, both the *Handbook* and Interpretation Bulletin have two aims:

1. To establish that a lease which is essentially a purchase by the lessee will be treated as a purchase for accounting and tax purposes.
2. To establish symmetry of accounting (and tax) treatment resulting from the lessee's treating such agreements as purchases and the lessor's treating them as sales and/or financings.

There are significant differences, however, between the principles to be applied in the accounting area and those to be applied for tax purposes outlined in IT-233R. For this reason, it is frequently beneficial and sometimes essential to design carefully the lease contract to achieve the most advantageous accounting and income tax result for both the lessor and the lessee.

CRITERIA FOR A CAPITAL LEASE

Both paragraph 3 of IT-233R and the *CICA Handbook* Section 3065.06-.08 appear to set out discrete rules for determining whether or not a lease contract will be treated as a sale for tax purposes and as a capital lease for accounting purposes. In fact, these sources establish only guidelines which appear to indicate when substantially all of the benefits and risks of ownership have been transferred to the lessee. Exhibit 4-1 summarizes these guidelines.

Exhibit 4.1

Criteria That Indicate a Capital Lease

For accounting

A lease is probably a capital lease if it meets any of the following criteria:

(a) There is reasonable assurance that the lessee will obtain ownership by the end of the lease term, e.g., if:
   (i) ownership of the leased property is transferred to the lessee by the end of the lease term; or
   (ii) the lease contains a bargain purchase option.
(b) The lease term is equal to a major portion of the estimated economic life of the leased property (usually 75% or more).
(c) The present value of the minimum lease payments, excluding executory costs, is equal to substantially all of the fair value of the leased property at the inception of the lease (usually 90% or more).

For the lessor, the transaction must pass two additional tests:
   (i) The risk associated with the collection of rentals is not greater than the normal credit risk associated with the collection of similar receivables.
   (ii) The amount of any unreimbursed costs likely to be incurred by the lessor under the lease can be reasonably estimated.

For federal income tax

A lease is deemed a sale if it meets any one of the following criteria:

(a) The lessee automatically acquires title to the property after payment of a specified amount in the form of rentals.
(b) The lessee is required to buy the property from the lessor during or at the end of the lease, or is required to guarantee full option price.
(c) The lease contains a bargain purchase option.
(d) There is evidence that the lessee will be allowed to acquire the property for less than fair market value.

APPLICATION OF THE GUIDELINES

The application of the guidelines can be illustrated by examining the acquisition of two large processing machines having a fair value of $3,200,000 by two medium-sized companies: Alpha Limited and the Omega Corporation. Alpha has experienced growth, but because of an inflationary environment, has had to borrow rather heavily. Its borrowing agreements contain a number of restrictive financial covenants which are to be measured by using Alpha's annual audited financial statements prepared in accordance with generally accepted accounting principles. Consequently, there are restrictions on the annual amount of capital expenditures, working capital ratio, debt/equity ratio, and interest coverage. In addition, Alpha has relatively little taxable income. Omega Corporation, in contrast, has little external debt and is generating significant taxable income.

Let's now assume that both Alpha and Omega wish to obtain the machines at the lowest possible cost. How should they deal with the supplier and financier? How will their arrangements affect their financial statements and their tax positions? Can they negotiate a bargain that avoids unfavourable financial side effects?

STRUCTURING THE LEASE AGREEMENT

The differing constraints on Alpha and Omega highlight the differences between operating leases (those that give one the use of an asset without the risk of ownership) and capital leases (those through which one assumes the risks and rewards of ownership). If it is to be in accordance with generally accepted accounting principles, a capital lease must be reflected on the statements of the lessee as the acquisition of an asset and an equal liability. This could be disastrous for Alpha because of the covenants in its borrowing agreements; the same lease would have no adverse effect on Omega, however.

Alpha wants assurance that, for accounting purposes, the contract will qualify as an operating lease. In all likelihood, this means that the company will have to lease from a manufacturer or dealer, since a financier would not usually be willing to accept any of the "risk" associated with ownership. For income tax purposes, Alpha would like to be able to capitalize the lease because, in the calculation of taxable income, the capital cost allowance (CCA) permits flexibility that does not exist for operating leases. This option is not available, however, because the lease conditions that permit this favourable income tax treatment would probably also create a capital lease for accounting purposes and thereby adversely affect the company's borrowing agreements. The best remaining course of action is for Alpha to trade off its inability to claim CCA to a lessor who has taxable income and who, therefore, can use the CCA on the acquisition of the machine. Alpha can then negotiate an acceptable after-tax yield to the lessor, which also reduces the company's rent.

21

Omega's position is quite different from Alpha's. Omega prefers a capital lease for income tax purposes and is not concerned about the impact on its financial statements. The corporation can take advantage of the present favourable treatment of capital leases under IT-233R, which permits (or, perhaps, requires) a lessee to reflect a lease which is, in effect, a purchase, as a purchase. Omega will, therefore, see to it that the lease either transfers title after payment of a specified amount of rent, or else that it provides a bargain purchase option. The corporation might then claim CCA and interest for income tax purposes. Note, that because many manufacturers' lease contracts are cancellable with little penalty, the lease will probably have to be arranged through a third party. The cancellation clause will usually disqualify the agreement as a capital lease for accounting purposes. In addition, the asset would have to qualify for fast write-off. Otherwise Omega would have a larger deduction for tax purposes through claiming rent over the term of the lease rather than interest and CCA on cost. This brief analysis emphasizes the necessity for preplanning both tax and accounting results if cost is to be minimized and the effect on financial statements controlled.

The need becomes even more apparent when we consider the results if the agreements were reversed. Alpha would then have a capital lease for tax and accounting purposes, and Omega would have an operating lease. Alpha would have a higher final cost and unused CCA. Furthermore, the required capitalization of the lease would likely offend all of the restrictive covenants in its borrowing agreements. The contract would result in the acquisition of an asset, thereby affecting the capital expenditure test. The principal portion of the rents due within a year would be included in current liabilities, reducing working capital. The debt/equity ratio also increased because the lease obligation is reflected as debt. Finally, the interest element of the rent payments, along with the fact that depreciation plus interest is greater in the early years of the contract than are rental payments, results in lower income, higher interest, and consequent deterioration in the interest coverage test.

The effect of reversing the agreements would be less severe for Omega. The charge against taxable income in the early years would be reduced, which means higher tax payments and reduced cash flow. Finally, the company would probably incur a higher interest cost by borrowing from the lessor on an operating lease basis and might not have control over the asset at maturity since there is no bargain purchase agreement.

CONTROLLING THE IMPACT OF THE LEASE AGREEMENT

The accounting and taxation aspects of leasing are complex, but careful planning can turn them to an advantage. How does one go about it? How does one secure a lease compatible with the desired tax and accounting treatment?

Exhibit 4-2 shows the possible combinations of treatments that different companies might want.

Exhibit 4-2

Desired Treatment of a Lease

Types of Lease	For Tax Purposes	For Accounting Purposes
(a) Operating lease	X	X
(b) Operating lease	X	
Capital lease		X
(c) Capital lease	X	X
(d) Capital lease	X	
Operating lease		X

Now, what basic criteria must the lease meet to obtain the desired treatment?

(a) if the objective is to have an operating lease for both accounting and tax purposes, the terms of the contract should specify:
- no "reasonable assurance" that the lessee will acquire ownership of the leased property, e.g., no bargain option to purchase and no automatic transfer of title on payment of stipulated total rent;
- a term running less than 75% of the useful life of the property;
- the present value of the total rent to be less than 90% of the property's fair market value;
- no guarantee to the lessor.

(b) If the objective is to have an operating lease for tax purposes and a capital lease for accounting purposes, the terms of the contract will include:
- no bargains, as above;
- no guarantee to the lessor.

The contract should, however, also specify either a term running more than 75% of the useful life of the property or a present value of the total rent of more than 90% of the property's fair market value. In addition, there should be nothing in the contract to show that the benefits of ownership are retained by the lessor.

(c) If the objective is to have a capital lease for both accounting and tax purposes, the terms of the contract will include, for the accounts, any one of the following and, for tax purposes, any one of the first two:
- bargains, such as the option to purchase, or the transfer of title on payment of a stipulated total rent;
- a guarantee by the lessee to buy the property, or that the lessor will receive the option price;
- a term running more than 75% of the useful life of the property;
- the present value of the total rent must be more than 90% of the property's fair market value.

(d) Finally, if the objective is to have a capital lease for tax purposes and an operating lease for accounting purposes — no deal. In all likelihood, the conditions to meet the requirements for a capital lease will result in the same treatment for accounting and income tax purposes.

Most often, the objective is for the lessee to have an operating lease, since it is generally less of a concern to the lessor that the lease should be a "capital lease" (more properly, for income tax purposes a sale and financing lease). The special election in s. 16.1 of the *Income Tax Act* referred to in Chapter 3 provides the lessee with an opportunity to have an operating lease for accounting purposes and, if desired, either an operating lease or a purchase and financing lease, assuming that the property is leased and the lessor conforms with the requirements of s. 16.1. This may well make the drafter's job easier than it was before the April 1989 tax changes were enacted.

Some Problem Areas

These suggestions condense the details of IT-233R and *CICA Handbook* Section 3065. They also imply that the determination of capital versus operating lease treatment is based on a set of "rules", whereas the CICA's position is that these are only guidelines. The distinction between capital and operating turns on whether a lease transfers the benefits and risks of ownership. One cannot have a capital lease merely by including language that meets a specific criterion, say the "75% rule", if other clauses require the lessor to assume the substantial risks and benefits of ownership. If large amounts are involved, one should seek a ruling from Revenue Canada as to the tax treatment and confirmation from an accountant on the accounting treatment.

Non-cancellable Term and Contingent Rentals

One should also bear in mind that the CICA includes the non-cancellable term (Section 3065.03(o)) in the capital lease criteria and excludes contingent rentals (Sections 3065.03(g); 3065.19). This provides an opportunity to control the accounting outcome. For example, if an operating lease is required, a lessor may permit the lessee to cancel at some point before receiving "substantially all" of the economic benefits. This turns what might otherwise have been a capital lease into an operating lease.

Similarly, when the present value of the minimum lease payments represents a higher proportion of the leased asset's fair value, it may be possible to reduce the lease payments by making some of the rents contingent, again producing an operating lease. Rent that is a function of the prime interest rate is contingent for the rental variance caused by a change in the prime rate from that in effect at the inception of the lease. Other examples of contingent rates would include rents which are a function of sales (common in real estate leases) or leases which make the rent a function of production, e.g., in a factory.

24

An attempt to clarify this was made in EIC-19, October 1, 1990. The conclusion of that discussion is that lease payments that vary with factors measurable at the inception of the lease (e.g., an index such as the consumer price index or the "prime rate") are not contingent and should be included in minimum rents based on the rate in effect at inception of the lease.

The EIC discussion also dealt with rents which depend on a factor based on future events (e.g., sales or production). They concluded, quite rightly in my view, that you should not predict the future when calculating such minimum rents. Some accountants had suggested that a minimum production level (perhaps the "break-even point") should be used to calculate minimum rent. However many lessors of real estate, plants, retail outlets, etc. have found that during severe recessions such as those of 1982 and 1991 the minimum is frequently below "break-even" and, regrettably for both lessors and lessees, it becomes zero when the businesses fail.

Accordingly, the EIC conclusion that such rents are contingent and therefore not included in minimum lease payments is appropriate.

Residual Value

If one wants a capital lease, one can use the bargain purchase option to meet both accounting and tax criteria, but note that the residual value to accrue to the lessee must also be estimated. The *Handbook* anticipates that a lessor will review the estimated residual value annually and write it down if it decreases; it cannot be written up later. Presumably, the same applies to the lessee, though the *Handbook* does not state this explicitly.

"Tax-trade" Sale/Leaseback

This is a lease in which a lessee negotiates a lower rental by giving up the CCA that would be deductible by purchasing the asset and the lessor reduces taxable income by claiming the CCA that the lessee was unable to use as effectively.

In recording income, the lessor may recognize the carefully negotiated tax position in a tax-trade lease (*Handbook*, Section 3065.37-.38). This permits the lessor to record the economic bargain that has been struck. It seems, however, that the lessee may not reflect tax factors in his or her accounting treatment. Yet the tax effect may be particularly significant to *a lessee* in the sale and leaseback of real property. Recaptured CCA and any capital gain earned by the vendor/lessee will usually result in tax payments, for example, but these are not included in the *Handbook* calculation of the leasing obligation and the interest rate implicit in the lease, even though the lessee clearly takes them into account when the lease calculations are made.

CICA Research Report on Leasing Issues (September 1989)

Both U.S. and Canadian accounting authorities have spent considerable time dealing with the complexities of lease accounting and the ingenious designs which have been developed to have transactions treated as financings on the books of the lessor and as operating leases on the books of the lessee. In general, the lessor has not been interested in assuming any financial risk and the lessee has not been interested in recording a purchase and a liability on the balance sheet; however, at the same time the lessor often wishes to control the asset at conclusion of the lease (for example, many airlines like to control their equipment when they come off lease because they have a heavy investment in maintenance in the specific aircraft and in fleet balancing in general). As a result of the multitude of changes in leasing that have been put into effect particularly in the United States, the CICA commissioned a research study which reported in 1989. The author was privileged to be one of the members of this study group which eventually issued a lengthy report dealing with the main problem areas in leasing; particularly, confusion in the definitions, the question of how a lease should be properly classified for accounting purposes, and problems relating to sale/leaseback transactions, subleases, lease inducement and leveraged leases. The study group also tried to highlight the major differences in practice between generally accepted accounting principles for leases in Canada and the United States. It is clear that there are a wide variety of interpretations of the current *Handbook*. Some use a "rules approach" similar in many respects to the United States' material while others use a judgmental approach which appears to have been contemplated when the initial *Handbook* was written. These differences will be ironed out by the Accounting Standards Board of the CICA in due course. In the meantime the study group recommended the publication of a "Question and Answer Book" to deal with practical problems encountered, the issuance of an accounting guideline to clarify more important problems, a short-term *Handbook* project to deal with substantive practice problems and a long-term *Handbook* project to reconsider the accounting of leases from first principles. In addition, some of the most contentious points were recommended to be referred to the Emerging Issues Committee for resolution. The following summary, extracted from the *CICA Research Report on Leasing Issues* (published by The Canadian Institute of Chartered Accountants, September, 1989) illustrates some of the problems:

Exhibit 4-3

Research Report on Leasing Issues — April 1989

Major Problems in Lease Accounting

A. The problem leading to the greatest diversity in practice is differing interpretations of the material contained in *Handbook* paragraph 3065.06. Some believe that this material was intended to provide guidance on the application of the recommendation in paragraph 3065.09: others believe that it was intended to be prescriptive. If the latter view is adopted, leases can be designed to avoid capitalization by precisely adhering to the letter of conditions in paragraph .06.

B. Contingent rentals — Leases can be structured such that significant rental payments meet the *Handbook* definition of "contingent rentals". This avoids capital lease treatment, although in substance it may be highly probable that these rentals will be paid.

C. Minimum lease payments — The definition of the amounts to be included in minimum lease payments is not complete. The most serious problem is the failure of the definition to recognize the differences in the risks associated with various portions of guaranteed residual amounts. Handling fixed price purchase options appropriately is also a significant problem. Also, the definition does not deal with initial direct costs to the lessee.

D. Investment in the leased property — This term is not defined, and there is no indication of whether it should be considered net of investment tax credits in applying lease classification tests.

E. Third party participation — Lessees and lessors are entering into many new forms of sales and financing arrangements with third parties. No criteria are provided to help distinguish a sale from a financing transaction.

F. Sale-leaseback transactions — There is likewise no discussion of the impact of continuing involvement with the leased assets by the seller-lessee on accounting for sale-leaseback transactions. Practice with respect to income recognition by the seller-lessee is at best described as mixed. Some people believe that a literal reading of the *Handbook* recommendation requires that *all* of the gain on a sale-leaseback transaction be deferred. Others use various methods to allocate the gain when the property being leased back is small in relation to the property sold. Still others follow the standards contained in SFAS 28.

G. Penalties and changes in lease provisions — There is insufficient discussion of penalties that may be incurred if a lease is not renewed, changes in lease provisions and their potential effects on:

- the classification of leases as capital or operating; and
- subsequent accounting.

Exhibit 4-3 (cont'd.)

H. Implicit/incremental borrowing rates — Although there do not appear to be any problems with the definitions, there are a number of problems and concerns with their use in practice. There also appear to be fundamental differences in practice in applying *Handbook* paragraph 3065.06(c).
I. After-tax income recognition— There is a Canada/U.S. GAAP difference in that Canadian standards permit the consideration of income tax factors in income recognition by lessors.

Since the publication of the study, the EIC have dealt with these problem areas:

EIC-19 October 1990

Minimum Lease Payments and Contingent Rentals — referred to above under Non-Cancellable Term and Contingent Rentals.

EIC-21 December 17, 1990

Accounting for Lease Inducements by the Lessee.

In this case the EIC concluded that lease inducements should be accounted for as a reduction of rental expense over the term of the lease. The EIC dealt specifically with such inducements as rent-free periods, periods of reduced rent, cash payments to the lessee from the lessor (whether earmarked for moving costs, leaseholds or other reasons), and assumption by the lessor of pre-existing leases. The benefit of such inducements should be estimated by the lessee and recorded at inception of the lease. The corresponding costs should be accounted for as they would have been if incurred directly by the lessee. Presumably this is to be the case for all inducements. See Exhibit 4-4 for three examples of accounting for lease inducements.

Accordingly, moving costs paid by a lessor for a lessee are expected to be expended when the cost would have been incurred by the lessee, by a charge to expense and a credit to deferred lease inducements. The credit would be amortized, usually straight-line, over the new lease period.

Similarly, if the lessor assumed an unfavourable lease, the lessee would calculate the present value of the difference between the current market rent and the rent in the lease. This would be recorded as a deferred charge to be amortized over the term of the *old* lease. The offsetting credit to deferred lease inducements would be amortized to income over the term of the *new* lease.

This results in somewhat cumbersome accounting: however it would presumably only be applied in cases where the lease inducements were significant in amount.

Exhibit 4-4

Accounting for Lease Inducements (EIC-21)

Illustrative Examples

Example 1

A company entered into a five year lease incurring monthly lease payments of $10,000 and receiving the first six months rent free.

Accounting Treatment

Calculation of rent expense:

$$\frac{54 \text{ months} \times \$10,000}{60 \text{ months}} = \$9,000/\text{month}$$

The annual rent expense would be $108,000 which spreads the benefit of the rent free period over the lease term rather than expensing $60,000 ($10,000 × 6 months) in the first year and $120,000 each year thereafter.

Example 2

A company entered into a five year lease with the following lease payment schedule:

Year	Monthly Rent	Total Annual Rent
1	$ 5,000	$ 60,000
2	7,000	84,000
3	9,000	108,000
4	11,000	132,000
5	13,000	156,000
Total Lease Payments		$ 540,000

Accounting Treatment

Calculation of rent expense

$$\frac{\$540,000}{60 \text{ months}} = \$9,000/\text{month}$$

The annual rent expense would be $108,000 which allocates the benefit of the reduced rent payments in the early periods over the lease term rather than expensing the amounts actually paid out each year. (i.e. $60,000 in year 1)

Example 3

A company moved to a new location and incurred moving expenses of $25,000 and leasehold improvement costs of $200,000. The lease in the new location requires monthly lease payments of $10,000 for a period of five years. The lessor agreed to reimburse the company for the following costs:

Example 4-4 (cont'd.)

Moving costs	$ 25,000
Leasehold improvements	50,000
	$ 75,000

Accounting Treatment

i) Moving Expenses
  - $25,000 paid by the lessee would be expensed in the year incurred.
  - $25,000 received from the lessor would be accounted for as a reduction in the annual rent expense allocated over the lease term.

ii) Leasehold Improvements
  - $200,000 paid by the lessee would be capitalized and amortized over the lease term.
  - $50,000 received from the lessor would be accounted for as a reduction in the annual rent expense allocated over the lease term.

Example

Monthly reduction in rent expense

Total monies received from lessor

Lease term

$$\frac{\$75,000}{12 \times 5} = \$1,250/\text{month}$$

The annual rent expense would be $105,000 (($10,000 − $1,250) × 12) which spreads the benefit of the reimbursed costs over the lease term rather than recognizing $75,000 in income in year one with rental expense of $120,000 per year over the next five years.

EIC-25 April 22, 1991

Accounting for Sale with Leasebacks.

This material deals with the issue of when it is appropriate to record a gain on a sale/leaseback. If only a minor part of the property is leased back (with a cut-off of 10% to identify "minor"), then the entire gain or loss should be recorded (assuming rent to be charged is current market rate).

If more than a minor part but less than "substantially all" of the property is leased back, then the gain on sale to be recorded at the date of sale is the total gain less the present value of the rentals under the leaseback. The amount deferred is then amortized to income over the term of the lease (usually straight-line if an operating leaseback and in proportion to the amortization of the leased asset if a capital leaseback).

It should be noted that the EIC pertains to leases of equipment as well as to real property.

Exhibit 4-5

Accounting for Sales with Leasebacks

Illustrative Examples from the "Emerging Issues Committee" Recommendation 25

Example 1

An enterprise sells an existing 20-storey office tower. At the same time, the seller leases back three floors of the office tower, estimated to be approximately 15% of the total rental value of the office tower, for 20 years, which is the remaining life of the building. Pertinent data are:

Sales price of the office tower	$ 5,000,000
Carrying value of the office tower	$ 1,000,000
Monthly rentals called for by leaseback	$ 8,250
Interest rate implicit in the lease	12%

The lease would be accounted for as a capital lease pursuant to the transfer of risks and benefits, particularly the economic life criterion of *CICA Handbook* Section 3065. The seller-lessee would compute the gain to be recognized as follows:

Gain on the sale	$ 4,000,000
Recorded amount of leased asset[1] (capital lease)	749,260
Gain to be recognized at time of sale	$ 3,250,740

The deferred gain of $749,260 would be amortized in proportion to the amortization of the leased asset over the term of the lease at a rate of $37,463 per year.

Example 2

An enterprise sells an aircraft with an estimated remaining economic life of 20 years. At the same time, the seller leases back the aircraft for ten years. Pertinent data are:

Sale price of the aircraft	$ 2,000,000
Carrying value of the aircraft	$ 300,000
Monthly rental under the leaseback	$ 22,000
Interest rate implicit in the lease	12%

The leaseback does not meet the criteria for classification as a capital lease; hence, it would be classified as an operating lease. The seller-lessee would compute the gain to be recognized on the sale as follows:

Gain on sale	$ 1,700,000
Present value of operating lease rental[1] ($22,000 for 120 months @ 12%)	1,533,411
Gain to be recognized at time of sale	$ 166,589

Exhibit 4-5 (cont'd.)

The deferred gain of $1,533,411 would be amortized over the lease term at a rate of $153,341 per year.

Illustrative Examples

Example 1 does not consider the treatment of the portion of the rent applicable to common area and land (Section 3065.72). Since these items have different attributes than the rest of the building it may not be appropriate to treat them as capital leases. They could be treated as operating leases and accounted for in the same manner as Example 1.

The capital lease portion would include the asset under capital lease, the liability for the capital lease obligation and the deferred gain on the balance sheet. The operating lease portion would only include the deferred gain on the balance sheet.

---

[1] Calculated as the present value of the minimum lease payments to a maximum of the leased asset's fair value using a discount rate being the lower of the lessee's incremental borrowing rate and the interest rate implicit in the lease.

EIC-30 October 16, 1991

Transfer of Ownership of Leased Property

This EIC emphasizes that paragraph 3065.06(a) of the *CICA Handbook* is designed to cover all circumstances when there is reasonable assurance that the lessee will obtain ownership of the leased properties by the end of the lease term, even if the lessee has only a fair market value option at the end of the lease.

This is an important recognition that the specific examples referred to in 3065.06(a) (bargain purchase and automatic transfer of title) are only examples of where the general principle might apply. Other circumstances could also ensure that the lessee would acquire title. For example, there may be an effective penalty through requiring an environmental cleanup to be made if title is not transferred, onerous maintenance costs could apply, rail cars spread across the continent might have to be recovered, refurbished and moved to a central location, etc. Any of these might be expected to result in substantial costs to be incurred by the lessee. If, at inception of the lease, it is reasonable to assume that the lessee will exercise the purchase option as a result of these or other lease provisions, then the lease is probably a capital lease.

While this is a welcome clarification that the provisions of 3065.06 were not intended to be all-inclusive, those assessing such conditions should not now jump to the conclusion that economic circumstances existing at the inception of a lease will exist at the termination of the lease. In the case of rail-cars, for example, the lessee may reduce the size of his operation over the lease term, change the kind of traffic carried, be unable to finance the purchase due to borrowing covenant restrictions or high interest rates, and so on. We should not be quick to assume that there will be no change in the operation of a business over the term of a long-term lease. Conditions which are in effect at inception of the lease should not be presumed to be in effect at termination. A lessee always needs the leased property at inception and usually it is in reasonable demand. But one of the reasons the property is leased (rather than bought) is to permit the lessee to walk away at the end of the lease if he or she wishes. This option is central to leasing and we should be careful not to project current demand a long way into the future when assessing the "reasonable assurance" that a lessee will acquire title to leased property by the end of the lease term.

Another area of research should be included in addition to those highlighted by the research report. With the introduction of the Goods and Services Tax (GST) there is a new opportunity for differences in classification between a lessor and a lessee. For example a lessor who receives an input credit for any GST paid therefore would exclude GST from the cost for purposes of accounting classification. An institution which does not receive the input tax credit or only receives a partial tax credit would have to include the tax in its asset cost for purposes of lease classification and this might increase the cost to the extent that the minimum rents no longer met the "90% test". In general, this will affect financial institutions (no input tax credit received) and the so-called MUSH-group — municipalities, universities, schools and hospitals. These groups receive varying credits of less than 100%.

THE BEST OF BOTH WORLDS

Canadian accounting and income tax guidelines on the treatment of leases are complex. The accounting definitions must be read carefully because the terms normally encountered (inception of the lease, minimum lease payments, term of the lease, and so on) have precise meanings. Although the Canadian acounting material is close to that of the American pronouncement in Statement of Financial Accounting Standards No. 13 (as amended), it differs in its recognition of "tax-trade" leases in lessor accounting. The U.S. body recognizes these only for leveraged leases. The Canadian position differs, too, in that it offers guidelines for the determining of capital leases, whereas the United States provides rules.

It is possible that, in the future, IT-233R will be amended to bring the tax treatment of leases more into line with the accounting treatment. Until then, it is wise to determine the accounting and tax results before the contract is signed. With astute planning, both lessor and lessee may achieve what everyone would like to have — the best of both worlds.

Chapter 5

Certain Real Estate Leases:
How Do You Measure the Useful Life
of a Shopping Centre?

The *CICA Handbook*'s accounting for leases closely parallels that of the Statement of Financial Accounting Standards No. 13, issued by the Financial Accounting Standards Board, except that, as noted, the Canadian material provides guidelines, whereas the U.S. material sets down rules. Both, however, take the position that a transaction that transfers substantially all of the risks and benefits of ownership to a lessee should be recorded as a sales-type or direct financing lease by the lessor and as a capital lease by the lessee.

This position seems quite appropriate for leases of equipment with a limited life which decline in value over their useful life. It seems less appropriate, however, for real estate leases because of the difficulty of estimating the useful life and residual value, as well as for leases covering only part of a property, for example, a retail store in a shopping centre.

This chapter, therefore, discusses the application of *Handbook* Section 3065 to long-term leases of real property, the difficulty of assessing the useful life, the application of the cost recovery guidelines (Section 3065.06(c) — the 90% test), the effect of appreciation in property values on these tests, and accounting for the leases of only parts of real property.

THE PROBLEM

Some lessees have used one of the cost recovery tests given in Section 3065.06(b) and (c) to classify leases as capital leases, while the lessors have pointed to the general tests of Section 3065.09 dealing with transfer of risks and benefits of ownership (at the end of the lease in particular) to classify lease agreements as operating leases.

It was exactly this lack of uniformity (or "symmetry") in accounting approaches that the Statement of Financial Accounting Standards No. 13 was trying to avoid. For example, in paragraph 61 it states: "because of this divergence in both concept and criteria a particular leasing transaction might be recorded as a sale or as a financing by the lessor and as an operating lease by the lessee. This difference . . . has been the subject of criticism as being inconsistent conceptually, and some of the identifying criteria for classifying leases, particularly those applying to lessee's accounting, have been termed vague and subject to varied interpretation in practice.'' The ''symmetry of accounting'' concept was also one of the main reasons for the Canadian pronouncement on leasing. In Canada, however, the principle adopted in the *Handbook* material was one of the transfer of risks and benefits of ownership. Calculations to indicate such transfers in Section 3065.06(a), (b), and (c) are presented as guidelines only.

THE USEFUL LIFE AND COST RECOVERY TESTS

Most of the difficulty from the point of view of real estate companies arises from paragraphs (b) and (c) of Section 3065.06. The intent of these two paragraphs appears to be to clarify whether the lessee will receive substantially all of the economic benefit from the leased asset and whether the lessor will have little or no financial interest in the property when the lease term ends. Paragraph (b) suggests that, if according to the lease term, the lessee receives substantially all the economic benefits expected from the leased property over its useful life, the lessee should treat the agreement as a capital lease. Similarly, paragraph (c) indicates that the lessee should also treat the agreement as a capital lease if the lessor recovers substantially all of the investment in the leased property, as well as a return on investment. Both these guidelines indicate situations where the lessor will have little or no interest in the property when the lease has expired.

These guidelines are quite useful when dealing with equipment having a well-defined life span; they are much less useful when dealing with real property, particularly shopping centres and office buildings. These may appreciate substantially in value over the initial 30- to 40-year lease term, and the lessor will continue to have significant interest in the property even if the initial investment has been recovered. In addition, there is a free choice — whether to rent or buy — with equipment; such choice generally does not exist with a store that is part of a shopping centre. Here, the owner may offer only leasing, no matter what the lessee wants. Therefore, in these instances, the ''cost recovery'' test does not reflect that there is no free market for a floor of a building or a desirable shopping location.

In both these cases, the test set out in Section 3065.06 may fail to reflect what the lessor and lessee intended. We must, therefore, look to the general statement of Section 3065.09 as the key determinant of what accounting treatment to use if the economic substance of the lease transaction is to be properly recorded.

WHO HAS THE RISKS AND BENEFITS OF OWNERSHIP?

The problems in lease accounting centre around one question: Who has the risks and benefits of ownership when leases of real property run from 30 to 60 years or more? To be specific, let us consider the position of an anchor tenant in a large, enclosed modern shopping mall. The tenant may well have some influence on who the other tenants will be, the lease will be noncancellable, and there will be an obligation to provide a replacement if the tenant has to move out. The rent may well be at a lower base rate than that charged to smaller tenants, and the term will extend for 30, 40, or more years. Over the lease term, the present value of the rents will, in all probability, ensure recovery of the lessor's investment. This meets the test in Section 3065.06(c), and indicates a capital lease for the lessee.

The lessor, on the other hand, may well be looking at this property over a longer time span than 30 years. The lessor may feel that, at the end of 30 years, the residual value of the land and building will be greater than the original cost. The lessor may conclude, therefore, that the agreement is clearly an operating lease since, as the legal owner of the property, he or she will continue to reap the rewards of ownership. Thus, the lessor will treat the transaction as an operating lease and the lessee will treat it as a capital lease.

If the tenant has a bargain purchase option or automatically acquires title to the real property when the lease ends, the lease ought to be treated as a capital lease. The same conclusion may be reasonable if the tenant had an equity position in a company that owns only the shopping centre where (1) the equity participation reflected the proportionate interests in the shopping centre, and (2) the agreement for the equity interest was an integral part of the lease agreement. Even in this case there is some question about whether we have a capital lease, and in fact, joint venture accounting may be more appropriate.

There is a more apparent problem when the lease is of a medium term — 30 to 40 years — and the tenant has no equity interest in the property. In this case, some people look at the lease term and the cost recovery tests to clarify the intent of the parties concerned. These factors may not give the right answer.

It is difficult to estimate the useful life of a shopping centre. Shopping centre complexes in urban centres have passed through at least three stages. The first, having an anchor store and relatively few additional shopping sites with outside access only, may now have reached economic obsolescence as a result of the development of sites with large, competing anchor tenants at either end and a variety of different shopping locations between. This second shopping centre design may, in turn, have been rendered technically or economically obsolete by the advent of enclosed malls with large, competing anchor tenants, several competing retail outlets, entertainment and food centres, etc., where it is easy to go from location to location irrespective of weather. Yet, few developers have built any of these sites with the expectation that they will be uneconomic in 30 years.

In addition, the successful centres may well increase in value, and unsuccessful centres may decline. In 1991-2, the recession may well result in serious losses because of apparent overbuilding in the 1980s. There is, therefore, no objective answer to the question "What will be the useful life?" at the beginning of the lease.

The subjectivity in the determination may be what is leading some people to use the investment recovery test (the so-called 90% test in Section 3065.06(c)) as a means of determining whether or not they are dealing with a capital lease.

Assessing the 90% recovery contemplated in Section 3065.06(c) does, however, present a problem: How are rents over land, common areas, and the property rented allocated? Particularly in a shopping centre, a significant portion of the base rent must be allocated to the shared machinery and equipment (heating, ventilating, air conditioning, etc.) and the common areas. Assuming that the land is expected to increase in value and the building to decrease, one would also expect that the rent applicable to the land would gradually increase and that applicable to the building would gradually decrease. If this assumption is correct, then the allocation of rent over the operating lease for the land (see section 3065.73), the operating lease for the common areas, and the possible capital lease for the rented space should perhaps not be allocated on a pro rata basis, but on a basis that reflects the expected change in the values of the separate areas. Accordingly, the amount allocated to rented premises would decline over time and the "90% test" would be met less often. If it is assumed, on the other hand, that the land and building both appreciate equally over time and that the rent is fixed, then apportioning over land and building based on the value at the beginning of the lease is appropriate.

Basically, symmetry of accounting and the lessor's and lessee's intent in drawing up the contracts ought to be given significant weight in determining the accounting treatment. If the owner leases the property, even over a long term, intending to enjoy what is anticipated to be the property's significant residual value, and if the tenant merely wants to occupy a space for a period long enough to recover the costs associated with entry into the market or to enjoy the benefits of growth opportunities, then each intends to sign an operating lease. The lessor should properly reflect the entire shopping centre as an asset in financial statements, and the lessee would properly consider the agreement an operating lease and account for it accordingly.

There should be persuasive evidence against such intentions before the lease is considered to be a capital lease. The mere recovery of the original dollar investment plus a return to the lessor seem inadequate reasons to upset the general position that the lessor expects to retain the benefits of ownership once the lease has expired. In addition, this approach would be in harmony with the general trend towards requiring purchasers of real estate to have a significant equity (downpayment) in property prior to the seller recognizing a sale. A flaw in lease capitalization and the complement — sales-type lease recording by the lessor — is this failure to require a significant "equity" or downpayment before recording the sale. This may lead to overstatement of profit since there is a risk of loss to the lessor from having an anchor tenant fail with little financial risk, through no downpayment. This becomes more than academic when considering anchor tenants who have suffered financial reverses to the detriment of the shopping centre as, for example, during the severe recession and high interest rates of the early 1980s or the 1976 bankruptcy of the W.T. Grant Co. in the United States. In more recent times, there have been widespread problems facing retailers and shopping centre owners. Town and Country stores in ladies' wear, Jack Fraser stores in men's wear, Zale Corp. in jewellery have all announced major restructuring and/or store closures in December 1991 alone. If lessors have to use Section 3065.07 (which deals with uncertainty as to collection of rents as a reason for the lessor to treat the contract as an operating lease rather than as a sales-type lease) to avoid recording a sale, symmetry is lost. Yet, if the "sale" is recorded, the transaction may not conform to the requirements of securities commissions or recommended practices for land development companies. It may also result in the ludicrous position of reflecting bits and pieces of a shopping centre as sold, while the rest, including common areas, is retained by the lessor.

WHAT IS HAPPENING IN THE "REAL WORLD"?

As one might expect, published annual reports reflect the difference of opinion over lease capitalization. Exhibit 5-1 indicates the position of several retail chains (which were public companies when Section 3065 of the *Handbook* was published) who are also anchor tenants in a number of shopping centres. It appears that most have determined that their long-term leases are predominantly operating leases. Only Canada Safeway has decided that its leases are predominantly capital leases, and presumably, a portion of the operating lease payments is for the operating portion of the capital lease (i.e., land and common areas). Unfortunately, this cannot be determined for any of the companies included. The chains appear to use the general principles of the *CICA Handbook* (transfer of risks and benefits) and consider that their agreements are not equivalent to ownership. The legal owner will continue to control the property and realize the residual value. Food retailers may be in a somewhat different position. Some of their locations are designed as "one-purpose" properties, and their judgement is that the building will indeed depreciate over the lease term. This view would support capitalization for these agreements.

Finally, one would expect in any of the above that the companies might

39

adopt one practice and vary from that only if a sustantial number of leases failed to conform to the predominant form. This would seem to be a sensible approach since a variety of treatments results in considerable accounting work for little apparent effect on equity, earnings, or debt ratios.

The Canadian accounting profession attempts to bring some uniformity to accounting for leases. This will occur only if both lessors and lessees use the same criteria for establishing whether a lease is capital or operating. It is important, therefore, to adhere to the concepts in the *Handbook* material and not merely rely on clerical calculations for recovery of investment or estimated useful life to determine the correct accounting treatment for long-term leases of real estate.

Exhibit 5-1

Selected Public Company Retail Chains Lease Data

Company	Year End	Total Obligations Under Capital Leases	As % of Total Liabilities	Current Obligations Under Capital Leases	Assets Under Capital Leases	As % of Total Assets	Total Liabilities to Equity % Before Capitalization	Total Liabilities to Equity % After Capitalization	Net Minimum Lease Payments Payable During Subsequent Periods Operating Leases	Net Minimum Lease Payments Payable During Subsequent Periods Capital Leases
Canada Safeway Limited	29/12/85	$ 57,951,000	13.2	$ 3,228,000	$ 44,287,000	8.1	47.5	56.5	$ 189,892,000	$ 114,669,000
	29/12/84	79,246,000	17.9	4,142,000	63,514,000	5.6	53.0	65.0	232,899,000	156,850,000
	30/12/78	64,529,000	37.6	3,905,000	50,631,000	9.5	29.5	48.2	127,400,000	154,221,000
Woodward Stores Limited	26/01/91	7,667,000	2.7	N/A	6,363,000	2.3	170.2	177.7	623,321,000	N/A
	26/01/85	8,742,737	2.3	529,713	7,878,307	1.4	156.0	160.3	317,124,000	31,180,956
	27/01/79	5,296,800	2.7	7,400	5,310,021	1.6	154.5	158.7	149,150,000	38,279,194
Loblaw Companies Limited	29/12/90	72,300,000	5.6	N/A	49,400,000	2.4	152.7	158.8	596,000,000	N/A
	29/12/84	76,900,000	9.6	7,300,000	61,100,000	4.8	156.0	171.0	504,100,000	163,200,000
	29/12/79	46,311,000	8.6	1,759,000	43,622,000	5.0	198.3	217.6	796,782,000	101,917,000
A&P(c)	23/02/91	241,336,000	11.6	20,444,000	173,726,000	5.2	151.1	170.8	1,562,798,000	467,090,000
Argen Incorporated (Dominion Stores)	31/12/84	54,714,000	8.4	2,231,000	50,960,000	4.7	136.0	149.0	270,642,000	162,282,000
Dominion Stores	22/03/80	14,655,000	5.9	209,000	14,459,000	3.2	130.2	138.5	480,792,000	41,246,000
Hudson's Bay Company(b)	31/01/90	NIL	0.0	NIL	NIL	0.0	164.5	164.5	1,890,700,000	NIL
(inc. Simpsons, Zellers)	31/01/85	NIL	0.0	NIL	NIL	0.0	282.0	282.0	1,309,000,000	NIL
Hudson's Bay Company	31/01/80	NIL	0.0	NIL	NIL	0.0	N/A	N/A	716,800,000	NIL
Simpsons Limited	31/01/79	NIL	0.0	NIL	NIL	0.0	N/A	N/A	6,700,000	NIL
Zellers Limited	26/01/80	14,884,546	9.0	(a)	8,911,530	3.2	155.5	169.5	180,345,294	26,810,532

(a) Not disclosed separately in financial statements.
(b) Hudson's Bay Company acquired Simpsons Limited and Zellers Limited subsequent to 1979.
(c) Great Atlantic and Pacific Tea Company (A&P) acquired Dominion stores subsequent to 1984.

Chapter 6

Accounting for Leases — Lessor

The basis for classifying leases as operating or capital is outlined in Chapter 2. In general, the accounting pronouncements expect that an operating lease for a lessee will be treated similarly by the lessor. Accordingly, if a lease is classified as operating by a lessee, it is expected that the lessor will reflect the leased asset in its financial statements and write the cost of the asset off over its useful life, generally reducing the cost to estimated residual value at the conclusion of the lease term. Capital leases, on the other hand, are divided into two general categories for the lessor, defined as sales-type and direct financing leases. This division recognizes the two major sources of leasing:

- manufacturers who lease their product and thereby earn both a profit margin over cost and a financing and leasing margin; and
- financial intermediaries who acquire the leased asset for purposes of leasing to a specific third party and expect to realize a financing margin.

The basic tests for determining whether a lease is operating or not are the same for the lessor and the lessee. In addition, the guidelines for determining whether the benefits and risks of ownership have been passed to the lessee are the same as those to determine whether the lease is a capital lease from the viewpoint of the lessee. These criteria are:

- that there is a reasonable assurance that the lessee will obtain title to the leased asset during or at the end of the lease term;
- that the lessee will receive substantially all the economic benefit of the leased property over its life span (the "75% test"); and
- that the lessor would receive over 90% of his or her investment in the leased property plus a return on the investment as a result of the lease agreement.

In addition, the Canadian Institute of Chartered Accountants (CICA) recognizes two other tests which a lease must pass if it is to be treated other than as an operating lease by the lessor:

- the credit risk associated with the lease is normal when compared to the risk of similar receivables; and

- the amount of nonreimbursable costs that are likely to be incurred by the lessor under the lease can be reasonably estimated.

These tests are generally included to guard against the situation where a lessor would attempt to record a profit on sale of a leased asset under a capital lease when the lease conditions make the eventual profit on the lease difficult to compute at the inception of the lease. Accordingly, if a vendor is leasing to poor credit risks, there is a concern that the leased asset will have to be repossessed and perhaps an alternative lessee located before the lessor can recover full cost. Prudence therefore dictates that the lessor treat such transactions as operating leases and not record any sales margin at the time of signing the lease agreements. Similarly, if the lessor guarantees the performance of the leased asset or undertakes to provide automatic upgrades in the event of technological change (as sometimes occurs in the computer leasing business), then the lessor's costs associated with the lease are not known, and it would again be imprudent to record a gain on sale at inception of the lease.

ACCOUNTING FOR AN OPERATING LEASE

After the lessor has classified a transaction as an operating lease, the accounting treatment is straightforward. The rental revenue would normally be recognized as income over the term of the lease as it becomes due. Ordinarily, income is recognized on a straight-line basis, irrespective of the actual cash payments falling due. However, if another "systematic and rational basis is more representative of the time pattern in which the benefit from the leased property is utilized" (*CICA Handbook*), then this other basis should be used. This latter treatment might occur where the utility of the leased asset is a function of hours of use, rather than the passage of time. In that case, it may be appropriate to reflect the lease income over the usage of the leased asset, assuming it could be determined by the lessor.

In addition, if the lessor has incurred "initial direct costs" such as commissions, legal fees, or documentation costs in connection with the lease, they should be deferred and amortized to expense in proportion to the rental income recorded. In practice, these costs are often minor compared to the total income of the lessor and are normally charged to expense as incurred, rather than deferred. Although this tends to understate earnings for the leasing company somewhat, it serves to offset the occasional bad debt or late payment costs incurred by the lessor. It also avoids the significant cost of computing and amortizing initial direct costs over the term of the lease.

The lessor will, of course, write off the cost of the leased asset over the lease term or write it down to its estimated residual value at the end of that term. If the lessee has an option to buy the asset at a fixed price at the conclusion of the lease term, the lessor would normally amortize the leased asset to an amount not exceeding the option price. The amortization or depreciation would ordinarily be on a straight-line basis, to coincide with the recording of the rental income. If it had been determined that the rental income should be recorded on something other than a straight-line basis, the amortization should be recorded on a comparable basis.

DIRECT FINANCING LEASES

These occur where a financial intermediary acts as lessor and expects to earn finance income rather than a gross margin on sale plus finance income. In general, such agreements are full-payout leases, with the lessee having the option of acquiring the asset at the conclusion of the lease term for a nominal amount or a "bargain purchase". In some cases, there can be an unguaranteed residual value which will increase the yield to the financial intermediary. If there are "executory costs" included in the lease payment, these would be in addition to the finance income. Since the financial intermediary is interested in a yield on its investment, any "initial direct costs", particularly legal fees and registrations, are recoverable from the lessee at the time of closing the transaction. If not, it would be normal practice to record these as an expense and to record sufficient finance income to offset them.

In summary, the financial intermediary earns a return on its cost, or occasionally on the carrying value of the leased asset at the interest rate implicit in the lease. The intermediary's net investment at any time would be represented by the minimum lease payments receivable, less any executory costs (and related profit therein if any), plus the unguaranteed residual value accruing to the lessor, less unearned finance income, which will be net of initial direct costs.

There are a variety of methods to record the income on such contracts, including:

- straight-line recording of income on a monthly basis over the lease term;
- the "sum-of-the-digits" basis; and
- the actuarial method.

Of these, only the actuarial method provides a constant rate of return on the net investment of the financial intermediary. Since the leases are written on the basis of a fixed rate of return, the third method is clearly the most relevant.

The straight-line method merely allocates the finance income in equal monthly instalments over the lease term. It ignores the effect of residual value and the fact that the lessor's funds invested in the lease are declining monthly. If the financial intermediary has financed the purchase of the leased asset on a basis which is designed to provide the lessor with a fixed "spread" between lending rate and borrowing rate, and the loan is paid down in equal instalments of principal and interest, then the straight-line method will result in large losses in the early life of the contract when the investment and risk

45

are the greatest and large profits in the latter months of the contract when the investment and risk are least.

The sum-of-the-digits method was common in the periods prior to the advent of the computer. It was primarily used for short-term contracts at rates which, when compared to today's rates, were relatively low. For example, it was relatively common in the financing of cars over 24 and 36 months and in the small loan business. For short-term (under 36 months) and low interest rate contracts, the sum-of-the-digits method is relatively close to the actuarial method (see *Neifeld's Guide to Instalment Computations* (Mack-Publishing Co., Easson, Penna., 1953). In its general application, the method is insufficiently accurate for longer-term contracts to justify its use, and it does not handle variations in the investment balance from month to month due to:

- initial skip payments or balloon payments (a higher than normal payment, at some time, usually the end of the contract);
- seasonal payments, which are common in the farming, fishing, and lumber industries, among others;
- payments that are uneven in amount, such as declining or ascending payments; and
- payments reflecting guaranteed residual value at the end of the lease and the unguaranteed residual value amount recorded by the lessor.

The assumption behind the sum-of-the-digits method is that the principal invested in the lease will be repaid by equal monthly instalments starting one month after the amount of the investment. This is, in fact, a relatively rare occurrence in leasing, and for this reason and because of the timing of payments referred to above, the method is unlikely to provide a constant rate of return on the investment; therefore, it is likely to give misleading results. This problem is aggravated for contracts over 36 months, for contracts with higher interest rates, and for contracts with any irregular payment.

The actuarial method provides not only a fixed rate of return on funds from time to time invested in the leased asset, but it also will handle any irregularity of payment, assuming that the payment schedule is properly recorded. A computer program is virtually essential for this activity, even for just a few contracts.

A direct financing lease is shown in the Appendix in Example 1(b) on an actuarial basis. The straight-line and sum-of-the-digits methods are shown in Example 1(b), direct financing (lessor). The accounting reflected in these examples is aimed at recording the asset and income on the assumption that the contract is written on a yield basis. This ignores the incidence of bad debts and changes in the estimate of residual value of the leased asset. It is important to review the future collectability of the remainder of the lease payments and to establish an adequate allowance for doubtful accounts if they are in jeopardy. In addition, it is important to review the residual value of the leased assets to see if the original estimates should be revised. Accounting practice requires a write-down where there has been a decline in residual value which is other than temporary. On the other hand, anticipated increases in residual value cannot be recorded until realized. This is an example of the doctrine of conservatism, which is an important part of accounting thought. In essence, it is designed to record losses when they are recognized, but not to reflect gains until they are realized.

SALES-TYPE LEASE

These transactions normally occur when a dealer or a manufacturer offers customers an opportunity of buying or leasing its products. If the lease is other than an operating lease, the lessor generally realizes two types of income: the first, profit on sale of the product; the second, finance income earned over the lease term.

To split the cash flow anticipated from the lease into its components, it is necessary to establish the sales value. This is the present value of the minimum lease payments (net of any executory costs and related profit included therein), computed at the interest rate implicit in the lease. This present value normally approximates the usual selling price for the asset. The cost of sale is the cost of the asset being leased or its carrying value, if for some reason it has been written down, net of the present value of the unguaranteed residual accruing to the lessor, calculated at the interest rate implicit in the lease. As is the case with any sale, the cost of sale can be greater than the sale value.

The finance portion of the income is the difference between:

(a) the total minimum lease payments, again net of any executory cost and related profit included therein, plus;
(b) the unguaranteed residual value; and
(c) the present value of those two amounts. The discount rate for determining the present value of the minimum lease payments and the unguaranteed residual is the interest rate implicit in the lease.

As with a direct financing lease, the residual value which is not guaranteed to the lessor would be reviewed annually to determine whether a decline in value has occurred. If the decline in value is other than temporary, the accounting for the lease transaction would be revised using the changed lower estimate. The reduction in net investment in the lease would be charged to income, and a later upward revision could not be made. In contrast to direct financing leases, however, "initial direct costs" are considered to be part of the cost of incurring the sale, rather than the cost of incurring the finance income, and are accordingly expensed at the inception of the lease.

Financial statement presentation usually reflects the amounts receivable under long-term, sales-type leases as a separate asset. The amount is the sum of the minimum lease payments, less any executory costs and related profit therein, plus the unguaranteed residual value accruing to the lessor, less unearned income remaining to be allocated over the lease term. An example of the financial statement presentation for a sales-type lease and calculation relating thereto is shown in the Appendix as Example 1(c).

SALE OF LEASE PROPERTY OR ASSIGNMENT TO A THIRD PARTY

There are a number of circumstances under which lessors may wish to obtain financing for some of their leases. They may sell the leased assets to a financier or they may receive funds in exchange for an assignment of the lease payments. Where the substance of the transaction is that the lessor retains substantial ownership risks in connection with the leased property, a transaction is treated as a loan to the lessor. For example, the lessor may guarantee all of the lease payments to the financier and may guarantee the residual value. In addition, the lessor may undertake to remarket the leased property in the event that the lessee returns it for any reason during the term of the lease. In these cases, the asset remains on the books of the lessor and the rents received are recorded, either by the lessor or by the financier if they have been assigned, as revenue. Interest expense will be recorded at a rate which would be comparable to that which an unrelated lender would negotiate with the lessor for a loan under similar terms and conditions. In addition, the remaining asset value would be amortized over the term of the loan.

Note that this treatment would only be applicable to the sale of property which is subject to an operating lease, since for both the sales-type lease and a direct financing lease substantially all of the risks and benefits of ownership are transferred to the lessee. Therefore, the lessor does not have any of the risks of ownership in connection with the leased property.

The requirement appearing in the *CICA Handbook* in paragraph 3065.62 that the interest rate applicable to the loan be that which an unrelated lender would negotiate with the lessor for a loan under similar terms and conditions gives rise to practical difficulties. The lessor is required to amortize the asset over the loan period. At the same time, it is anticipated that there will be a considerable unguaranteed residual value over the loan period (or the transaction would not have been an operating lease). In addition, there is only one interest rate which will equate the principal sum received from a financier to the stream of rents coming in from the lessee. If we assume that the appropriate interest rate under paragraph 3065.62 would be higher than the rate represented by these cash flows, then the rent will not amortize the principal balance and there will be an unpaid liability at the conclusion of the loan period, yet there will be no more payments to be received by the financier and no payment due by the lessor.

Similarly, if the assumed interest rate is lower than the rate which will amortize the cash flows against the funds actually received, more of the payment of rent will be attributed to principal, and the loan balance will therefore be amortized below zero. Presumably, a rate other than that equating the rents to the amount of funds advanced would be appropriate if the lessor has in fact sold the residual value to the financier as well. Although that could be the case in transactions of this type — which are actually financings — in practice, the lessor generally has a right to obtain title to the equipment at the conclusion of the loan period for a nominal value. The lessor could then realize on the residual value, and there would be no need to alter the amortization originally established under the operating lease. Lessors beware, however, that non-recourse assignments of lease payments to a lender may be treated for income tax purposes as a sale of a right, with the proceeds fully taxable. This risk can be mitigated by documentation of the entire transaction as a financing with the assignment of rents merely for collateral security, along with clear title resting in the lessor on payment of the debt.

A common situation in a real estate transaction involving franchisees is to have the franchisor as the head-lessor and franchisees as sub-lessees. In these circumstances it is common for the franchisee to make the payments directly to a landlord or to a lender in the case of leasehold improvements and equipment which have been leased and financed. In general, the transactions qualify as capital leases since they are full pay out leases to the lender and generally permit the head-lessor to acquire title for a nominal amount. Similarly the sub-lease provides for the franchisee to obtain title for a nominal amount at the end of his sub-lease. Accordingly, the head-lessor will generally record the transaction as a purchase of an asset and a funding until the sub-lease is signed. At that time the asset has been ''sold'' to the franchisee who should record it in its books as a purchase and financing. The sub-lessee has the bargain purchase option at the end of the lease and generally continues to use the leased assets in its business. The head-lessor generally has no interest in the assets at that stage; however, since the head-lessor remains contingently liable it would be normal to include a note in the financial statements indicating the contingency, if any.

It is clear that careful attention will have to be paid to such transactions to ensure that the accounting properly reflects the full agreement and that revisions to the original accounting for operating leases are properly recorded. This is particularly true if the lessor has in effect sold its residual value. If the financier has valued the residual value at an amount lower than has the lessor, that may require an immediate adjustment to recognize a permanent reduction in value of the residual.

TAX-ORIENTED LEASING

In the late 1950s and early 1960s, lessors priced their product somewhat higher than they were priced in conditional sales agreements, an alternative method of acquiring use of an asset. In addition, ''one dollar options'' were not uncommon, providing the lessee with the right to acquire the leased asset at the conclusion of the initial lease term for a nominal amount, often $1.00. If the lessor's portfolio of leases was growing, the lessor was able to increase income tax deferral each year as a result of claiming a whole year's capital cost allowance against, on average, only six months' rental income. Accordingly, from the position of the lessor, it appeared that leasing was more profitable than selling on a conditional sales agreement. The conditional sales agreement required income to be recorded each fiscal period, and tax was generally payable in each fiscal year, assuming the business was successful. As a result of this apparently favourable treatment of leasing, leasing portfolios expanded, and the variety of equipment under lease was almost limitless. In addition, the term of leases, particularly to first-rate credits, increased from the normal three or four years that was typical for equipment, to seven years or more for aircraft, and 15 years or more for railway rolling stock.

These transactions began to generate large income tax deferrals for several years. This resulted from the lessor's ability to claim a full year's capital cost allowance irrespective of the term of the lease. Therefore, if lessors sought to recover their dollar investment from a lessee, the principal they had to recover in a two-year lease was the same number of dollars as they had to recover in a ten-year lease. However, in the ten-year lease they needed to recover on average only one-tenth of the original cost, whereas in a two-year lease they had to recover one-half. Clearly, the annual rent charged to the lessee for a short-term lease was higher than the annual rent charged on a long-term lease. Since the capital cost allowance claimable each year is constant irrespective of the term, the capital cost allowance was much greater than the rental income in these long-term leases and tax deferrals built up.

The larger dollar value on long-term leases was often financed by the lessor through a specific funding of the cost of the leased asset. Accordingly, these leases were referred to as "leveraged leases." The lessor sought to recover the cost of borrowing plus a return over the life of the lease. Since the lease term was quite long and the asset was often "special use" to the lessee, the leases had to be non-cancellable; otherwise the lessors ran the risk of having the asset returned to them and having no ability to remarket it to realize the remainder of their investment. It was evident to the lessee that the lessor received considerable income tax advantage from this type of financing transaction. As a result, the lessee and the lessor negotiated the lease rate on a basis that recognized the significant income tax benefits achieved by the lessor. In some cases the income tax benefits were sufficient that the cash used to acquire the lease portfolio was recovered in the early years of the lease, often after two or three years. For the next few years of the particular lease, the lessor was in fact "borrowing" on an interest-free basis from the federal government through tax deferrals. The interest rate implicit in the lease to the lessee could be calculated at several percentage points lower than the lessor's normal cost of borrowing. However, the lessor computed its actual rate of return by deducting deferred income tax from net investment in the lease, thereby reducing investment from time to time outstanding and providing the lessor with a higher yield on investment than would be realized if the deferred income tax were not recognized.

As a result, a method of accounting for such leases was developed in practice and required the reduction of the cash invested in the lease by the investment tax credits and by deferred income tax realized by the lessor. This was recognized in the *CICA Handbook* in paragraphs 36 to 39 of Section 3065, which permits the recognition of the investment tax credit and deferred income taxes as reductions from the lessee's net investment for purposes of income recognition.

The *CICA Handbook* stresses that "when income tax elements that affect the cash flow are predictable with reasonable assurance, it may be appropriate to take these elements into consideration in accounting for income from the lease." In practice, it is very difficult to assess whether the expected gains from tax deferrals over long periods of time will be realized. For example:

1. For much of the late 1970s and early 1980s, substantially the entire leasing industry in Canada was tax-sheltered. That is, they had no taxable income from any source and therefore could not benefit in the short run from further tax deferrals.
2. The lessor might be quite profitable in the year the lease was written, but as a result of rising interest rates, high credit losses, or declines in other lines of business expected to generate taxable income, it might have no taxable income in later years.
3. Investment tax credits could be lost through inability to claim such deductions before they expired.
4. A number of leases have been challenged by taxation authorities as being, in effect, sales. This resulted in an *acceleration* of income tax rather than a deferral. Unfortunately, the acceleration was not known to the lessor until the income tax position was assessed, usually several years after the transaction was entered into.
5. Tax changes after the contract is written or changes in Revenue Canada's assessing practices after the contract is written can result in decreased returns to the lessor, particularly for changes in taxes based on capital and debt.

For reasons such as these, it is imprudent to assume that the tax deferrals anticipated in long-term leases will be realized in fact. It is advisable to be cautious when using tax-oriented lease accounting, and of course, it is equally a reason for the lessor to be cautious about trading off tax advantages that may never be realized. This subject is developed further in the next chapter and in Chapter 11.

Chapter 7

Tax Implications of Leases for the Lessor

Lessors in an operating lease enjoy two "tax advantages" which can reduce taxes otherwise payable and, therefore, their investment in the lease transaction. These are the ability to claim capital cost allowances (CCA) and the entitlement to investment tax credits (ITC). Over the years the amount of CCA claimable has been altered by redefining classes and by reducing the amount of CCA claimable in the first year by using a rate of one-half of the rate applicable to the asset class for the remaining years. Similarly, ITC rates vary for type of asset and region in which the leased asset is to be used, as well as the use to which the leased asset is to be put. Nevertheless, lessors still can obtain some income tax deferral which may be useful to them if they have otherwise taxable income. To be sure of this the lessor must be satisfied that the lease is an operating lease for income tax purposes. If taxation authorities can successfully maintain that the lease was in fact a sale to the lessee, the difference in the incidence of income tax to the lessor is dramatic and unfavourable.

Essentially, Revenue Canada will treat a lease as a sale either if ownership passes to the lessee during or at the end of the lease term, or if the lessee has the right to acquire the asset on terms which no reasonable person would fail to exercise, including "bargain purchase." In effect, Revenue Canada would like to see only those transactions where the lessee cannot acquire title to be treated as operating leases. In practice, it permits leases where the lessee option is at "fair market value" to be treated as operating leases, although the determination of what is fair market value is not straightforward. The option price must be a legitimate pre-estimate at inception of the lease of the expected fair market value at the time the lessee has the option to acquire the asset. Factors such as obsolescence, changing markets, changing interest rates, and rapid technological change all work to make a perfect pre-estimate of market value at termination of a long-term lease particularly difficult. Alternatively, the parties could agree to have a fair market value determination made at the option date. Nevertheless, it is in the interest of the lessor to ensure that the method of arriving at fair market value is rational and well documented if the lessor wishes to withstand any review of the transaction by Revenue Canada several years after inception of the lease.

INVESTMENT TAX CREDIT

The federal government provides a number of incentives for industry to re-equip and modernize, one of which is the investment tax credit mechanism. It is only available to purchasers, including lessors, and the terms change with each federal budget. From time to time the government has made amendments to the rates of investment tax credit, the type of equipment which is covered by the credits, the regions in which the equipment may be used to achieve the highest tax credits, and has made provision for a partial refund of the credit in cash rather than the more normal offset against federal income tax liabilities. The particular provisions are not critical for the purposes of this book, but would have to be reviewed by any lessor entering into a significant dollar value of transactions. If the lessor is not in a taxable position where advantage of the full investment tax credits can be taken, the option of receiving a reduced cash grant may exist, or if the lessee is in a taxable position it may be possible to effect a transfer of the credits to the lessee. This requires careful planning, as the credits are only available for new equipment of the required class. Accordingly, it may be necessary for the lessee to acquire the equipment in the first instance, have the lessor purchase the equipment from the lessee at a reduced price to recognize the receipt of ITC by the lessee, and then lease the equipment back to the lessee. With this step there is a risk that the equipment will be treated as inventory to the lessee.

It should be noted in dealing with ITC and CCA that the amount of investment tax credits claimed by a taxpayer reduces the CCA pool dollar for dollar. That is, if $100 of investment tax credit on a class 10 asset is claimed, the class 10 is reduced by $100.

CAPITAL COST ALLOWANCE

The Canadian tax system treats assets on a pool concept with many classifications, for each of which there is a separate capital cost allowance rate. In general, the lessor may claim up to the maximum CCA in each year except the first year when a rate up to 50% of the normal rate may be claimed. When an asset is sold the proceeds of sale are credited to the particular pool in an amount up to the original cost of the asset. If the lessor receives more than original cost for the asset (which has happened for some aircraft leases, but can happen for any appreciating asset), the excess over the original cost is taxed as a capital gain in the hands of the lessor.

The effect of this system is that the lessor continues to claim CCA at a fixed rate on a declining balance of unclaimed capital cost (UCC) until the asset is sold. At that point there may be a balance left in the pool for the particular asset, and capital cost allowance continues to be claimable on this net balance (original cost minus CCA claimed minus proceeds of sale) until all assets of the class are sold. At that time the lessor must claim the balance in the pool as a "terminal loss" if no other additions to the pool are made by the fiscal year end. Indeed, this introduces one of the difficulties in leasing. If lessors are not careful to match the amount of CCA claimed on a particular lease, they can find that they have been taxed on all of the lease rents (which usually equals their cost net of proceeds of sale on the leased asset), but have not been allowed to deduct all of their costs against taxable income as the UCC of the asset at termination of the lease will only be recovered by future CCA claims. This position can become quite serious for the lessor in short-term, full-payout operating leases where the UCC will be quite high (i.e., CCA rates are low in relation to the term of the lease).

In some cases it may be advantageous for a lessor to dispose of a leased asset to ensure that no more assets of that particular class are on hand. This will permit the lessor to claim a terminal loss which would otherwise not be available. Conversely, the lessor may wish to retain an asset so that it is not required to claim the terminal loss. If the pool of assets for any particular CCA class becomes negative, through sales of assets, the year-end negative balance is taxable to the lessor.

In May 1976, Revenue Canada introduced a restriction on the amount of CCA that could be claimed by a lessor. This restriction was put in place to avoid perceived abuses of leasing whereby individuals not in the leasing industry were claiming large amounts of capital cost allowance on individual leases as "tax shelters." The effect of the change (*Income Tax Regulations*, C.R.C. 1978, c. 945, s. 1100(15)) restricts the amount of CCA deductible to the amount of net leasing income. In effect, it precludes the claiming of a loss from leasing. There is an exception for a "principal business" corporation where 90% of the gross revenue of the company is from renting or leasing property. In addition, a company that both sells and services equipment of the same kind as it leases gets relief from the CCA restrictions.

The definitions relating to property are quite complex and may well provide either a tax trap or a tax opportunity in a particular situation. There is apparently no definition of what constitutes gross revenue from renting or leasing property, and presumably normal accounting practice would prevail.

As a result of the restriction, leasing is often done through a subsidiary. If the subsidiary is financed substantially by share capital, much of the tax advantage of leasing is retained. Since the leasing subsidiary is a principal business corporation, it has no restriction on its ability to claim CCA. In addition, since it has no interest expense, its only expenses are administration and CCA. If the parent company has borrowed funds to finance the subsidiary, the tax shelter normally available to a leasing company has been, in effect, transferred to the parent company through the higher interest expense incurred to fund the subsidiary. Accordingly, the restriction on CCA has been effective in limiting the use of leasing as a tax shelter by individuals, but should have a relatively minor effect on companies. Individuals could also start their own principal business leasing corporation which is funded entirely by capital borrowed personally by the individual. Since the interest on such debt is currently tax deductible to the individual, they would also have transferred much of the leasing tax shelter to themselves.

An example of a lease, contrasting the income tax position of the individual and a company, the claiming of CCA, and the effects on the pool on disposition is given in Example 4 of the Appendix. (In Example 4 a class 29 write-off as it was in 1986 has been used. Current write-offs, although differing, would still show a comparable restriction to the individual.)

"STRETCH" LEASES

One form of lease agreement that has given rise to a disproportionate amount of difficulty with Revenue Canada is the "stretch" lease. In this agreement the lessee may lease a particular asset over, say, a 48 month period. At the end of the primary lease term, the lessee has the option of acquiring the asset or leasing for a further six months, at which point the lessee has no option to acquire. The rentals for the six-month period will be arranged so that their present value is very close to the option price at the end of the 48th month when discounted for the six months at the interest rate implicit in the lease. The question from an income tax perspective is twofold:

(a) Is the option price a "bargain purchase option"?

(b) Is the option not certain to be exercised, since the lessee will incur the same cost whether the option is exercised or the lessee continues to pay rent for the six-month period, but, if the option is exercised, the lessee will realize the residual value at the end of the stretch period?

Under either (a) or (b) the tax department feels that the lessee is going to acquire title to the leased asset in a manner that meets its requirements for the lease to be treated as a purchase in the first instance. Its feeling is that the lessee will always exercise the option to acquire the asset at the end of the 48th month since by doing this the lessee will enjoy whatever residual value the leased asset has at the end of the 54th month. If the lessee does not exercise the option, this residual value is lost. Accordingly, "any reasonable person" would exercise the option. In practice, there are a number of reasons for this not to be a foregone conclusion:

1. If the lease term is fairly long and the asset value is fairly high, the lessee may not in fact be able to borrow the funds necessary to acquire the leased asset at the end of the primary lease term.

2. If interest rates have changed dramatically so that the cost of borrowing has increased, the lessee may decide that it is not financially sound to borrow at the then-current interest rates merely to enjoy a residual value at the end of the stretch period.

3. Finally, the asset may have no commercial value to the lessee at the end
    of the stretch period, and the lessee will be in a position where it will
    have to arrange for disposition, rather than having the lessor do that.
    In some cases, ownership of the asset could be a liability if, for exam-
    ple, an owner is obligated to maintain a standard of repair, security,
    environmental clean-up, or similar obligation to incur an ongoing cost.
    This might be the case with aircraft, hazardous materials, etc.

In all of these cases the action of the lessee at the end of the primary
lease term cannot be determined with assurance at the inception of the lease.
On the other hand, if it is expected that the leased asset will have a significant residual value at the end of the stretch period and this is contemplated
at the inception of the lease, it would be difficult to argue that the lessee
would not ordinarily exercise the option to acquire the leased asset at the
end of the primary lease term. Under these circumstances, there is a strong
argument that the transaction should be treated as a purchase by the lessee
and a sale by the lessor, for income tax purposes.

What If the Lease is a Sale?

In the event that the lease is determined to be a sale under this or other terms
of a lease agreement, the lessor is taxable on the sale price under the agreement. This would be computed as the present value of the lease payments;
however, the lessor may be permitted to defer the profit on the sale by claiming a "reserve" under s. 20 of the *Income Tax Act*, S.C. 1970-71-72, c. 63.
The amount and calculation of such reserves change from time to time;
accordingly, these should be reviewed regularly. The lessor would then take
the interest element into income annually, as a payment on account of interest.
Any such deemed interest is deductible to the lessee, assuming the amount
is reasonable and incurred for business purposes. If the allocation of the rents
between selling price and interest is unreasonable, when, for example, the
objective is to have high interest and a low selling price, Revenue Canada
would probably treat a larger portion of the total payments as on account
of the sale and a smaller portion as on account of interest. The interest element would be that appropriate to the lessee's borrowing position for assets
of similar type under similar conditions.

This may well yield a higher interest rate than the lessor would incur
on its own borrowing and a higher interest rate than the lessee would pay
on normal borrowings, since the "lender" has access only to the leased asset
as security and the lease may well provide for 100% financing rather than
financing on a basis whereby the lessee has significant equity in the asset
being acquired.

In the event that the transaction is treated as a sale, the lessee claims
CCA on the "purchase." It should be noted that the current Bulletin
(IT-233R) indicates the total of the rents, is up to "fair market value," are

included as "cost," with the difference to be treated as interest. In any event, the lessor and the lessee have some opportunity to ensure that the allocation of the rents is on a basis that provides them with the maximum tax benefits. Presuming that the lessor and the lessee agree on the allocation and the amount allocated to interest is defensible under the circumstances, then it is not likely to be upset by Revenue Canada.

RENTAL CREDITS

Some lease agreements provide for an option price to the lessee with the price reduced by all or a portion of the rental paid. In general, the rental credits really reduce the option price to the expected fair market value. For income tax purposes this concept has been accepted in paragraph 13 of IT-233R, which provides that the actual cost rather than the cost plus rental credits is the basis for determining cost for income tax purposes. If this provides for the acquisition of the asset at less than fair market value, the "deemed cost" of the asset in accordance with s. 13(5.2) of the *Income Tax Act* may still be the fair market value. In this case, the difference between fair market value and the price actually paid is treated as capital cost allowance previously allowed to the taxpayer and is therefore subject to recapture.

SALE OF OPTIONS

In some circumstances the lessee may have an option to acquire property, but does not wish to exercise the option because of the deemed cost provisions referred to above or for other reasons. If the lessee elects to sell the option, the option price will be included in the taxpayer's income, less the cost of acquiring the option, if any, if the lessee had been entitled to deduct the rent in computing income.

REVISED LEASING REGULATIONS — APRIL 26, 1989

The leasing proposals announced by the Department of Finance on April 26, 1989 created significant uncertainties for lessors. Between that date and their final enactment in 1991 there were a number of important changes to the regulations which reduced the adverse impact on lessors. The leasing industry, through the Equipment Lessors' Association of Canada, worked diligently to place the problems before the Finance Department and was successful in obtaining a number of substantive revisions to the original proposal. Nevertheless, the reforms as enacted represent a major increase in complexity of the tax. They introduce a number of technical terms (specified leasing property, exempt property, prescribed property) and the amendments contained detailed, complex wording. The changes impose a significant information system and accounting requirement on lessors who must maintain information on the normal CCA basis for assets which do not qualify as "specified leasing property". In addition a separate class has to be maintained for each specified leasing property and calculations made under both the old and a new system.

It should be noted that, in this case, property refers to each individual item in a lease. For example if a lessor were providing a lease of furnishings for a hotel, each individual item of furniture — chair, chesterfield, bed, television receiver, radio receiver, and so on — would have its own CCA class. For each such property the lessor must maintain:

(a) the fair market value when the property became a "specified leasing property" (presumably this is normally the cost to the lessor);

(b) "prescribed interest rate" applicable to each such property (or a track of the floating rate where that was chosen);

(c) an amortization schedule to show the CCA calculation under the new rules on both an annual and cumulative basis;

(d) the CCA available under the "old" rules (without the half year convention if the lessor is a principal business corporation) on both an annual and a cumulative basis;

(e) the amount claimable in the year under the regulation and the amount actually claimed.

While it should not be difficult to allocate costs of a variety of assets acquired at one time and leased, the lessor must also allocate proceeds of sale to individual assets since a terminal loss would be claimable at the end of the lease or the CCA would be recaptured if the individual asset were disposed of for more than its undepreciated capital cost.

It is anticipated that Revenue Canada would not require a separate cost allowance schedule to be filed for each individual asset with the lessor's income tax return since, for a large leasing company, this could be an enormous list. Presumably the data can be filed in a summary form; however, the background information supporting the calculation will have to be retained for many years to support an audit by Revenue Canada or perhaps to amend an income tax return once filed.

Similarly most leasing companies will categorize their leased assets into four types:

I   Specified Leasing Property;
II Exempt Property;
III Prescribed Property (only needed at the inception of the lease for filing with the joint election of the lessee);
IV Other Property.

The capital cost allowance for specified leasing properties is subject to the new restrictions under the Act. All other property leased falls into the normal CCA classes and calculations.

Specified Leasing Property — CCA Calculation

The regulations are designed to split the payments on leases of specified leasing property into an interest element and a principal element. The calculation starts with the fair market value of the leasing property and computes interest at a "prescribed rate" (one percentage point higher than the long-term Canada bond rate for the last Wednesday of the second month prior to the lease date, for bonds with remaining maturity of over ten years). The rate is based on semi-annual compounding, not in advance.

The regulations provide that payments be applied first to interest on principal, second to unpaid interest and the remainder to principal. The CCA payable by the taxpayer in respect to the property is the lesser of:

(a) the principal payments on the synthetic loan; and

(b) the CCA which would have been deductible had the asset not been a specified leasing property.

In addition it should be noted that the calculation is on a cumulative basis for each property. Accordingly, in the year of acquisition, the CCA is limited to the lesser of the so-called principal payments referred to above and the CCA that would have been deductible had the property not been a "specified leasing property". In the next year, the amount of CCA claimable for the year is restricted to the lesser of the cumulative principal payments for the two years and the cumulative CCA otherwise claimable. For a principal business corporation, the cumulative calculation would not include the "half year convention" for CCA in the year of addition of an asset. The following example, based on a principal business corporation, will show the operation of this rather complex calculation.

Exhibit 7-1

The New Rules

Example

Showing CCA Restriction and Terminal Loss

Cost of property to Lessor	=	$1,000,000
Term of lease	=	60 months
Usual CCA rate	=	25%
Interest rate on debt	=	12%
Prescribed interest rate (per new rules)	=	10%
Rate in rents	=	14%
Rent	=	$23,000/month
Residual value at end of term	=	$23,122

Start rent on June 30, 1991. Apply all payments to debt. Assume a December 31 year-end for the lessor. Asset is sold for residual value in 1996.

Exhibit 7-1 (cont'd.)

Lessor Position

	Total	1991	1992	1993	1994	1995	1996
Rent	$1,380,000	$138,000	$276,000	$276,000	$276,000	$276,000	$138,000
Interest	318,829	58,024	100,984	78,788	53,777	25,593	1,663
CCA (See notes)	976,878	90,848	195,550	215,594	181,602	79,102	214,182
	1,295,707	148,872	296,534	294,382	235,379	104,695	215,845
Net income	$ 84,293	(10,872)	(20,534)	(18,382)	40,621	171,305	(77,845)

Data Required for CCA Calculation:

	Restricted CCA			Regular CCA	
Year	*Annual*	*Cumul.*		*Annual*	*Cumul.*
1991	$ 90,848	$ **90,848**		$250,000	**$250,000**
1992	195,550	**286,398**		187,500	**437,500**
1993	215,594	**501,992**		140,625	**578,125**
1994	237,692	**739,684**		105,469	**683,594**
1995	260,316	**1,000,000**		79,102	**762,696**
1996	0	**1,000,000**		59,326	**822,022**

Notes

1991: Restricted CCA is less than regular CCA, therefore claim restricted

1992: **Cumulative** restricted CCA is less than cumulative regular CCA, therefore claim restricted CCA

1993: (Same as 1992)

1994: Cumulative restricted CCA is greater than cumulative regular CCA, therefore claim the amount to bring the cumulative total up to the cumulative regular CCA ($683,594 – 501,992 = $181,602 to be claimed)

1995: Claim regular CCA

1996: Claim terminal loss

The above example shows the restriction of CCA in Year One under the new Regulations, with a continuing restriction in Year Two and Year Three. After that point of time the "Old Rules" CCA will apply until the year of termination, when, under the new rules a terminal loss is allowed on a property by property basis. The terminal loss of $214,182 is calculated by deducting the cumulative CCA ($762,696) from the original cost ($1 million) which gives you the undepreciated capital cost or UCC at the end of 1995. From this you deduct the residual value proceeds assumed to be received in 1996 of $23,122, giving undepreciated capital cost of $214,182, all of which is deductible in 1996 following termination of the lease.

A few points are of interest from this calculation. First, in the restricted

CCA you will note that the annual CCA increases each year. This is because it is essentially the principal payment of an amortized loan and the principal element of combined payments of principal and interest increase over the life of the loan. This is contrasted with regular CCA which is on a diminishing balance basis. Therefore, the CCA each year is declining. The new rules may well provide some companies with greater flexibility in balancing their taxable pool in the future since the new system would permit you to claim a large amount of CCA in say Year Four. For example by Year Four the cumulative CCA under the old system would have been $683,594. If on this asset no CCA had actually been claimed, then the claim for 1994 could have been as high as $683,594. Under the regular CCA system, if no CCA had been claimed on an asset the maximum claim in any one year would have been $250,000. In addition, of course, the new CCA system allows you to claim a terminal loss at the end of the lease. This was not available under the pre-April 26, 1989 basis. In fact it is instructive to look at the resulting tax position had the older system been used (the system prior to April 26, 1989) as opposed to the new system (the after April 26, 1989 system). From the perspective of the lessor, the comparison is as follows:

Exhibit 7-2

Taxable Income (loss)

Year	Prior to April 26/89	After April 26/89	New System More (Less) Favourable
1991	$(45,024)	$(10,872)	$(34,152)
1992	(43,734)	(20,534)	(23,200)
1993	33,149	(18,382)	51,531
1994	99,176	40,621	58,555
1995	158,122	171,305	(13,183)
1996	72,904	(77,845)	150,749
Taxable Income	274,593	$ 84,293	$190,300
Less: UCC Claimable over future years	190,300		
Eventual taxable income	$ 84,293		

On a cumulative basis the new system is less favourable in the first two years but more favourable on an annual or a cumulative basis thereafter and much more favourable by the end of the term. It should be noted that the calculation prior to April 26, 1989 required a half year CCA deduction in the first year. Accordingly the CCA used for that calculation is $125,000 rather than the $250,000 used in the "Regular CCA" calculation above. This is due to one of the changes in the regulations that permit a principal business corporation when using the new rules to avoid the "half year convention" in calculation of the cumulative CCA.

It should be noted that s. 1100(1.12) of the Income Tax Regulations provides that if the lessor acquired property for lease but the property was not leased by the end of the taxation year in which it was acquired, the CCA otherwise deductible is reduced to NIL.

A principal business corporation can elect to have all "exempt property" included in separate classes (therefore eligible for terminal loss) similar to the result above for the specified leasing property. Accordingly principal business corporations can, if they wish have a separate class for each leasing property which is either specified or exempt property. Furthermore if a principal business corporation wishes to have all property treated as "not exempt" the taxpayer may elect to have all of the property that is the subject of leases entered into it in those years deemed not to be exempt property. It should be noted that this provision permitting the taxpayer to substantially simplify the record keeping by keeping only one CCA calculation set for all leases entered into after the year of election, does not deem all property "specified leasing property". It merely deems it to be "not exempt property". This is an important distinction since it means that to have the new rules applied the property must still pass the test of being a "specified leasing property". Essentially that means that, at the time, the property must meet the following tests:

Specified Leasing Property

1. Depreciable property
2. Used mainly to produce rent or leasing revenue
3. Arm's length lease
4. Term of lease > 1 year
5. Property subject to the lease has an aggregate fair market value > $25,000

Does not include:

- Intangible property
- Certified films
- Certified productions
- Systems software
- Exempt property

What's Exempt Property?

The new Act provides a specific definition of exempt property which is *not* subject to the new CCA calculation. The definition is quite detailed; however, for our purposes we might summarize it as:

1. General purpose office furniture (Class 8)
2. Mobile office equipment
   • cellular telephones
   • pages
3. General purpose electronic data processing equipment (Class 10)
   • cost < $1,000,000
4. Ancillary data processing equipment (Class 10)
   • cost < $1,000,000
5. Equipment designed for residential use
   • furniture
   • appliances
   • television and radio receivers
   • etc.
6. Vehicles
   • passenger vehicles
   • vans
   • pick-up trucks
   • trucks or tractors designed for hauling freight on highways
   • highway trailers for the above
7. Buildings, parts of buildings or component parts
   • *other than* those leased to a person exempt from tax under s. 149 of the Act (which includes charities, non-profit organization, universities, etc.), a person who earns income which is exempt under the Act, or a Canadian government, municipality or other Canadian public authority *and* who previously owned the building!
8. A vessel mooring space
9. A railway car

After you have considered specified leasing property and exempt property and have noted that the principal business corporation can elect to have either separate class treatment for exempt property or all leased property deemed to be "not exempt", what is left over?

Essentially this list would include:

1. property which is not depreciable (such as land);
2. intangible property;
3. certified films and productions, for which special rules apply which are beyond the scope of this book;
4. systems software.

Leases of these kinds of properties are subject to the restrictions on rental properties (Income Tax Regulations, C.R.R. 1978, c. 945, reg. 1100(11)) and the general restriction for leasing properties (reg. 1100(15)) (other than for principal business corporations) which still exist in addition to the April 26, 1989 amendments.

With all of these restrictions the question may arise, if the CCA in an organization is restricted, as to which claims should be cut back? It used to be that you made sure that you claimed 100% of the CCA on the low CCA classes (buildings — 5% or 10% for example). This allowed you the more rapid write-off classes should your situation improve. Since the specified leasing property restrictions permit you to catch up in future years what you are unable to claim in early years, it may well be desirable to claim full CCA on all regular CCA classes, and less CCA on specified leasing properties. It will be interesting to see how this unfolds in practice.

LEASING AND THE GOODS AND SERVICES TAX

Introduction

Goods and Services Tax ("GST") legislation is part of the *Excise Tax Act*, R.S.C. 1985, c. E-15 and is new and quite complex. This summary is intended only to give a broad explanation. Reference should be made to the legislation if any action is to be taken concerning the GST.

The principal of the GST is to impose tax on all goods and services supplied unless specifically "exempt" or "zero-rated". Supplies are divided into three categories: taxable, zero-rated and exempt. Taxable supplies are subject to a tax rate of 7% on the total consideration for the supply. Taxable imports are charged GST on their duty-paid value at the time of importation. Zero-rated supplies include basic groceries, exports, prescription drugs, medical devices, etc. Exempt supplies include health services, educational services, financial services, etc.

The difference between a zero-rated supply and an exempt supply is that the GST paid on purchases made for the provision of a zero-rated supply or a taxable supply is recoverable by a business making the payments, whereas GST paid on purchases used in the provision of an exempt supply is not recoverable.

Input Tax Credit

An important feature of the GST is the input tax credit. The input tax credit enables the payer of the GST to recover up to 100% of the GST paid in respect of any purchases used to provide a taxable or zero-rated supply provided they are registered. Only purchases or expenses incurred in the provision of an exempt supply are not entitled to an input tax credit. However, some restrictions do apply with regards to certain expenses, i.e., employee benefits, automobiles, etc. Accordingly, a lessor will recover all GST via the input tax credit route.

Compliance Requirements

The GST requires most suppliers providing taxable supplies be registered and to submit GST returns on a regular basis. The actual GST to be remitted in a reporting period will be GST collected less input tax credit.

Operating vs. Capital Lease

GST is paid by the lessor (on equipment purchased) and charged to the lessee (on rent) on either an operating or capital lease. But there is a difference in the lessee's ability to recover input tax credit. The input tax credit claim by a lessee other than a financial institution for an operating lease is available based on the percentage of the leased asset's commercial use. In the case of leases capitalized in a CCA pool for income tax purposes, being most capital leases, 100% of the input tax credit is available provided the leased property is used over 50% for commercial purposes. However, the lessees will be denied any input tax credit when the commercial use drops to 50% or less.

Some problems may occur with leases which are capital leases for accounting and purchases for tax purposes. Property is defined for GST purposes as that on which CCA is claimed. On these transactions GST should likely be charged on the deemed purchase price by the lessor and *not* charged on the "rents". However for leases which are capitalized for accounting purposes only (not for tax), GST should presumably be charged in the same manner as for operating leases.

Real Property Leases

Most leases of real property are subject to GST. In the case of net leases, the GST is applicable not only on the net lease payment, but also on the "additional rent" and "percentage rent", if any. Lease of property for use as a residence to the same person for a period of a month or more is exempt from GST. While the lessee will not pay GST on the rent, the lessor/landlord will not be able to claim input tax credits on the expenses related to the residential lease.

As it is quite common for buildings to be used for both commercial and residential purposes, the GST legislation contains complex provisions which regulate the determination and recapture of input tax credits under such circumstances.

De-minimis Test for a Financial Institution

In general, registrants for the collection of GST who gross either more than 10% of their revenue or $10 million from interest, dividends or other financial services are defined as a "financial institution" for GST purposes. Financial institutions are required to allocate their input tax credit claim based on their percentage of use for commercial activities, whereas registrants who are not financial institutions may claim 100% of the GST paid on all eligible expenses used substantially for commercial activities. Hence, it is crucial for lessors to keep a close watch on their interest and dividend income to ensure that it does not jeopardize their claim for input tax credit.

Transitional Rules

The transitional provisions of the GST legislation provide "grandfathering" to certain leases that were entered into prior to 1991. Lease payments due or made before September 1990 are not subject to GST regardless of the period to which the payment relates. There will be no GST on all equipment operating leases entered into prior to August 8, 1989 until renewed or altered. Lease payments for automobile and equipment for use by medical practitioners, leased before 1991, will not be taxable until 1994. These grandfathered transactions are not "exempt" supplies; therefore, the lessor will be entitled to claim the ITC on the expenses incurred for the lease.

Chapter 8

What You Should Know About Your Lease

When evaluating a lease, one should review the terms of the lease as well as the rental payments and contrast these to the terms for an outright purchase. This analysis will require knowledge of the fair market value of the property at the inception of the lease as the starting point for a lease or buy decision. In addition, however, the following factors have to be considered in determining whether the lease or the purchase is the appropriate vehicle to acquire the right to use the asset.

LENGTH OF TERM/RENEWAL

If the term of the lease is for a period less than that during which the lessee expects to require the use of the asset, then the lessee would like to ensure that there are sufficient renewal terms in the lease to provide the option to continue having the use of the asset over the needed time. If the asset is purchased, the lessee will have exclusive benefit for as long as wished. The term and the amount of the rents are, of course, intertwined. If the lessee is paying nominal monthly rent when compared to the value of the asset and the rental rate is protected in the renewals, it may be sufficient to lease the asset rather than purchase it. However, if the lessee is expected to reimburse the lessor substantially for the full cost of the asset over the initial term of the lease, then the decision between lease and buy becomes germane.

PAYMENT FREQUENCY

Most leases provide for equal monthly payments. However, it may be desirable for lessees to arrange their lease payments to meet normal cash flow cycles. On the assumption that their credit rating is adequate, this is a point that can usually be negotiated with the lessor. For example, a lessee may wish to have payments made quarterly or to skip months of particularly low cash flow and increase payments in periods of high cash flow.

The lessor may request a number of months' advance rental or a security deposit to protect itself against late payments and to ensure that the leased asset is returned in reasonable condition. The practice of requiring advance rentals has varied from one month's rental for each year of lease to no prepaid rentals at all. Different businesses also have different practices. For example, in automobile leasing it is common to provide at least one month's advance rent. On high-value "luxury" cars this may increase to several months' rent aggregating several thousand dollars. The amount of the rent may well reduce the lessor's risk, but it also reduces the amount of funds that have to be paid out by the lessor at the point of acquisition of the asset, and this should be taken into account in the analysis of the cost of renting to the lessee. In addition, most leases provide for the rent to be payable in advance rather than in arrears. This not only ensures that the lessor has its rent for each particular rental period, but also provides a faster pay-back of investment and should likewise be taken into account when assessing the cost of leasing.

CONTINGENT RENTS, INSURANCE, AND OTHER COSTS PAYABLE BY THE LESSEE

Some leases will provide for a basic rent and additional rent which is a factor of the utility of the asset to the lessee or the use of the asset by the lessee. For example, in retail-space leases it is common to have a base rent plus a "percentage rent" which varies with the sales of the location. Other leases may provide for added rent with added use, as in some automobile leases. These additional rental amounts are usually referred to as "contingent rentals".

The lessee will be required to pay taxes incurred by the lessor (excluding income and capital taxes) as a result of the lease. This would usually include only sales tax or equivalent, except for leases of real property, when property tax may also be included.

Some leases call for the lessee to pay maintenance costs, to return the equipment in fully maintained condition at conclusion of the lease, and to carry out all work necessary to maintain the manufacturer's warranty.

The lessee is generally responsible for risk of loss or damage to the equipment during the lease and will be required to cover the risk with insurance, with the lessor as named insured. In the event of default or late payment, a variety of charges may be provided for in the lease. These are at high rates, to act as a deterrent.

PURCHASE OPTION/RESIDUAL VALUE

The lessee may have an option to acquire the asset at agreed prices during the term of the lease or at expiry. In some cases the lessor will also seek a "residual guarantee", that is, the lessee will guarantee the lessor a minimum resale value at termination of the lease or will recover the difference from the lessee.

Various option points during the lease will have, generally, a declining option price as the lease term progresses, reflecting both depreciation and obsolescence as well as the recovery by the lessor of its investment.

EARLY TERMINATION/BUYOUT

If the lessee terminates the lease prematurely, compensation to the lessor for unrecovered investment and profit will likely be required. If yields have declined, there may also be a "reinvestment fee" charged. Some leases provide for a sliding scale purchase price, whereby the termination cost or payout can be made at any time. In the early months, there will be a price set above fair value to act as a deterrent or penalty. In large leasing transactions where the lessor is counting on significant tax benefits, early payout might require the lessor to incur a large tax liability. If this has to be met out of high cost borrowings, the cost will be passed on to the lessee as an increased payout charge. In later months, the buyout price will reduce until at termination it equals the guaranteed residual. Except for these provisions, leases are generally not cancellable.

UPGRADE PRIVILEGE

Some lessors, particularly of computer equipment, permit automatic replacement of original equipment with improved equipment as manufacturers make it available. This provision, called an "upgrade", permits the lessee to have modern equipment of newest technology while also avoiding the necessity to dispose of the outdated equipment.

The lessor can frequently remarket the used equipment at a better price due to the broader market available through the lessor's contacts. As a result, the lessor provides the upgrade at a monthly or other rental which recognizes the fair value of the new equipment plus the unrecovered cost of the replaced equipment.

OWNERSHIP/CCA RIGHTS

There will be a specific clause confirming that ownership rests with the lessor. In some cases it will be agreed that the lessee will have the right to claim CCA. The lease will have been drafted as a capital lease, with provisions that transfer title at the conclusion of the lease (automatically or by exercise of a bargain purchase option). It is convenient if the lessor and lessee agree when the lessee will claim CCA and that the lessor will not treat the lease as an operating lease for income tax purposes. Conversely, the lessor may wish formal agreement with the lessee that the lessor will claim CCA and that the lessee will not attempt to do so. This is designed to ensure that both parties consider the lease, including residual guarantees and options, as an operating lease.

71

Assignment

If the lessee does *not* wish the lease to be assignable, this should be clear in the documentation. Otherwise the payments and credit data provided to the lessor may well find their way to a funder to the lessor. Therefore, data provided to the lessor may lose its confidentiality.

Leases will contain other clauses to reflect the particular needs of the agreement, to confirm receipt of the equipment in usable form, and so on. The lessee should look on the standard agreement provided by the lessor as a starting point in arriving at a "custom agreement" which meets its needs. Particular attention should be paid to:

- those clauses which incorporate the lessee's needs (payment timing and frequency, prepayments and deposits, purchase options, prepayment rights, upgrade rights, term of lease and renewal options, warranty);
- those clauses which protect the lessor's investment (maintenance, prepayment penalties, events of default and the rights and obligations in event of default, late payment charges, guaranteed residual value, return of property at termination, insurance coverage, location of equipment during lease).

Once the form of agreement has been reached in principle, the lessee should have the agreement reviewed by a lawyer, who should alert the lessee to legal matters that should be addressed prior to completing the agreement in final form. No agreement or letter of intent should be signed prior to completion of the review by the lawyer.

Most leases contain a clause that the "agreement shall constitute the sole and entire agreement. . . ." In some cases, lessees have "side letters" of agreement providing options or guaranteeing residual values to the lessor. Such letters are of dubious value as part of the lease and may well prejudice the tax treatment or accounting treatment of the lease. Moreover, if not reflected in the accounting and tax treatment, they can lead to unfavourable tax assessment and the potential charge of tax fraud if Revenue Canada considers that concealment of such agreements was to provide more favourable tax treatment to either the lessor or lessee.

Exhibit 8-1 shows two standard lease examples, reprinted with permission of Scott Computer Leasing Inc. and PB Leasing, a division of Pitney Bowes of Canada Ltd.

Exhibit 8-1

Standard Lease Examples

Equipment Lease

MASTER EQUIPMENT LEASE

LEASE NUMBER	CUSTOMER NUMBER

The undersigned SCOTT COMPUTER LEASING INC., an Ontario Corporation, with its principal offices at 6711 Mississauga Road,

Mississauga, Ontario L5N 2W3 (hereinafter called "Lessor")and _____

a corporation, with its principal offices at _____

_____ (hereinafter called "Lessee").

In consideration of the mutual promises and covenants herein, hereby agree as follows:

1. LEASE: Lessor hereby leases to Lessee and Lessee hereby leases from Lessor, the personal property (herein called "Equipment") described in the Master Equipment Lease Schedule(s) (herein called "Equipment Schedule") executed concurrently herewith or executed hereafter and made a part of this Master Equipment Lease (hereinafter called the "Agreement"). The parties may from time to time by mutual agreement lease other items of Equipment pursuant to this Agreement for such terms and at such rates as may be agreed, by execution of additional Equipment Schedule(s) covering such items and such Equipment Schedule(s) shall constitute part of this Agreement for all purposes as if the provisions thereof were set forth at length herein.

Each Equipment Schedule, as and when executed, shall form a separate agreement of lease, and shall stand, subject to the supremacy of terms and conditions of this Agreement, as a separate and independent contract and agreement between the Lessor and the Lessee.

It is acknowledged and agreed that the agreement of lease hereunder shall be commenced by the Lessee sourcing and selecting the equipment to be leased hereunder, and providing to the Lessor an Authorization and Indemnity Agreement in connection therewith, pursuant to which the Lessor will issue the appropriate purchase order and complete the necessary arrangements so as to provide for acquisition of the said equipment (subject to the provisions of this Agreement and the Authorization and Indemnity Agreement) forthwith upon completion of delivery and installation of the equipment and acceptance by the Lessee, the Lessee will sign and deliver an Acceptance Certificate which will authorize payment upon delivery of suppliers invoice(s), Lessee shall permit acquisition of the equipment from time to time, the Lessor may thereafter execute and complete the Equipment Schedule(s), as described herein, the Equipment Schedule(s) to be completed by notation by Lessor, and upon such completion, the Lease Agreement hereunder to have commenced for the specified equipment.

2. RENTAL TERM: The term of the lease of the Equipment covered by each Equipment Schedule hereunder shall commence on the effective date specified in the Equipment Schedule describing such Equipment regardless of the date of actual delivery from the Supplier to the Lessee or regardless of the date of acceptance and shall continue until the last day of the calendar month which is the last of the number of whole calendar months specified on the Equipment Schedule. From the expiry date provided in the Equipment Schedule, the within Agreement shall continue, on a month-to-month basis unless terminated as hereinafter provided, the Equipment Schedule may be terminated by either party at the end of the rental term or at the end of any calendar month thereafter upon one-hundred and twenty (120) days prior written notice by either party hereto to the other. The Equipment Schedule shall not be terminated or cancelled for any reason during the rental term, other than termination or cancellation by the Lessor upon default, as herein provided.

3. MONTHLY RENTAL: Monthly rental payable for the Equipment described in each Equipment Schedule shall be the amount set forth in such Equipment Schedule and shall be payable in advance on the first day of each month during the rental term. All rental payments must be received by Lessor on the due date at the address specified above or at such other address as Lessor or its assignee, if any, may specify in writing to Lessee. Subject to the rights and remedies of the Lessor, as provided herein and at law, if Lessee fails to pay any rental or additional charges when due, Lessee agrees to pay a delinquency charge (which compensates for administrative costs and is not a penalty) of 5 per cent of the total amount past due.

4. TAXES: There shall be added to the monthly rental, and Lessee shall pay all taxes, assessments, and other governmental charges, howsoever designated, levied, assessed or based upon such rentals or upon this Agreement or the Equipment, its use (including provincial and local privilege or excise taxes based upon gross revenue), and all taxes or amounts in lieu thereof paid or payable by the Lessor in respect to the foregoing, exclusive, however, of taxes based upon the net income of the Lessor arising under this Agreement. Lessee specifically agrees to pay such additional charges at the same time as the monthly rental provided, however, taxes assessed on an annual or semi-annual basis, such as personal property taxes, shall be paid upon request of Lessor. Lessee further agrees to promptly file all reports and returns, including, but not limited to, any applications for exemption, if applicable, associated with Lessee's obligations under this Agreement required by any governmental authority.

5. MAINTENANCE: Lessee shall enter into a maintenance agreement with the manufacturer of the Equipment. Lessee will, during the term of each Equipment Schedule, keep or cause to be kept, the Equipment in good working order in accordance with the provisions of manufacturer's maintenance agreement and shall make any necessary repairs, adjustments and perform any maintenance for such purposes. Lessee shall allow the manufacturer reasonable access to the Equipment to effect such repairs and to perform such maintenance, preventative or otherwise, as may be necessary. Notwithstanding such maintenance agreement. Lessee specifically acknowledges that the repair and maintenance of the Equipment is Lessee's sole responsibility. All repairs or replacements shall be deemed accessions to the Equipment and shall enure to the benefit of Lessor hereunder. Lessee agrees to comply with any instructions specified by the manufacturer with reference to the installation of the Equipment, including, but not limited to, Lessee's providing suitable electric current to operate the Equipment and providing a suitable place of installation within the manufacturer's specifications, at all times meeting the minimum standards of insurance Underwriters for the protection of electronic computer systems. All other supplies consumed or required for the operations of the Equipment shall be obtained or furnished by Lessee at Lessee's expense.

6. EQUIPMENT TO REMAIN PERSONAL PROPERTY: The Equipment shall be and remain personal property, notwithstanding the manner in which it may be attached or affixed to any real estate and upon termination of the Equipment Schedule, the Lessee shall have the duty and the Lessor shall have the right to remove the Equipment from the Lessee's premises where the same shall be located, whether or not affixed or attached to the realty or any building at the sole cost and expense of the Lessee. Title to the Equipment shall at all times remain with the Lessor, and Lessee, at the request of Lessor shall take such steps as the Lessor may reasonably request to disclose and maintain its ownership interest therein. Lessee shall keep the Equipment free and clear of all claims, liens, levies, attachments and other legal processes of whatsoever nature which may arise in favour of the creditors of Lessee. During the term of the Equipment Schedule, the Equipment shall be located at the Lessee's address shown above unless otherwise agreed to in writing by the Lessor, the Lessee shall provide to the Lessor, at the request of the Lessor, an acknowledgement of the Landlord of any address to which the equipment shall be delivered or affixed, acknowledging that title shall remain with the Lessee, and that the Lessee, and the Lessor upon realization pursuant to this lease, shall have the right to remove such equipment from the premises, without interference by the Landlord.

7. RISK OF LOSS: During the term of all Equipment Schedules, Lessee shall be solely responsible for loss or damage to the Equipment resulting from any and all causes, including, but not limited to fire, lightning, sprinkler leakage, tornado and windstorm, explosion, smoke and smudge, aircraft and motor vehicle damage, strikes, riots, civil commotion, burglary, and theft. In order to protect Lessor's interest, Lessee agrees that commencing on the day of its delivery to the Lessee and continuing thereafter during the term of the Equipment Schedule, the Equipment shall at all times be at the Lessee's risk and at the Lessee's sole expense shall be covered and insured by an all risk insurance policy to the full insurable value of the Equipment. Lessee further agrees to cause the insurer, who shall be acceptable to Lessor, to name Lessor and any assignee designated by Lessor as additional named insureds and/or loss payees. Lessee shall furnish a certificate of insurance from the insurer as evidence of compliance with this paragraph. Lessee shall further cause the insurer to give Lessor, its assigns and/or mortgagees thirty (30) days advance notice of any cancelation of the insurance coverages. In the event there is a lapse of insurance coverage, or in the event Lessee fails to provide the coverage set forth above, Lessor shall have the right to procure such insurance coverages which, in its sole discretion, it may deem appropriate and Lessee agrees to immediately reimburse Lessor upon notification by Lessor of the costs thereof. Any damage to the Equipment shall not abate the monthly rental or other payments due or to become due under this Agreement. If the Equipment, or any part thereof, is damaged by any cause, Lessee shall promptly cause such damage to be repaired at its expense returning the Equipment, or any part thereof which may be damaged to its previous condition. If the Equipment, or any part thereof which may be damaged, cannot be repaired, or is lost or destroyed, Lessee shall promptly replace such equipment, or any part thereof, with similar equipment by the same manufacturer, whether new or used, acceptable to Lessor.

8. ALTERATIONS AND ATTACHMENTS: No alterations, attachments or additions to the Equipment may be made without the prior written approval of Lessor. When such approval is obtained for alterations, attachments or additions the expense of effecting said alterations, attachments or additions shall be at the sole cost of the Lessee. All alterations, attachments or additions to the Equipment shall be the property of the Lessor and shall be deemed incorporated in the Equipment and subject to the terms of this Agreement and the applicable Equipment Schedule, unless otherwise agreed in writing by Lessor.

9. TRANSPORTATION AND INSTALLATION EXPENSES: All charges for the transportation, drayage, unpacking and rigging of the Equipment, to Lessee's premises, shall be paid by Lessee. Charges for the discontinuance, packing, transportation, drayage and rigging of the Equipment at the expiration or termination of the Equipment Schedule shall be borne by Lessee to a terminal in Mississauga, Ontario designated by Lessor. Unless otherwise specified in the Equipment Schedule, Lessee shall be responsible for all equipment installation charges.

10. DISCLAIMER OF LIABILITY:

Selection - Lessee acknowledges, represents and warrants that it has made the selection of the Equipment based on its own judgment and expressly disclaims any reliance upon statements made by the Lessor. Lessee authorizes Lessor to insert in each Equipment Schedule the serial number and other identifying data of the Equipment.

Warranty and Disclaimer of Warranties - Lessor warrants to Lessee that, so long as Lessee shall not be in default of any of the provisions of the applicable Equipment Schedule, neither owner, Lessor, nor any assignee or secured party of Lessor will disturb Lessee's quiet and peaceful possession of the Equipment and Lessee's unrestricted use thereof for its intended purpose. Lessor makes no other warranty, express or implied, as to any matter whatsoever, including, without limitation, the design or condition of the equipment, its merchantability or its fitness or capacity or durability for any particular purpose. The quality of the material or workmanship of the equipment or conformity of the equipment to the provisions and specifications of any purchase order or orders relating hereto and, as to Lessor, Lessee leases the equipment "as is". Lessor shall not be liable, to any extent whatever, for the selection, quality, condition, merchantability, suitability, fitness, operation or performance of the Equipment. Without limiting the generality of the foregoing, Lessor shall not be liable to Lessee for any liability, claim, loss, damage or expense of any kind or nature (including strict liability in tort) caused, directly or indirectly, by the Equipment or any inadequacy thereof for any purpose, or any deficiency or defect therein, or the use or maintenance thereof, or any repairs, servicing or adjustments thereto; or any delay in providing or failure to provide any part thereof, or any interruption or loss of service or use thereof, or any loss of business, or any damage whatsoever and howsoever caused except for any such loss or damage caused by wilful misconduct of Lessor, or its agents and representatives. Lessor hereby appoints Lessee as Lessor's agent to assert, during the term of the applicable Equipment Schedule, any right Lessor may have to enforce the manufacturer's warranties, if any, provided, however, that Lessee shall indemnify and hold Lessor or its assignee harmless from and against any and all claims, costs, expenses, damages, loses and liabilities incurred or suffered by Lessor as a result of or incident to any action by Lessee in connection therewith.

11. ASSIGNMENTS AND SECURITY INTERESTS: Lessee acknowledges that Lessor might pledge the Equipment and grant a security interest therein so long as such security interest shall not interfere with the right of Lessee hereunder and as long as Lessee shall not be in default hereunder. The Lessee agrees that Lessor's grant of the security interest in the Equipment, or the assignment of any Equipment Schedule, shall not be construed to be an assumption by the secured party or the assignee of Lessor's obligations under this Agreement. Lessee agrees that upon notice by any assignee or secured party, Lessee shall begin making payments under the Equipment Schedule directly to the secured party or assignee, or such other persons as they shall direct. It is specifically acknowledged that a direction by the Lessor to the Lessee, or by a secured party or an assignee, to begin making payments directly to the secured party or assignee, shall not constitute an assumption by the secured party or the assignee of the Lessor's obligations under this Agreement. It is hereby agreed by Lessor that Lessee shall be entitled to rely upon notice from the secured party or assignee of Lessor's default as being conclusive evidence of such default without the necessity of contacting Lessor, and Lessee may begin making payments in accordance with the foregoing without further notice to Lessor.

12. QUIET POSSESSION: Lessor agrees that so long as Lessee is not in default under the terms of the Equipment Schedule, Lessee shall and may quietly and peaceably have, hold, enjoy and possess the Equipment subject to and in accordance with the provisions of this Agreement and Equipment Schedule.

13. DEFAULT: Lessee acknowledges that Lessor has or will have purchased the Equipment at the specific request of Lessee for the purpose of this Agreement and that rent hereunder and loss to Lessor in the event of default is dependent upon the cost of the Equipment to Lessor, the term of the lease of each item of Equipment and the return, if any, expected by Lessor from the sale of the Equipment at the end of the original lease term. If (i) Lessee shall fail to make any rent payment within 5 days after such payment has not been made when due; if (ii) Lessee shall fail to make any other payment or perform or observe any other covenant, condition or agreement to be performed or observed by it hereunder and such failure shall continue unremedied for a period of 15 days after written notice thereof by Lessor provided that, the period of time hereunder, shall be the lesser of the period of fifteen (15) days noted and such lesser period of time as shall be provided for rectification prior to such default jeopardizing cost or continued existence of any warranty by any manufacturer or supplier of the Equipment or any insurance in relation to the Equipment; or (iii) any representation or warranty made by Lessee herein or in any document or certificate furnished Lessor in connection herewith or pursuant hereto shall prove to be incorrect at any time in any material respect; or (iv) Lessee shall become insolvent or bankrupt or make an assignment for the benefit of creditors or consent to the appointment of a trustee or receiver; or a trustee or a receiver shall be appointed for Lessee or for a substantial part of its property without its consent and shall not be dismissed within a period of 15 days, or bankruptcy, reorganization or insolvency proceedings shall be instituted by or against Lessee and, if instituted against Lessee, shall not be dismissed within a period of 15 days, then, upon the occurrence of any such event, Lessor may at its option declare this Agreement to be in default and may do one or more of the following:

(a) terminate this Agreement and Lessee's right to possession of the Equipment and enter upon the premises where such Equipment is located without demand or notice, and without court order or other process of law, and take immediate possession thereof, whether it is affixed to the realty or not, and remove such Equipment, without liability to Lessor for or by reason of such entry or taking of possession, whether for damage to property caused by such taking or otherwise;

(b) sell or sub-lease the Equipment at public or private sale or sub-lease as Lessor in its sole discretion may determine without notice to Lessee or advertisement; and

(c) demand and recover as damages the present value of the aggregate of all unpaid amounts payable hereunder as rental to the expiration of the term of the lease of the Equipment (calculated by discounting such amounts at a rate of 6% per annum) together with all additional rental and other amounts due hereunder to Lessor, and Lessee agrees that such amounts are a genuine pre-estimate of the damages that would be suffered by Lessor and are liquidated damages and not a penalty.

Lessee shall be liable for any and all unpaid additional rent due hereunder before, after or during the exercise of any of the foregoing remedies and for all legal fees and other costs and expenses of any nature whatsoever incurred by reason of the occurrence of any event of default or the exercise of Lessor's remedies in respect thereof, including all costs and expenses incurred in connections with the placing of such Equipment in the condition required by Clause 17. The sale by Lessor of any Equipment as aforesaid shall terminate the lease of the sold Equipment, but no entry, possession, sub-lease or sale of any Equipment or any repudiation shall otherwise terminate the lease of any Equipment or terminate this Agreement or prejudice the right of Lessor to recover damages as aforesaid or otherwise affect its rights and remedies hereunder. Except as otherwise expressly provided above, no remedy referred to in this Clause is intended to be exclusive, but each shall be cumulative and in addition to any other remedy referred to above or otherwise available to Lessor at law or in equity. The obligations of Lessee under this Clause shall survive any termination of this Agreement.

14. RIGHT OF INSPECTION. Lessee shall permit persons designated by Lessor to examine the Equipment from time to time during the Lessee's regular business hours. Lessee will immediately notify Lessor of any occurrence affecting the proper operation of the Equipment. Lessee agrees to co-operate with Lessor, its assigns or any secured party, including any insurer, in providing the names and addresses of any persons injured, witnesses and owners of property damaged, and such other information as may be known to Lessee or its employees and SHALL PROMPTLY ADVISE Lessor of all correspondence, paper, notices and documents whatsoever received by Lessee in connection with any claim or demand involving or relating to the improper manufacture, operation or functioning of the Equipment or any part thereof charging Lessor with any liability and shall aid in the investigation and defense of all such claims and aid in the recovery of any damages to the Equipment from third persons who may be liable therefor.

15. ASSIGNMENT: This Agreement and all Equipment Schedules shall be binding upon and enure to the benefit of the parties hereto and their respective successors and permitted assigns. Lessee, however, may not assign any interest in this Agreement or any Equipment Schedule, or sublet the Equipment or any part thereof, without first having secured the prior written consent of Lessor, its successors or assigns. Lessee acknowledges that the terms and conditions of this Agreement and the Equipment Schedules to be executed in connection therewith have been fixed in anticipation of the possible assignment or assignments of all or a portion of Lessor's rights under each Equipment Lease and Lessor's granting of a security interest in the Equipment, or any part thereof, to secure such assignment.

16. NOTICES: Any notices of demand required or permitted by law or any provisions of this Agreement or any Equipment Schedule shall be in writing and shall be deemed to have been delivered by depositing same in the Canadian mail addressed to the party concerned at the address set forth above, or at such other address as Lessor or Lessee may designate in writing hereafter.

17. SURRENDER OF EQUIPMENT: Upon termination of the Equipment Schedule, Lessee will surrender possession of the Equipment to Lessor in the same condition as when taken, ordinary wear and tear expected, at such place in Mississauga, Ontario as Lessor may reasonably direct and any cost of removal incurred by Lessor and all transportation charges shall be paid by Lessee.

18. MISCELLANEOUS:

A. The parties hereto agree that this Agreement and each Equipment Schedule shall be governed by the laws of the Province of Ontario. If any portion or provision shall be deemed to be unenforceable such unenforceability shall not affect the remaining terms and provisions hereof.

B. All of the covenants, agreements, provisions and conditions of this Agreement and Equipment Schedules shall enure to the benefit of and be binding upon the parties hereto and to their successors, legal representatives, and permitted assigns.

C. Each party represents to the other that this Agreement and all Equipment Schedules have been authorized by all necessary corporate, partnership or other necessary action and each has the full power and authority to enter into and perform the terms thereof.

D. This Agreement and any Equipment Schedule and any attached schedule, rider, or addenda thereto shall constitute the sole and entire agreement between the parties regarding the subject matter thereto. Neither this Agreement nor any Equipment Schedule may be altered, modified, terminated or discharged except in writing signed by the party against whom such alteration, modification, termination or discharge is sought.

E. Lessee hereby agrees to furnish such other documentation as may be reasonably required by Lessor, including, but not limited to, certificate of status, corporate resolutions, opinions of counsel, financial statements and the like, in such form as may be reasonably acceptable to Lessor. The parties hereto agree that information contained in this Agreement and all Equipment Schedules is confidential and may not be disclosed by any party except for purposes of enforcement of this Agreement and any Equipment Schedules or as may be required by law or as may be reasonably required by the Lessor for purposes of undertaking financing arrangements with any secured party or assignee.

F. No omission or delay, by Lessor at any time to enforce any right or remedy reserved to it, or to require the performance of any of the terms, covenants or provisions hereof by Lessee at any time designated, shall be a waiver of any such right or remedy to which Lessor is entitled, nor shall it in any way affect the right of Lessor to enforce such provisions thereafter.

19. SPECIAL PROVISIONS AND DELETIONS:

IN WITNESS WHEREOF, the parties have caused this Agreement to be executed on _____ , 19 ____
by duly authorized representatives.

SCOTT COMPUTER LEASING INC., (Lessor)   _____ (Lessee)

                                              _____

                                              _____

BY: _____   BY : _____

TITLE: _____   TITLE: _____

ACCEPTANCE CERTIFICATE

LEASE NUMBER _____

CUSTOMER NUMBER _____

SCHEDULE NUMBER _____

Equipment Supplier _____

Invoice Number(s) _____ _____

_____ _____

_____ _____

EQUIPMENT

LOCATION	QUANTITY	MAKE /MODEL & DESCRIPTION	SERIAL NUMBER	COST

The undersigned hereby authorizes Scott Computer Leasing Inc., to purchase and pay for the above described equipment and agrees to lease said equipment subject to the terms and conditions set forth in that certain Master Equipment Lease, Lease No. _____ entered into between Lessor and Lessee as of the _____ day of _____, 19_____ and pursuant to the terms and conditions of the Authorization and Indemnity Agreement entered into between the Lessor and the Lessee as of the _____ day of_____, 19_____. It is specifically acknowledged and agreed that pursuant to the provisions of the Master Equipment Lease and the Authorization and Indemnity Agreement, that Lessor may, at such time as it shall determine, following delivery of the within Acceptance Certificate, complete payment of the invoice numbers noted above. It is acknowledged that the Authorization and Indemnity Agreement shall govern the relationship of the undersigned and Lessor in relation to the Equipment until such time as the relevant Schedule to the Master Equipment Lease has been completed by Lessor. The undersigned declares that the Installation Date as provided for in paragraph 4 of the Authorization and Indemnity Agreement is _____, 19_____.

THE UNDERSIGNED CONFIRMS THAT SCOTT COMPUTER LEASING INC., HAS MADE NO WARRANTY OR REPRESENTATION, EXPRESS OR IMPLIED, OF MERCHANTABILITY, FITNESS, DESIGN, CONDITION, WORKMANSHIP OR OTHERWISE OF THE EQUIPMENT. THE UNDERSIGNED ACCEPTS SUCH EQUIPMENT AS IS AND WHERE IS. IT IS SPECIFICALLY ACKNOWLEDGED AND AGREED THAT THE TERMS AND CONDITIONS WITH REGARD TO THE EXCLUSION OF LIABILITY AND THE ACCEPTANCE OF THE EQUIPMENT BY THE UNDERSIGNED AS SET OUT IN THE MASTER EQUIPMENT LEASE IS HEREBY INCORPORATED AND ACKNOWLEDGED IN FULL.

The undersigned acknowledges that it shall be solely responsible for loss or damage to the Equipment resulting from any and all causes.

Agreed to this _____ day of _____ 19_____.

Company _____

By _____

Title _____

LOCATION	QTY	MAKE/MODEL & DESCRIPTION	SERIAL NUMBER

MASTER EQUIPMENT LEASE SCHEDULE

LESSEE: _____ (herein called "Lessee")

          _____

SCHEDULE NUMBER _____

LEASE NUMBER _____

CUSTOMER NUMBER _____

LESSOR: SCOTT COMPUTER LEASING INC. (herein called "Lessor")

          6711 Mississauga Road, Suite 702, Mississauga, Ontario L5N 2W3

1. Lessor hereby leases to Lessee, the Equipment hereinafter described, in consideration of the rental and for the term hereinafter set forth, the whole pursuant to and subject to the terms and conditions set forth in that certain Master Equipment Lease, Lease No. _____ entered into between Lessor and Lessee as of the _____ day of _____ , 19 _____

2. Rental Payments in advance will be made monthly at the rate shown below starting with a payment due on the Effective Date shown below and payments thereafter on the 1st day of each month during the term hereof.

Effective Date shall be: _____

Expiry Date: _____

Term: _____

Monthly Rental: _____

3. Special Provision(s):

4.

EQUIPMENT

LOCATION	QTY	MAKE/MODEL & DESCRIPTION	SERIAL NUMBER

5. The within Schedule constitutes an agreement to lease in accordance with, and subject to, the provisions of the Master Equipment Lease Agreement. The within Schedule shall constitute a separate and independent agreement to lease, subject to the application of the terms and conditions of the Master Equipment Lease Agreement. The terms and conditions of the Master Equipment Lease Agreement shall govern the relationship, and the agreement of lease, as between the Lessor and the Lessee, other than as modified by the specified terms and conditions herein set forth.

In WITNESS WHEREOF, the parties have caused this agreement to be executed on this _____ day of _____ , 19 _____

SCOTT COMPUTER LEASING INC. (LESSOR)

_____ (LESSEE)

_____
Authorized Signature

_____
Authorized Signature

Title: _____

Title: _____

79

Pitney Bowes Leasing

A Division of Pitney Bowes of Canada Ltd.
Suite 200, The Promontory I, 2695 North Sheridan Way, Mississauga, Ontario, L5K 2N7

MASTER EQUIPMENT LEASE

LEASE NO. _____

LESSOR: PITNEY BOWES LEASING
    A Division of Pitney Bowes of Canada Ltd.   (herein called "Lessor")

LESSEE: ....(herein called "Lessee")

ADDRESS: ....

1. LEASE. Lessor hereby leases to Lessee and Lessee hereby leases from Lessor, the personal property (herein called "Equipment") described in the Schedule(s) executed concurrently herewith or executed hereafter and made a part of this Master Equipment Lease (hereinafter called the "Agreement"). The parties may from time to time by mutual agreement lease other items of Equipment pursuant to this Agreement for such terms and at such rates as may be agreed, by execution of additional Schedule(s) covering such items and such Schedule(s) shall constitute part of this Agreement for all purposes as if the provisions thereof were set forth at length herein.

2. TERM. The term of the lease of the Equipment covered by each Schedule hereunder shall commence on the Effective Date specified in the Schedule describing such Equipment regardless of the date of actual delivery by the Supplier to Lessee or regardless of the date of acceptance, and shall continue for the period specified in such Schedule.

3. RENT. The monthly rent payable for the Equipment described in each Schedule shall be the amount set forth in such Schedule and shall be payable on the dates specified therein to Lessor at the above address or as otherwise specified in such Schedule. Unless otherwise specified in such Schedule, rent shall be payable monthly in advance.

4. WARRANTIES. There are no representations, conditions or warranties, express or implied, statutory or otherwise, with respect to the Equipment or this Agreement or affecting the rights of the parties hereto other than as specifically contained herein, and without limiting the generality of the foregoing, Lessor shall not be deemed to make, now or hereafter at any time, any representation or warranty, express or implied, as to the quality of the material or workmanship of the Equipment or the conformity of the Equipment to the provisions and specifications of any lease hereunder or to any purchase order or orders relating to the Equipment, or to the condition, design and merchantability, durability, operation or fitness for use or for any particular purpose of any Equipment or the freedom thereof from liens, encumbrances or rights of others, or any other representation or warranty whatsoever, express or implied, with respect to any Equipment except as provided herein. Lessor nevertheless agrees to assign or otherwise make available to Lessee such rights as Lessor may have under any warranty with respect to any Equipment made by any manufacturer, vendor or supplier thereof.

5. TAXES. Lessee agrees to comply with all laws, regulations and orders relating to this Agreement and the Equipment and to pay when due, all license fees, assessments and sales, use, property, excise and other taxes, levies, fees, duties, charges or withholdings of any nature now or hereafter imposed by any federal, provincial or municipal or local taxing authority upon this Agreement or any Equipment, or the purchase, installation, shipment, ownership, delivery, leasing, possession, use, operation and return or other disposition thereof. Lessee shall assume the risk of liability arising from or pertaining to the possession, operation or use of such Equipment. Lessee does hereby agree to indemnify, hold safe and harmless from and against and covenants to defend Lessor against any and all claims, costs, expenses, damages and liabilities, arising from or pertaining to the purchase, installation, ownership, delivery, shipment, leasing, possession, use, operation and return or other disposition of such Equipment. Any fees, taxes or other lawful charges paid by Lessor upon failure of Lessee to make such payments, shall at Lessor's option become immediately due from Lessee to Lessor. The indemnities contained in this clause shall survive the termination of this Agreement.

6. DELIVERY. Delivery of each item of Equipment shall be made pursuant to the provisions of the Schedule applicable to such item. Lessee acknowledges that each item of Equipment listed or otherwise described in each Schedule hereto has been or will have been selected by the Lessee prior to the execution by the Lessee of the applicable Schedule and that Lessee at its expense shall be responsible for all necessary inspections and tests of each item of Equipment to determine if such item is in compliance with the requirements of Lessee. The provisions of the clauses hereof entitled "Lessee's Obligations Unconditional" and "Warranties" shall apply if upon delivery of any such item it is not in compliance with the requirements of Lessee or is unsatisfactory for any other reason.

7. USE. Lessee will permit the Equipment to be operated only by competent and duly qualified personnel in accordance with applicable manufacturer's manuals and instructions and in accordance with applicable governmental regulations, if any. Lessee will use the Equipment for business purposes only and, unless specifically permitted to do so in the applicable Schedule, will not change the location of any item of Equipment from the place or places specified in such Schedule without the prior written consent of Lessor. Lessee shall have quiet possession of the Equipment and shall have unlimited use of the Equipment without extra charge for such use, but Lessee shall be solely responsible for the operation and control of the Equipment and any applicable programs.

8. LIENS, ENCUMBRANCES AND RIGHTS OF OTHERS. Lessee will not directly or indirectly create, incur, assume or suffer to exist any mortgage, pledge, lien, attachment, charge, encumbrance or any other rights of others whatsoever on or with respect to any Equipment, title thereto or any interest therein or permit its assets to vest in or be subject to the rights of any trustee or receiver or become insolvent or bankrupt.

9. INDEMNITY. Lessee does hereby assume liability for, and does hereby agree to indemnify, protect, save and keep harmless Lessor and its agents and servants, officers and directors, from and against any and all liabilities, obligations, losses, damages, penalties, claims, actions, suits, costs, expenses and disbursements, including legal expenses, of whatsoever kind and nature, imposed or assumed by, incurred by or asserted against Lessor in any way relating to or arising out of the manufacture, order, acceptance or rejection, purchase, ownership, delivery, lease, possession, use, importation, installation, condition, sale, return or other disposition of the Equipment (including, without limitation, any costs or expenses incurred by Lessor in the acquisition by Lessor of any Equipment which are in excess of or not included in the acquisition cost indicated in the Schedule applicable to such Equipment, any claim relating to any latent and other defects, whether or not discoverable by Lessee, any claim in tort for strict liability and any claim for patent, trademark, design or copyright infringement). Lessee agrees to give Lessor prompt notice of any claim or liability hereby indemnified against. This clause shall be effective and in full force and effect from the date of the execution of this Agreement even though the rental term of any Equipment under this Agreement has not yet commenced. The indemnities contained in this clause shall continue in full force and effect notwithstanding the expiration or other termination of this Agreement and shall be payable on demand.

10. ASSIGNMENT BY LESSEE AND LESSOR. Without the prior written consent of Lessor, Lessee will not assign any of its rights hereunder or sublet any Equipment or permit any Equipment to be in the possession of anyone but Lessee. Lessor may at any time without notice to Lessee, but subject to the rights of Lessee hereunder, transfer or assign this Agreement or any Equipment or any rent or other moneys and benefits due or to become due hereunder.

11. IDENTIFICATION. No right, title or interest in the Equipment shall pass to Lessee other than, conditioned upon Lessee's compliance with and fulfilment of the terms and conditions of this Agreement, the right to maintain possession of and use the Equipment for the full lease term. Lessor may require plates or markings to be affixed to or placed on the Equipment indicating Lessor is the owner.

12. NOT PART OF REALTY. It is agreed that the Equipment shall be and at all times remain personal property, and that the Equipment shall not be located on any land subject to mortgage or any land owned other than by Lessee without the consent and waiver of the mortgagee or owner in form satisfactory to Lessor. Without limiting the generality of the provisions of the clause hereof entitled "Loss and Destruction" and the clause hereof entitled "Liens, Encumbrances and Rights of Others" (i) Lessee agrees to take such action (including the obtaining and registration of waivers) at its own expense as may be reasonably necessary to prevent any third party from acquiring any right to or interest in any Equipment by virtue of such Equipment being deemed to be real or immoveable property or a part of any real or immoveable property or a fixture and (ii) if at any time any person shall claim any right or interest referred to in clause (i) above, Lessee shall at its own expense cause such claim to be waived in writing or otherwise eliminated to Lessor's satisfaction within 15 days after such claim shall have first become known to Lessee.

13. DEFAULT. Any of the following shall each constitute an "event of default": (i) the failure of Lessee to pay any instalment of the rental payment or any other sum due under the terms of this Agreement; (ii) the breach of any covenant or condition contained in this Agreement; (iii) the subjection of the Equipment to any lien, levy, privilege, seizure or attachment; (iv) any assignment by Lessee for the benefit of creditors; (v) the admission of Lessee in writing of its inability to pay its debts generally as they become due; (vi) the appointment of a receiver, trustee or similar official for Lessee or for any of its property; (vii) the filing by or against Lessee of a petition in bankruptcy or a petition for the reorganization or liquidation of Lessee under any Federal or Provincial laws; (viii) any other act of bankruptcy by Lessee.

Upon the occurrence of any event of default, Lessor shall be entitled at its option, exercisable by written notice to Lessee, to declare Lessee to be in default, whereupon Lessee shall be obliged to return the Equipment to Lessor and shall also be liable to Lessor for the payment of liquidated damages, which shall be calculated as follows: (i) by calculating the entire amount of the then unpaid rental payments for the remainder of the term of the lease of the Equipment, each such rental payment to be subject to a discount equal to interest at the rate of 5% per annum on each rental payment calculated and compounded monthly over the period commencing on the date of the aforesaid notice and ending on the date on which such rental payment would have bcome due and payable under the terms of the lease of the Equipment; and (ii) by adding to the sum calculated according to (i), any amount due and unpaid hereunder; and (iii) by deducting from the sum calculated according to (ii) the net proceeds of the sale, leasing or other disposition of the Equipment after deduction of expenses as hereinafter defined. Said liquidated damages shall be conclusively deemed to be a genuine pre-estimate by the parties hereto of the damages suffered by Lessor in the circumstances and not a penalty. The said expenses shall include, without limiting the generality of the foregoing, all legal fees and other expenses incurred by Lessor in attempting to enforce the provisions of this Agreement or to recover damages for a breach thereof, including costs and expenses associated with the sale of the Equipment.

14. TIME OF ESSENCE. Time shall be of the essence of this Agreement and of the lease of each item of Equipment hereunder.

15. NOTICES. All demands or notices hereunder shall be in writing and shall become effective and be deemed to have been given when delivered to the other party or alternatively when deposited in a post office with proper postage for ordinary mail prepaid, addressed to the respective party at its address set forth in the opening clause hereof or at such other address as such party shall from time to time designate in writing to the other party by written notice given in the manner prescribed in this clause.

16. MAINTENANCE, REPAIR AND REPLACEMENT. Lessee, at its own expense, will cause the manufacturer of the Equipment to keep the Equipment in good working order and provide all maintenance and service and make all repairs necessary for such purpose. If the Equipment or any item of Equipment or any parts, components or accessories forming part of any item of Equipment shall from time to time become worn out, lost, stolen, destroyed, damaged beyond repair or otherwise permanently rendered unfit for use, Lessee, at its own expense, will within a reasonable time replace such Equipment, item, parts, components or accessories, or cause the same to be replaced by replacement Equipment, items, parts, components or accessories which are free and clear of all liens, encumbrances or rights of others and which have a value and utility at least equal to the Equipment, items, parts, components or accessories replaced and be acceptable for maintenance upon the same terms by the manufacturer of the Equipment, items, parts, components or accessories replaced. All such replacement Equipment, items, parts, components and accessories shall immediately upon acquisition by the Lessee become the property of Lessor for all purposes hereof in place of the original Equipment, items, parts, components and accessories and such Equipment, items, parts, components and accessories shall thereafter form part of the applicable item of Equipment for all purposes hereof; but the Equipment, items, parts, components or accessories replaced thereby shall no longer be the property of Lessor. Notwithstanding the foregoing, Lessee may, with consent in writing of Lessor, have the Equipment or any item of Equipment maintained and serviced by someone other than the manufacturer. Lessee may from time to time add parts, components or accessories not leased hereunder to an item of Equipment only if such addition does not impair the value or utility of such item or affect any warranty relating thereto; and any parts, components or accessories so added to such item shall remain the property of Lessee or other owner thereof and may be removed by Lessee at any time prior to the termination of the lease of such item hereunder only if such parts, components or accessories are not required to be added as a replacement as above provided and if such removal does not impair the value or utility of such item and no event of default hereunder shall then have occurred and be continuing. Any parts, components or accessories not so removed upon the termination of the lease of such item shall thereupon become the property of Lessor.

17. LOSS AND DESTRUCTION. Lessee hereby assumes and shall bear the entire risk of loss, damage to or destruction of the Equipment. If the Equipment or any item of Equipment shall be lost, damaged or destroyed by any cause whatsoever or be stolen or rendered permanently unfit for use for any reason, or if the use by Lessee of such Equipment or item shall be substantially interfered with by any third party for a period of more than 10 days, Lessee shall promptly give Lessor written notice of such event, and shall promptly pay to Lessor the aggregate unpaid rent payments for the full term of the lease of such item, and in addition shall provide proof to the satisfaction of Lessor of compliance with the clause

7-009 R 12/90

hereof entitled "Maintenance, Repair and Replacement."

18. INSURANCE. Lessee shall obtain and maintain for the entire term of the Agreement, at its own expense, property damage and liability insurance and insurance against loss or damage to the Equipment including, without limitation, loss by fire (including so-called extended coverage), theft, collision and such other risks of loss as are customarily insured by "all risks" policies on the type of Equipment leased hereunder and by businesses in which Lessee is engaged, in such amounts, in such form and with such insurers as shall be satisfactory to Lessor; provided, however, that the amount of insurance covering damage to or loss of the Equipment shall not be less than the greater of the full replacement value of the Equipment or the instalments of rent then remaining unpaid hereunder. Each insurance policy will name Lessee as an insured and Lessor as an additional insured, and loss payee thereof, and shall contain a clause requiring the insurer to give to Lessor at least 10 days' prior written notice of any alteration in the terms of such policy or of the cancellation thereof. At Lessor's request, Lessee shall furnish to Lessor a certificate of insurance or other evidence satisfactory to Lessor that such insurance coverage is in effect; provided, however, that Lessor shall be under no duty either to ascertain the existence of or to examine such insurance policy or to advise Lessee in the event such insurance coverage shall not comply with the requirements hereof. Upon failure of Lessee to provide evidence of insurance satisfactory to Lessor, Lessor may purchase or otherwise provide such insurance and the cost thereof to Lessor shall be deemed additional rent hereunder and shall be payable by Lessee on demand. Lessee hereby appoints Lessor its agent and attorney to make claims and receive payment in accordance with the provisions of such policies. Lessee further agrees to give Lessor prompt notice of any damage to, or loss of, the Equipment, or any part thereof.

19. RETURN OF EQUIPMENT. Upon the expiration or earlier termination of the lease of each item of Equipment hereunder, Lessee, at its own risk, will return such Equipment forthwith to Lessor at such address in Canada as may be designated by Lessor by notice to Lessee. Lessee shall bear all expenses in connection with the return of the Equipment including dismantling, packing, crating, loading, rigging, transportation, drayage, insurance and other costs and charges but not any charges or expenses in connection with de-crating or installation of such Equipment at such address designated by Lessor. If the transportation charges to the place designated by Lessor exceed the amount Lessee would normally have otherwise incurred in transporting such Equipment to Toronto, Ontario, Lessor shall reimburse Lessee upon return of such Equipment for such excess. Lessee shall at its expense cause the manufacturer of the Equipment to supervise the dismantling, packing, crating and loading of the Equipment and shall use a carrier approved by Lessor. Lessee agrees that upon return of the Equipment, the Equipment will be in such condition that the manufacturer thereof will accept it for maintenance under the standard maintenance agreement of the manufacturer. Lessee agrees that any name or other identification of Lessee will be removed from the Equipment upon its return and that such Equipment will be in the same condition as delivered to Lessee hereunder, ordinary wear and tear excepted, and free and clear of all liens, encumbrances or rights of others whatsoever except liens or encumbrances resulting from claims against Lessor.

20. FURTHER ASSURANCES. Lessee will promptly and duly execute and deliver to Lessor such further documents and assurances and take such further action as Lessor may from time to time request in order to more effectively carry out the intent and purpose hereof and to establish and protect the rights, interests and remedies intended to be created in favour of Lessor hereby, including without limitation (i) the filing or recording of this Agreement including any Schedule or amendment hereto, or a financing, renewal or continuation statement with respect hereto or thereto, in accordance with the laws of any applicable jurisdiction and (ii) the taking of such further action as Lessor may deem desirable to fully protect Lessor's interest hereunder. Lessee hereby authorizes Lessor to effect any such filing or recording as aforesaid (including the filing of any such financing statements without the signature of Lessee). Lessee shall also upon the request of Lessor provide evidence satisfactory to Lessor of the due authorization, execution and delivery of any Schedule hereto.

21. NON-CANCELLABLE LEASE. This Agreement cannot be cancelled or terminated except as expressly provided herein.

22. LESSOR'S PAYMENT. If Lessee fails to make any payment of rent required to be made by it hereunder or fails to perform or comply with any of its agreements contained herein, Lessor may itself make such payment or perform or comply with such agreement, and the amount of such payment and the amount of the reasonable expenses of Lessor incurred in connection with such payment or the performance of or compliance with such agreement, as the case may be, shall be deemed additional rent hereunder and shall be payable by Lessee upon demand.

23. LESSEE'S OBLIGATIONS UNCONDITIONAL. Lessee hereby agrees that Lessee's obligation to pay all rent and any other amounts owing hereunder shall be absolute and

unconditional under all circumstances. Lessee agrees to pay all rent and such other amounts regardless of any claim in the nature of set off or compensation which may be made by Lessee. Lessee shall not be entitled to any abatement of rent or other amounts payable hereunder by Lessee or any reduction thereof including, but not limited to, abatements or reductions due to any present or future claims of Lessee against Lessor or any assignee, under this Agreement or otherwise, or against any manufacturer, vendor or supplier of the Equipment; nor, except as otherwise expressly provided herein, shall this Agreement or lease hereunder terminate, or the respective obligations of Lessor or Lessee be affected by reason of any defect in or damage to or loss or destruction of all or any of the Equipment from whatsoever cause, the interference with use by any private person, corporation or governmental authority, the invalidity or unenforceability or lack of due authorization of this Agreement or Schedule hereunder, or for any other cause, whether similar or dissimilar to the foregoing, any present or future law or regulation to the contrary notwithstanding, it being the intention of the parties hereto that the rents and other amounts payable by Lessee hereunder shall continue to be payable in all events unless the obligation to pay the same shall be terminated pursuant to the express provisions of this Agreement. Lessee acknowledges that the manufacturer, vendor and supplier of the Equipment and the Equipment and its specifications have all been determined and selected by Lessee and that Lessor has or will have purchased the Equipment at the request of Lessee for the purposes of this particular Agreement. Lessee also acknowledges that it is satisfied with the specifications pertaining to the Equipment. Lessee agrees that if the Equipment or any part thereof, or any machinery, equipment or other property intended by Lessee or by the manufacturer, vendor or supplier thereof to constitute Equipment hereunder, is not properly installed, does not operate as intended by Lessee or as represented or warranted by the manufacturer, vendor or supplier thereof, totally fails to function or perform so as to give rise to a fundamental breach or alleged fundamental breach with respect to the Agreement or the Equipment or such part, or is unsuitable or unsatisfactory or unacceptable for any other reason whatsoever, Lessee shall make claim and any complaint thereto solely and directly against the manufacturer, vendor or supplier of the Equipment and shall nevertheless unconditionally pay Lessor all rent and other amounts expressed to be payable hereunder.

24. MISCELLANEOUS. No waiver by Lessor of any default shall constitute a waiver of any other default by Lessee or waiver of Lessor's rights. Should Lessee fail to perform any obligation hereunder, Lessor may cause such obligation to be performed and the cost thereof shall be considered as additional rental to be paid by Lessee. Should Lessee fail to pay when due any rental payment or any sum required to be paid to Lessor, Lessee shall pay interest on such delinquent payment from the due date thereof until paid at the rate of 1 1/2% per month. If this Agreement is placed in the hands of a lawyer for collection or enforcement, Lessee agrees to pay all costs, charges and expenses incurred by Lessor as well as reasonable legal fees which Lessor will be obliged to pay its lawyer. This Agreement may not be amended except in writing and shall be binding upon and enure to the benefit of the parties hereto, their permitted successors and assigns. Any provision of this Agreement which is unenforceable in any jurisdiction shall, as to such jurisdiction, be ineffective to the extent of such prohibition or unenforceability without invalidating the remaining provisions hereof and any such prohibition or unenforceability in any jurisdiction shall not invalidate or render unenforceable such provision in any other jurisdiction. The captions in this Agreement are for convenience only and shall not define or limit any of the terms hereof. This Agreement shall in all respects be governed by and construed in accordance with the laws of the Province wherein the Equipment is to be located according to the terms hereof.

25. LESSOR'S INSPECTION. Lessee agrees that Lessor or its authorized representatives may at all reasonable times inspect the Equipment and the books, manuals and records of Lessee relative thereto, but that Lessor shall have no duty to make any such inspection and shall incur no liability by reason of not making the same.

26. WAIVER OF LESSEE. To the extent permitted by law, Lessee hereby agrees that, in British Columbia, the provisions of Sections 11 and 43(15) of the Personal Property Security Act, in Saskatchewan, the Limitation of Civil Rights Act and, in Alberta, the provisions of Section 43(11) of the Personal Property Security Act, as the said Sections or Acts may from time to time be amended or replaced, shall have no force, effect or application to this Agreement or any agreement or instrument renewing, amending or extending this Agreement, and hereby releases and waives any and all rights and benefits and the protection given by the said Acts or Sections thereof.

This Agreement consisting of the foregoing, and the Schedule(s) correctly set forth the entire Agreement between Lessor and Lessee. No agreements or understandings shall be binding on either of the parties hereto unless in writing and executed by authorized representatives of both parties. The term "Lessee" as used herein shall mean and include any and all Lessees who sign hereunder, each of whom shall be jointly and severally bound thereby.

Executed this _____ day of _____ 19 ____

By execution hereof, the signer hereby certifies that he/she has read this Agreement, and that he/she is duly authorized to execute same on behalf of Lessee.

LESSEE: _____ C/S

By _____
Authorized Signature and Title

_____
Witness

LESSOR: PITNEY BOWES LEASING
      A Division of Pitney Bowes Of Canada Ltd.

By _____
Authorized Signature and Title

81

7-009 R 12/90

Pitney Bowes Leasing

A Division of Pitney Bowes of Canada Ltd.
Suite 200, The Promontory I, 2695 North Sheridan Way, Mississauga, Ontario, L5K 2N7

MASTER EQUIPMENT LEASE SCHEDULE

Schedule No. _____   Lease No. _____

Lessor: PITNEY BOWES LEASING
      A Division of Pitney Bowes of Canada Ltd.   (herein called "Lessor")

Lessee: . . . . (herein called "Lessee")

Address: . . . .

. . . .

Effective Date shall be _____, or the date upon which Lessor has received Lessee's Delivery and Acceptance Certificate establishing that Lessee has accepted the Equipment, whichever shall first occur.

1.   The term of the lease for the Equipment covered by this Schedule shall commence on the Effective Date specified above and shall continue for a period of _____ months.

2.   For the use of the Equipment covered by this Schedule, Lessee shall pay to Lessor at the Lessor's office at Suite 200, The Promontory 1, 2695 North Sheridan Way, Mississauga, Ontario, L5K 2N7, a total rental payment equal to the amount of each rental payment specified below multiplied by the number of rental payments specified below. The first rental payment shall become due on the Effective Date specified above and subsequent rental payments in every calendar month or other calendar period after the month of shipment on the 1st of such month or period.

PAYMENTS WILL BE MADE	NUMBER OF PAYMENTS	RENTAL PAYMENTS EXCLUDING TAXES	GOODS AND SERVICES TAX	PROVINCIAL SALES TAX	TOTAL OF EACH RENTAL PAYMENT
☐ Monthly					
☐ Quarterly					
☐ Annually	_____	_____	_____	_____	_____

Lessor's Goods and Services Tax No: **R104212717**

3.   The following items of Equipment are hereby leased on the terms specified in this Schedule and this Schedule becomes a part of and subject to the terms and conditions of that certain Master Equipment Lease, Lease No. _____ dated _____ 19 _____ (h e r e i n called the "Lease Agreement").

QUANTITY	DESCRIPTION	MODEL NO.	SERIAL NO.

Place of Installation

7-010 R 12/90

4.   Lessee acknowledges that Lessor has ordered the Equipment designated by this Schedule for purchase from the seller thereof at the request of Lessee for the purposes of the lease of such Equipment to Lessee by Lessor. Lessee acknowledges that it has notice and has taken communication of the purchase order (herein called the "Purchase Order") for the purchase by Lessor of the Equipment covered by this Schedule, and that Lessor has signed the Purchase Order at the request of Lessee. The said Equipment is scheduled for shipment to Lessee as set forth in the Purchase Order and for installation at the location set forth herein. Lessor shall in no way be liable for any failure on the part of the seller named in the Purchase Order (herein called the "Seller") to ship, deliver and/or install such Equipment or any part thereof, or for any other default with respect to the Purchase Order or such Equipment.

5.   Lessee agrees that the Equipment shall be delivered to Lessee FOB the plant of the Seller and that the Equipment shall be at the risk of Lessee upon such delivery. Lessee shall be responsible for all transportation charges for delivery of the Equipment to Lessee's premises specified above and for all unloading, rigging, unpacking, assembly and installation of the Equipment. Notwithstanding that the Effective Date of the term of the lease of the Equipment covered by this Schedule may not have occurred, the obligations of the Lessee under the Lease Agreement, other than the payment of the rent, shall apply in respect to such Equipment from the date of execution by Lessee of this Schedule.

6.   Lessee agrees that it will, on behalf of Lessor, take all necessary action in arranging with the Seller for the timely shipment, delivery and installation of the Equipment in accordance with the provisions of the Purchase Order and that Lessee will provide all necessary supervision and assistance to assure the proper installation of the Equipment in good working order. Notice from the Seller of the installation date, as defined in the Purchase Order, shall be conclusive evidence that Lessee has accepted the Equipment for all purposes of the Lease Agreement as being in accordance with specifications, properly installed and/or assembled, in good working order, repair and appearance and without defect or inherent vice in condition, design, operation or fitness for use, whether or not discoverable by Lessee. If the installation date has not occurred by _____ , Lessor shall be entitled to terminate all of its obligations arising from this Schedule without incurring any liability whatsoever to Lessee. Should Lessor so terminate its obligations hereunder, Lessee shall nevertheless indemnify Lessor against and hold it harmless from any and all liability, losses, costs and expenses of whatsoever kind and nature, incurred by Lessor in any way relating to the order or purchase of the Equipment from the Seller including, but without limitation, any damages for the cancellation by Lessor of the Purchase Order.

7.   The above specified terms and conditions constitute a formal supplement of the Lease Agreement and this Schedule shall form part thereof. Except as herein modified all specifications, terms and conditions currently applicable to the Lease Agreement shall remain in full force and effect.

In witness whereof the parties hereto have executed this Agreement as of the

_____ day of _____ 19 _____

By execution hereof, the signer hereby certifies that she/he has read this Agreement, and that she/he is duly authorized to execute same on behalf of Lessee.

LESSEE: _____ C/S

By _____
         Authorized Signature and Title

LESSOR: PITNEY BOWES LEASING
              A Division of Pitney Bowes Of Canada Ltd.

By _____
         Authorized Signature and Title

7-010   6/90

||||| Pitney Bowes Leasing

A Division of Pitney Bowes of Canada Ltd.

SUITE 200, THE PROMONTORY I
2695 NORTH SHERIDAN WAY, MISSISSAUGA, ONTARIO L5K 2N7

(LESSOR)

LEASE CONTRACT

CUSTOMER No.	
LEASE No.	

LESSEE NAME		
ADDRESS		PRESENTLY LEASING THROUGH PB LEASING ☐ YES ☐ NO
P.O. BOX		CORRESPONDENCE:
CITY AND PROVINCE	POSTAL CODE	ENGLISH ☐ FRENCH ☐
NAME AND TITLE OF LEASE SIGNOR	TEL No. (Inc. Area Code)	YEARS IN BUSINESS

Company Name . . . . Bank . . . .

Branch Address . . . . Address . . . .

Sales Representative . . . .

LOCATION OF EQUIPMENT
(if different than above)

LESSEE OWNS PREMISES ☐	NAME AND ADDRESS OF LANDLORD IF EQUIPMENT IS TO BE PLACED IN RENTED PREMISES IN THE PROVINCE OF QUEBEC		
QUANTITY	EQUIPMENT DESCRIPTION (Including Model and Serial No(s).)		PRICE $

LESSOR'S GOODS AND SERVICES TAX NUMBER R122592173	LEASE START DATE				TOTAL COST OF EQUIPMENT	$
		DD	MM	YY		

INITIAL TERM: No. of Months	PAYMENTS WILL BE MADE ☐ Monthly ☐ Quarterly ☐ Annually	No. OF PAYMENTS	RENTAL PAYMENT EXCLUDING TAX	GOODS AND SERVICES TAX	PROVINCIAL SALES TAX	TOTAL OF EACH RENTAL PAYMENT	RENEWAL RENTAL

TERMS AND CONDITIONS OF LEASE

For and in consideration of the covenants and agreements by the Lessee to pay the total rental payment herein provided for and to perform the terms, covenants and conditions on the Lessee's part herein contained, the Lessor hereby leases, and lets unto the Lessee, and the Lessee hereby leases and takes from the Lessor, each unit of equipment described above and hereinafter referred to as "said equipment", for the term set forth above (commencing on the date of the first delivery of any of the said equipment to the Lessee) and upon and subject to the covenants, conditions and provisions hereinafter set forth.

1. RENTAL. For the use of said equipment, the Lessee shall pay to the Lessor at the Lessor's office, at Suite 200, The Promontory I, 2695 North Sheridan Way, Mississauga, Ontario L5K 2N7, a total rental payment equal to the amount of each rental payment specified above multiplied by the number of rental payments specified above. The first rental payment shall become due upon the execution hereof by Lessee and subsequent rent payments in every calendar month, or other calendar period, after the month of shipment on the 1st of such month or period. Rental payment hereunder is payable without abatement.

2. EQUIPMENT DESCRIPTION. The Lessee authorizes the Lessor to complete the description of said equipment above with the insertion of serial numbers and other details specifically identifying said equipment.

3. REPRESENTATIONS AND WARRANTIES. Each unit of said equipment leased hereunder is of a size, design and capacity personally chosen and selected by the Lessee and the Lessee is satisfied that the same is suitable for its purposes and the Lessor has made no representation or warranty with respect to the suitability or durability of any such unit for the purposes or uses of the Lessee, or any other representation or warranty express or implied with respect thereto.

The Lessee acknowledges that said equipment hereby leased was personally chosen and selected by the Lessee for business purposes, and purchased at the Lessee's request from a supplier designated by the Lessee. Consequently, the Lessee takes full responsibility for the choosing and the selection, and will look only to the supplier for warranty against latent defects or other matters, the Lessor hereby conveying expressly and without reserve to the Lessee all warranties, if any, resulting from the sale of said equipment entered into with the supplier. The Lessee renounces the right to any claim or defence against the Lessor relating to said equipment. In the event of an action brought by the Lessor for default under the provisions of this Lease, the Lessee waives all defences predicated on the failure of said equipment to perform the function for which it was designed and further acknowledges and agrees that such failure shall not be deemed to be in breach of this Lease.

SEE REVERSE SIDE FOR ADDITIONAL TERMS AND CONDITIONS WHICH ARE PART OF THIS LEASE.

THE UNDERSIGNED ACKNOWLEDGES TO HAVE READ THE ENTIRE LEASE AND ACCEPTS THE TERMS AND CONDITIONS THEREOF.

Date of Execution . . . .
Pitney Bowes Leasing
A Division of Pitney Bowes of Canada Ltd.

BY: . . . .
　　　Authorized Signature

TITLE: . . . .

Name of Lessee . . . .

. . . .
The undersigned affirms that he/she is duly authorized to execute this LEASE CONTRACT

BY: . . . . TITLE: . . . .
　　　Authorized Signature

BY: . . . .

7-001 R 10/91

Lessor Copy

84

4. GOVERNING LAW. This Lease shall be interpreted and enforced in accordance with the laws of the Province wherein said equipment is to be located according to the terms hereof. Lessor and Lessee hereby acknowledge that they have required this Lease and all related documents to be drawn up in the English language. Le Locateur et le Locataire reconnaissent avoir exigé que le présent crédit-bail et les documents qui s'y rattachent soient rédigés en anglais.
5. EQUIPMENT OWNED BY LESSOR. This agreement is one of leasing only and the Lessee shall not have or acquire any right, title or interest in or to said equipment except the right of the Lessee and its competent employees to use or operate said equipment as provided herein.
6. LOSS OR DAMAGE TO EQUIPMENT. The Lessee assumes the entire risk of loss or damage to said equipment from any cause whatsoever. No loss or damage to said equipment or any part thereof shall affect or impair the obligations of the Lessee hereunder which shall continue in full force and effect. It is understood and agreed that this Lease shall not prejudice the subrogation rights of any insurance carrier.
7. NO SUBLEASE OR ASSIGNMENT OF LEASE BY LESSEE. The Lessee shall not transfer, deliver up possession of or sublet said equipment and this Lease shall not be assignable by the Lessee without written permission of the Lessor, which permission shall not be unreasonably withheld. Nothing contained herein shall prevent the Lessor from assigning, pledging, mortgaging, transferring or otherwise disposing, either in whole or in part, of the Lessor's rights hereunder.
8. MAINTENANCE AND INSPECTION OF EQUIPMENT. The Lessee shall at all times and at the Lessee's own expense keep said equipment in good and efficient working order and repair and shall furnish any and all parts, mechanisms and devices required to keep said equipment in good mechanical and working order. The Lessor, its employees and/or agents shall at all times have access to said equipment for the purpose of inspecting it. The Lessee shall not, without the prior written consent of the Lessor, make any alterations, additions or improvements to said equipment. All such alterations, additions or improvements so made shall belong to and remain the property of the Lessor.
9. COMPLIANCE BY LESSEE WITH ALL LAWS, ORDINANCES, ETC. The Lessee shall comply with and conform to all laws, ordinances and regulations present or future, in any way relating to the ownership, possession, use or maintenance of said equipment throughout the term of this Lease and to the perfect exoneration from liability of the Lessor.
10. EQUIPMENT TO BE KEPT FREE OF LEVIES, PRIVILEGES, LIENS, CHARGES, ETC. The Lessee shall keep said equipment free of levies, privileges, liens and encumbrances and shall pay all licence fees, registration fees, assessments, charges and taxes (Municipal, Provincial and Federal), which may be levied or assessed, directly or indirectly, against or on account of said equipment or any interest therein or use thereof. If the Lessee shall fail to pay such licence fees, registration fees, assessments, charges or taxes the Lessor may pay such licence fees, registration fees, assessments, charges and taxes as the case may be in which event the cost thereof shall be forthwith due and payable by the Lessee.
11. INDEMNIFICATION OF LESSOR BY LESSEE. The Lessee shall indemnify the Lessor against and hold the Lessor harmless from any and all claims, actions, suits, proceedings, costs, expenses, damages and liabilities, including legal fees, arising out of, connected with, or resulting from said equipment, including without limitation, the manufacture, selection, delivery, installation, possession, use, operation or return of said equipment or otherwise on account of any personal injury or death or damage to property occasioned by said equipment or the negligence of employees, servants or agents of Lessee, or on account of any infringement or alleged infringement of patent occasioned by the operation of said equipment.
12. INSURANCE. As and from the earlier of the date upon which the Lessor acquires ownership of, or title to, the said equipment or the date on which the Lessor may have any risk, responsibility or liability therefor, and thereafter throughout the term of this Agreement, the Lessee shall, at its sole expense, place and maintain, in a form, with an insurer, and with coverage and limits, in each case, acceptable to the Lessor: (a) "all risks" insurance against the loss of or theft of or damage to said equipment, for the full replacement value thereof, naming the Lessor as a loss payee; and (b) public liability and property damage insurance, naming the Lessor as additional insured, covering any liability in respect of the use, operation, possession and ownership of the said equipment. Such insurance policies shall contain a clause requiring the insurer to give to the Lessor at least thirty days' prior written notice of any alteration in the terms of such policy or of the cancellation thereof. At the Lessor's request, the Lessee shall furnish to the Lessor a certificate of insurance or other evidence satisfactory to the Lessor that such insurance coverage is in effect; provided, however, that the Lessor shall be under no duty either to ascertain the existence of or to examine such insurance policy or to advise the Lessee in the event that such insurance coverage shall not comply with the requirements hereof. Upon failure of the Lessee to provide evidence of insurance satisfactory to the Lessor, the Lessor shall have the right, but not the obligation, to purchase or otherwise provide such insurance protecting the Lessor's interest and the cost thereof to the Lessee (including without limitation, the full premium paid for such insurance and any customary charges or fees of the Lessor or the Lessor's designee associated with such insurance) shall be deemed additional rent hereunder and shall be payable by the Lessee on demand as and when directed by the Lessor. Notwithstanding the fact that there may be insurance required hereunder, or the proceeds from such insurance may be made available to the Lessee, any and all risk of loss or damage to the equipment arising from any cause whatsoever shall be borne by the Lessee and the Lessee, in addition to the obligations assumed under Clause 11 of this Agreement, agrees to indemnify the Lessor for any loss of or damage to the said equipment.
13. EQUIPMENT TO REMAIN PERSONAL PROPERTY. The said equipment shall at all times during the term of this Lease be and remain personal or movable property, regardless of the manner in which it may be attached to any real estate. The Lessee shall install said equipment in a manner which will permit its removal without material injury to the place of installation. The Lessee shall be responsible for any damage done to any real or immovable property, building or structure by the removal of said equipment and shall indemnify and save harmless the Lessor therefrom.
14. TERMINATION ON DEFAULT. Upon the occurrence of any event of default, the Lessor shall be entitled at its option, exercisable by written notice to the Lessee, to declare the Lessee to be in default, whereupon the Lessee shall be obligated to return said equipment to the Lessor and shall also be liable to the Lessor for the payment of liquidated damages, which shall be calculated as follows: (i) by calculating the entire amount of the then unpaid rental payments for the remainder of the term of this Lease, each such rental payment to be subject to a discount equal to interest at the rate of rental payment to be subject to a discount equal to interest at the rate of (5%) per annum on each rental payment calculated and compounded monthly over the period commencing on the date of the aforesaid notice and ending on the date on which such rental payment would have become due and payable under the terms of this Lease; and (ii) by adding to the sum calculated according to (i), any amount due and unpaid hereunder, and (iii) by deducting from the sum calculated according to (ii) the net proceeds of the sale, leasing or other disposition of said equipment after deduction of expenses as hereinafter defined. Said liquidated damages shall be conclusively deemed to be a genuine pre-estimate by the parties hereto of the damages suffered by Lessor in the circumstances and not a penalty. The said expenses shall include, without limiting the generality of the foregoing, all legal fees and other expenses incurred by the Lessor in attempting to enforce the provisions of this Lease or to recover damages for a breach thereof, including costs and expenses associated with the sale of said equipment.
15. EVENTS OF DEFAULT. Any of the following shall each constitute an "event of default": (i) the failure of the Lessee to pay any instalment of the rental payment or any other sum due under the terms of this Lease; (ii) the breach of any covenant or condition contained in this Lease; (iii) the subjection of said equipment to any lien, levy, privilege, seizure or attachment; (iv) any assignment by the Lessee for the benefit of creditors; (v) the admission of the Lessee in writing of its inability to pay its debts generally as they become due; (vi) the appointment of a receiver, trustee or similar official for the Lessee or for any of its property; (vii) the filing by or against the Lessee of a petition in bankruptcy or a petition for the reorganisation or liquidation of the Lessee under any Federal or Provincial laws; (viii) any other act of bankruptcy by the Lessee.
16. ASSIGNMENT BY LESSOR. Should the Lessor assign the sums due and to become due hereunder to any bank, insurance company or other lending agency (of which assignment the Lessee hereby waives notice and signification), the Lessee shall recognize such assignment and should the Lessor default in the performance of any of the terms and conditions of this Lease, the Lessee may not, as to such assignee, terminate this Lease or subject the Lessee's obligations to pay money under this Lease to any diminution or right of set-off or compensation. Nothing herein contained shall release the Lessor from its obligation to perform any duty, covenant or condition required to be performed by a Lessor under the terms of this Lease should the same be so assigned.
17. RETURN OF EQUIPMENT UPON TERMINATION. Upon termination of this Lease for any reason, the Lessee shall at its cost, return said equipment to the Lessor at a place designated by the Lessor and if the Lessee fails to do so, the Lessor shall have the right to enter upon the premises where said equipment may be and take possession of and remove if at the Lessee's expense, all without legal process. In the event that with or without the consent of Lessor, Lessee remains in the possession of or uses said equipment after the expiration of the Initial Term of this Lease or renewal thereof, all the provisions of this Lease shall apply thereto unless and until the same has been surrendered pursuant to the terms of this Clause, or Lessor has relieved Lessee from its obligations under this Lease with respect to said equipment. Nothing in this Clause shall have the effect of extending or renewing the term of this Lease.
18. WAIVER BY LESSOR. No covenant or condition of this Lease can be waived except by the written consent of the Lessor, and forbearance or indulgence by the Lessor in any regard whatsoever shall not constitute a waiver of the covenant or condition to be performed by the Lessee to which the same may apply, and, until complete performance by the Lessee of said covenant or condition, the Lessor shall be entitled to invoke any remedy available to the Lessor under the Lease or by law, despite said forbearance or indulgence.
19. INTEREST CHARGES. Should the Lessee fail to pay when due any rental payment or any sum required to be paid to Lessor, the Lessee shall pay interest on such delinquent payment from the due date thereof until paid at the rate of 11/2% per month.
20. TIME OF THE ESSENCE. Time is of the essence of this Lease and of each and all of its provision.
21. BINDING UPON SUCCESSORS, HEIRS AND ASSIGNS. This Lease shall enure to the benefit of and be binding upon the successors, heirs and assigns of the respective parties hereto, provided that nothing contained in this Clause shall impair any of the provisions herein set forth prohibiting transfer or subletting of said equipment by the Lessee, or assignment of this Lease by the Lessee.
22. HEADINGS. The headings in this Lease are for convenience of reference only and shall not affect the interpretation thereof.
23. INTERPRETATION. It is hereby agreed by and between the parties hereto that whenever the context of this Lease so requires, the singular number shall include the plural and vice versa, and that words importing the masculine gender shall include the feminine and neuter genders, and that in case more than one lessee is named as Lessee, the liability of such lessees shall be joint and several.
24. NON-CANCELLABLE LEASE. This Lease cannot be cancelled or terminated except as expressly provided herein and will remain in force for the full term indicated herein.
25. LEGAL EXPENSES. If this Lease is placed in the hands of a lawyer for collection or enforcement, the Lessee agrees to pay all costs, charges and expenses incurred by the Lessor as well as reasonable legal fees which the Lessor will be obliged to pay its lawyer.
26. LOCATION AND USE OF EQUIPMENT. The said equipment shall be located and used at the place of business of the Lessee or as designated on the reverse side hereof and shall not be removed therefrom without the prior written consent of the Lessor.
27. WAIVER OF LESSEE. To the extent permitted by law, the Lessee hereby agrees that, in British Columbia, the provisions of Sections 11 and 43(15) of the Personal Property Security Act, in Saskatchewan, the Limitation of Civil Rights Act, in Alberta, the provisions of Section 43(11) of the Personal Property Security Act and, in Quebec, the provisions of the Civil Code relating to the leasing or hiring of things, as the said Sections, Acts or Code may from time to time be amended or replaced, shall have no force, effect or application to this Lease or any agreement or instrument renewing, amending or extending this Lease, and hereby releases and waives any and all rights and benefits and the protection given by the said Acts, Code or Sections thereof.
28. RENEWAL. If this Lease is in good standing on the last day of the Initial Term the Lessee shall have the option to renew this Lease on the terms and conditions hereof from year to year at the Renewal Rental shown above, it having been determined and agreed by the parties hereto that such amount represents the expected fair market value of the said equipment at the end of the Initial Term of this Lease.

Chapter 9

Measuring Return to the Lessor

The most difficult tasks facing lessors are to ensure that they will recover their investment, to assess their rate of return on a lease, and to determine whether that rate is acceptable or too high or too low for the market. If the rate is too high for the market, in a competitive economy lessors will not be able to attract the lessees because the competition will bid the lease away from them. If the rate is too low, the lessors will obtain too much business at a low yield and will use up their financing capacity on low-yield business, prejudicing the viability of the organization in the long run. The lessor has two main concerns:

- Will the cash flows be received in the amounts and at the times contemplated when the lease is written?
- Is the yield in the lease sufficient for the long-term viability of the organization?

CASH-FLOW-RELATED RISKS

It is worthwhile from time to time to consider all the factors that can affect the likelihood that an organization will receive the cash from its leases that it anticipates when the leases are written. There are an amazing number of possible interferences with the cash flow. Over the years these have waxed and waned in importance. Some are controllable at the inception of the lease, and some are controllable during the lease term. They fall into two broad categories: risks associated with the lease, and those associated with funding. Those associated with the lease include the following:

1. The periodic payments may arrive late, resulting in increased borrowing cost to the lessor. Postal disruptions and delays alone can result in significant time loss during the course of a contract. Of course, this can be overcome today with either post-dated cheques or preauthorized payments. In addition, the lease can provide compensation for late payments, but it is difficult to enforce when the lateness is primarily due to postal delays.

2. Lessee stops payment altogether. This could result from dissatisfaction with the equipment, insolvency or bankruptcy of the lessee, or because the lessee has disappeared or, as they say, "skipped."

3. Courts fail to enforce payment on the lessee. This has been the cause of disproportionate credit losses to lessors. The legal system's view of a lease document may well be different from the view of the business person. The court may simply refuse to require the lessee to perform in accordance with the contract. The documentation may be poor, and therefore the contract may not be enforceable in accordance with its terms; registrations may have been imperfect or not renewed at the required times. In addition, a variety of legal defences can be put up by the lessee, a receiver, or a landlord. For instance, the leased asset may have melded into, or become attached to, other assets such as a building, a manufacturing line, etc. The court may not support removal of the leased asset under these circumstances. The leased asset may have nothing to identify it from other similar assets owned by the lessee. Accordingly, repossession may not be possible as against other creditors or the landlord.

4. Obsolescence results in reduction of the realizable value of the asset. This might occur during the term of the lease, and would be serious in the event the asset is repossessed; or at termination of the lease, the unguaranteed residual value on which the lessor was relying for a significant part of the overall cash flow may have declined.

5. The initial expenses are higher than expected and not recoverable from the lessee. These expenses could include credit investigation, funding costs, legal costs associated with the lease, etc.

6. In tax-oriented leases the conditions expected at the inception of the lease are not realized. The income tax resources expected to be saved by the organization are less than was anticipated when the lease was signed. This has generally occurred due to the lessor having insufficient taxable income to absorb all of the capital cost allowance available from the leased asset. However, a number of other situations could affect the after-tax cash flows. This would include having insufficient taxable income against which to claim investment tax credits in the time spans originally estimated, changes in the CCA rate which result in lower claimable amounts, or successful attack of the lease by Revenue Canada resulting in high taxable income at inception of the lease rather than a tax shelter. In addition capital tax and income tax rate changes can occur and a surtax could be imposed. This may be good or bad. If it is imposed during the period when the lease provides shelter, then the savings are greater. In the best of all worlds, tax rates are increased during the shelter period and decreased later when the leasing company becomes taxable. However, there is a risk that the opposite will occur and the company will face low tax rates during the shelter period and high tax

rates during the tax paying period. Finally, the tax department may not allow the offset of the leasing loss against other income of the lessor because it does not meet one of the tests in the *Income Tax Act*, S.C. 1970-71-72, c. 63, or because of other technical deficiencies.

There is a comparable list of factors relating to funding that can affect the cash flow of the lease compared to that which was contemplated at inception. This would include:

1. The initial borrowing costs exceed original budget and are not recoverable from the lessee.

2. Borrowing is done on a variable-rate basis, versus a fixed-rate lease basis. This exposes the organization to unlimited interest costs during periods of high interest rates. In fact, during the early 1980s several lessors were in the position of paying a higher rate for their borrowings than they were realizing on their lease portfolio. This condition is often referred to in the industry as "under-water" leases. As rates drop, of course this situation reverses and the lessor makes a "windfall" gain from lower interest costs.

3. If leases are funded by long-term, fixed-rate contracts with the repayment of the debt later than the cash flow from the lease, the lessor may run into the opposite position to that referred above. That is, as lease payments are made by the lessee, a portion is attributable to the funding capital. If repayment of the capital is not due, the funds have to be reinvested in new leases. If interest rates have generally dropped during this period, the lessor may not be able to realize the same rate of return as the cost of funds, and the lease will again be "under water".

4. If the term of the borrowing is less than the term of the lease, a refunding problem may arise mid-term. This is the classic "borrowing short, lending long" circumstance which can result in the demise of the organization through its inability to meet its debt requirements generally as they fall due.

5. The lessor may breach one or more borrowing covenants during the terms of the lease, resulting in required prepayment of portions or all of the borrowed funds.

6. Funding that has been committed does not arrive or does not arrive on a timely basis, and alternative borrowings, likely at higher costs, are required.

The above lists are not exhaustive, but they are sufficiently long to make it clear that lessors who wish to optimize their return must address all these factors in their financial planning, credit analysis, and rate setting. In addition, it is useful to differentiate between those cash flows which are *contractual* (lease payments, guaranteed residual payments, interest expense payments by the lessor and the repayments of the lessor's principal) and generally have a high probability of occurring, and those payments which are *conjectural*, such as the unguaranteed residual and the timing and amount of tax payment deferrals. In general, a lower probability, and therefore a lower value, might be placed on the latter cash flows, and the lease analysis would try to distinguish clearly between the flows which are likely to occur in the normal commercial sense and those which time and experience have proved to be less likely.

In addition, the longer the term of the lease, the greater is the uncertainty with respect to economic conditions, obsolescence, tax climate, etc. Accordingly, cash flows which are due a long time in the future and are conjectural rather than contractual should generally be ignored unless sufficient work can be done to raise their probability of occurrence to an acceptable level. What is acceptable will vary from company to company, since some managements are risk takers and some are risk-averse. Moreover, it should vary depending on the size of the transaction as compared to the size of the organization making the investment in the lease. Subjectively, one may give a rating of .95 to contractual cash flows, indicating that they are highly assured of occurring. Intuitively, one might also assign a probability of a residual value being achieved, for other than standard equipment such as an automobile, at .5 to .6. Similarly, income tax cash flows expected in periods after two years from the date of the lease would not have an assurance level greater than .5. There are a variety of techniques to assess the risk, and the basic aim is to arrive at a series of cash flows that have the same likelihood of occurrence. Only then can one begin to use the measurement techniques to determine the rate of return to be earned on the presumed risk level.

INVESTMENT AMOUNT — BEFORE OR AFTER DEBT (LEVERAGE)

In computing the actual return on a lease-by-lease basis, we are generally taking that lease in isolation from all others. This is to ensure that the yield on the particular lease is not intermingled with the yield from other investment decisions. In addition, the yield should be calculated on the net investment in the lease from time to time, without regard to the funding provided for the lease. Some analysts prefer to compute the return on "company funds" in use in the lease as opposed to total funds in use, including outside borrowing. There can be no clear-cut argument one way or the other. Those who prefer to include the borrowing on a lease and to compute the net return on company funds argue that the use of company funds and the return on these funds are of primary interest to the organization in the long run. In addition, they recognize that some transactions can be financed solely by a pledge on the particular leased assets without any additional call on the company's credit. Particularly in cases where the credit of the lessee is superior to that of the lessor, as often occurs in leveraged leases, funding secured by an assignment of lease rents and limited to specific leased assets leaves the company's other assets unencumbered; therefore, it does not limit future borrowing. In addition, the leverage allowed on such transactions may be significantly higher than the leverage which the company enjoys in the general operation of its business. Finally, the rate of return on the company's funds on leveraged leases will be markedly higher than the rate of return on the total investment, ignoring funding. To show a low return on what is essentially a high return transaction, some feel, is misleading. This is serious if it leads to incorrect management decisions.

The following points should be considered:

1. Shareholders should expect a reasonable return on assets employed, whether they are company funds or borrowed money, since the only reason to borrow is to provide a greater return to the investor.

2. Borrowing increases the risk of insolvency of an organization, and very high leverage has very high risks associated with it. Concentrating on the higher clerical calculation of a yield net of borrowings focuses the attention solely on the rate of return number without clarifying the risk associated through the borrowings. Indeed, on a specific transaction, if one were to borrow all of the cost and always provide for the company to have no funds invested in it, the rate of return would be infinite. The risk associated with the transaction, particularly if repeated in the long run, is very high, and the probability of lenders funding the organization in the long run on this basis is remote.

3. While assets of the organization outside the particular investment may not be encumbered in a leveraged lease transaction, the company's equity in the investment is encumbered and therefore is not available to support general borrowings. In addition, in the event of default, the company loses its equity plus all of its general and administrative expenses associated with the transaction, since these are separate obligations outside the lease.

4. Many companies design a financial base that includes a reasonable debt/equity ratio. Large leveraged leases distort the ratio for the company and may preclude other desirable transactions needed to spread loss and absorb general and administrative expense.

5. Outside lenders frequently impose restrictions on individual transaction size and on overall debt/equity ratios. Accordingly, although the organization's general assets may not be at risk in a particular leveraged transaction, the company's general borrowing is restricted, and therefore its ability to acquire other desirable leases is restricted. In that sense, the acquisition of a large leveraged lease may have an "opportunity cost" through the inability of the organization to carry out other transactions.

6. Although the company may not have a contingent liability on the borrowing, it may be necessary or desirable for general corporate purposes (such as to maintain relations with lenders, suppliers, and customers)

for the company to assume some or all of the remaining risk on a leveraged lease transaction.

In summary, while there may be circumstances that will alter the general rule, it is preferable to compute return on the gross investment in a lease, without deducting borrowing related to the transaction. Leveraged lessors and those who are sophisticated in the industry in their assessment of returns on large transactions may disagree. It must be understood, therefore, that after calculating the return on the investment from time to time outstanding, it is also necessary to calculate the spread between cost of money and the investment yield. If the interest rate spread is acceptable, the leveraged lease transaction can be accepted. If it is too low, it would have to be rejected. In some cases, individual transactions demand special attention because of their size and unusual income tax ramifications. In these cases it may well be necessary to recognize that part of the economic rationale for the transaction is that income taxes that would otherwise be payable as a result of other taxable income will be reduced by the large lease transaction. In general, this reduction is temporary, and it is practice, therefore, to treat the delayed income tax payment as a non-interest bearing loan. Clearly, this will affect the overall interest associated with the particular transaction and therefore the interest rate spread. Of course, as indicated in the previous section, one must be sure that the income tax payments will actually be delayed for the period anticipated, in the amount anticipated.

TAX BENEFITS IN OR OUT OF THE CALCULATION?

On large transactions it is desirable to consider the incremental change in income tax position as a result of the particular lease transaction. If the leased asset is eligible for a high rate of investment tax credit and a fast write-off for income tax purposes, then the lessor will enjoy:

- the rentals, prepaid rents, security deposits provided for in the agreement with the lessee;
- investment tax credit on the cost of the leased asset; and
- accelerated capital cost allowance claims which permit a reduction in taxes otherwise payable;
- increased provincial capital taxes and the Large Corporation Tax (LCT) introduced by the federal government in 1989.

It should be noted that the LCT is a tax on capital in excess of $10 million. For this purpose there is a broad definition of capital, including borrowings. In general, the LCT definition is an "accounting" capital calculation rather than a tax-adjusted capital calculation which is common in some provincial capital tax calculations. In large transactions the LCT and provincial capital taxes become a very important part of the company's overall spread in the transaction. The LCT is currently at 0.2 of 1% of capital (compared to the province of Ontario capital tax, for example, which is 0.3 of 1%). However the LCT is not deductible in computing taxable income whereas other provincial taxes generally are. This situation may change, however, with the introduction of a proposal by the federal government to limit the deduction of provincial costs, including capital taxes to a formula basis. This could result in non-deductible provincial tax if a particularly large transaction is undertaken. The LCT is an example of a tax which, although not applied retroactively, did apply to capital outstanding from transactions which occurred in earlier years. Therefore the spread which a company had projected on a large transaction would be eroded by the LCT to a considerable extent. This should reinforce the danger inherent in calculating yields on transactions based on current income tax law assumptions if the transaction is to carry on for several years in the future. In addition, the federal Large Corporation Tax, since its inception in 1989, has already been increased once.

The lessor's net incremental investment can be calculated by reducing the original investment by the Investment Tax Credit and tax reduction from CCA in the periods they are to be realized. Cash inflow includes the after-tax rental income calculated by reducing the rental income by the incremental income taxes associated with the added rent. The lessor would also calculate the after-tax cash inflow from either the guaranteed or unguaranteed residual values. In some cases, this would simply be the residual value received minus the incremental income taxes resulting from the receipt, if there were no other assets in the particular CCA pool. If there are other assets in the pool, then the realization of the residual will not result in a current income tax payable by the lessor, but would reduce future CCA. The present value of that reduced tax shelter can be calculated using the formula ATR ÷ (R + i), where: A = the UCC of the leased asset less the proceeds of disposition, T = the income tax rate, R = the CCA rate, i = an appropriate after-tax discount rate.

The correct mechanics of the calculation require knowing the undepreciated capital cost of the leased asset prior to realization of the residual, since the undepreciated capital cost is first recovered by receipt of the residual and only the excess would give rise to a reduction in future CCA other than that applicable to the lease transaction.

In doing this kind of after-tax calculation of cash flows, it is important to differentiate between the cash inflow from the rental payments and realization of the residual, which are relatively assured by the lease contract and the credit assessment of the lessee, and the expected incremental income tax effects of the lease. Any cash tax savings or tax payable as a result of the lease transaction are less certain to be accurately reflected due to the potential for changes in taxable income of the lessor, income tax rates in the future, and possibly CCA rates and the handling for tax purposes of residual values.

Many lessors have found, to their disappointment, that some of the yield in a large transaction has not been realized as a result of the lessor being completely tax sheltered and therefore unable to obtain the cash savings of taxes otherwise payable as a result of entering into a particular lease transaction. This, along with diminution of unguaranteed residual values, has resulted in loss transactions rather than profitable transactions. Nevertheless, the calculation is worthwhile as a means of arriving at an estimate of the tax effects in the overall yield. If a transaction is unprofitable unless the tax effects are recognized, and the tax effects do not have the same degree of assurance as the cash flows from the lease and the repayment of borrowed funds, then the return on the lease transaction should be higher to compensate the lessor for the potential that it will be unable to realize some of the presumed income tax benefits.

It is equally important to know the lessee's after-tax cost of the asset:

• on the transaction as a lease;
• on the transaction as a purchase.

By doing this calculation, the after-tax cost of the leased asset will be known and an estimate made of the importance of the tax savings to the lessee as opposed to the lessor. This may well put the lessor in a position to negotiate a better lease transaction, or alert the lessor to the fact that the after-tax cost to the lessee of owning may be cheaper than the after-tax cost of leasing. Therefore, it may be more advantageous to the lessee to acquire the asset through a conditional sale contract than through a lease.

In summary, then, one should consider:

• assessing lease yields based on all of the cash flows associated with the transaction, including prepaid rents, security deposits, residual values, contingent rents, and regular rental payments;
• differentiating between those cash flows that are relatively certain, in that they are contractual and based on the lease agreement, and those that are anticipated but less certain, primarily the income tax benefits and unguaranteed residual values;
• calculating costs or return on both a pre- and post-tax basis.

There are a number of ways to measure rate of return; the following four will be reviewed:

• the pay-back period;
• net present value;
• internal rate of return (IRR);
• the after-tax rate of return.

PAY-BACK PERIOD

This title refers to a simple method of assessing one investment versus another.

The monthly cash inflows from the investment are calculated and these are divided into the total investment. The result is the number of months it takes to recover the original investment. For example, a $1,000 investment which generated $20 per month of income would have a payback period of $1,000 ÷ 20 = 50 months. This would indicate that the investor's investment would not be recouped from cash flows until the end of the 50th month. The same system is often used on an annual basis. For example, $1,000 investment generating $240 of annual cash flow would have a pay-back period of $1,000 ÷ $240 = 4.17 years. Of course, this only indicates when the investment has been recovered, without any return on the investment. To extend that further there is a more useful system called the "discounted pay-back method." This system requires the present value of each year's cash inflows to be calculated. These are then accumulated year by year until they equal the original investment. At that point, the investment has been recovered plus a return equal to the rate at which the cash inflows were discounted. For example, in the case of the $1,000 investment with the repayment of $20 per month and a discount rate of 1% per month, the monthly pay-back period would be 70 months, or the annual pay-back period would be 5.8 years.

The pay-back calculation is a rough method of assessing return on an investment, but it may be used if two otherwise similar projects are viewed as acceptable and the task is merely to differentiate between the two. In addition, if the pay-back period is rather high and the useful life of the asset is only a little longer than the pay-back period, then the risk of obsolescence increases.

A particular difficulty, however, is that this system will not differentiate between two cash flows of differing lengths. For example, if two investment proposals were to be viewed, one providing an investment of $1,000 with an inflow of $20 per month for 70 months, and the second with the same investment and inflow but for 100 months, rather than 70, the pay-back calculation would be identical for both. Clearly, the one with the longer income stream would be preferable.

NET PRESENT VALUE METHOD

This is a common method for assessing whether an investment provides an acceptable rate of return. It requires information on the original investment, any additional cash flows required by the investor, and all of the cash inflows related to the investment. These are spread out in time and their net present value calculated by using the discount rate which is felt to be acceptable to the company. If the cash inflows were discounted at the weighted cost of capital for the company and the net present value was equal to or greater than zero, then the investment would return sufficient to the corporation to repay the investment plus earn a yield equal to the weighted cost of capital.

For example, if an investment of $1,000 were made and a return of $20

95

per month expected to be realized for at least 70 months and a discount rate of 1% per month was acceptable to the company, then the net present value of the cash inflows and the cash outflows would be just over zero, indicating that the contract achieved the desired rate of return. In general, contracts with the higher net present value are superior to contracts with lower net present values.

The above example was quite simple. In practice, there may be additional cash outflows required at some time during the contract life, and there may well be residual values, deposits, security deposits, etc., associated with the contract which make the calculations more complex. For this reason, the net present value method is generally not used unless a computer is available to do the calculation. In addition, there are always non-monetary and non-quantified differences between investments. For example, one may have a high net present value and a short life span. If funds can be reinvested at the same high rate at conclusion of the original investment, the investment may be sound. If, however, interest rates are declining and the principal can only be invested in lower-yielding investments, then a contract with a lower net present value but a longer term may, in fact, provide more profit to the corporation. In addition, one contract may involve much higher risk than another contract, and so on. It is at least as important to come to grips with the non-quantified characteristics of a desirable investment as those which are quantified, as this brings into play management policy with respect to markets, target customers, and risk spreading among many customers (leading to higher administration) versus concentration in a few large accounts (which reduces administration and can either increase or decrease risk).

To summarize the net present value method, the following steps are performed:

1. Select the target rate of return which meets the company's objectives and which will be used for all similar contracts.
2. List all investments or cash outflows in the appropriate periods in time.
3. List all of the cash inflows in the appropriate period in time, including prepaid rents, security deposits, and residual values, recognizing that the security deposits may be returned at the end of the contract.
4. Find the present value of the outflows and the inflows and calculate the net present value.
5. If the net present value is equal to or greater than zero the contract meets the minimum monetary standards set by the company. It may also be necessary to summarize the non-monetary factors before a final decision on a particular investment is considered.

INTERNAL RATE OF RETURN (IRR)

This method is similar to the net present value method, except that the desired rate of return is an unknown and the actual rate of return which equates the cash inflows to the cash outflows is calculated. This rate is referred to as the internal rate of return, or IRR. The method is used when the target rate of return is not known, or when it is wished to compare the rate of return on two contracts to see which yields the higher return. The technique to calculate IRR requires the same cash information as the net present value. That is, one sets out the cash outflows and cash inflows as they occur in time. Then one finds the rate of return which discounts the inflows and outflows to zero. This is a difficult calculation and is ordinarily handled by one of the many computer programs available. It can be done by trial and error, where a discount rate is used to compute the present value of the inflows and outflows. Assuming that the outflows are negative and the inflows are positive, if the net present value is negative a lower rate of return is required. If it is positive a higher rate of return should be used.

Conceptually, the lease or investment with the highest rate of return is the most desirable. Again, this assumes that non-monetary factors have been considered and, when comparing two leases, that the non-monetary factors do not suggest that one is significantly better than the other. In using methods such as this, one has to consider the duration of the lease as well as its rate of return and perhaps the funding provided for the lease. If interest rates generally are high and the lessor has borrowed for a long term, a short-term investment with a high yield will generate cash in a short period of time which requires reinvestment. If interest rates have subsequently declined, it will be difficult to obtain the required yield to match the high cost of borrowing. Similarly, if interest rates are relatively low and borrowing is on a floating rate basis, a long-term lease would have an unsatisfactory yield as interest rates rose.

In summary the IRR method requires the following steps:

1. A spreading of the cash outflows and inflows in their correct positions in time, the same as for the net present value method.
2. A calculation of the rate of return which discounts the cash flows to zero. In general, the contract with the highest IRR is preferable.
3. Other considerations may be as important as the IRR. These could include credit factors, policy factors within the company, relative interest rates, particularly as between the lease and the related borrowings, term of the lease, etc.

When using both the net present value and the IRR calculations, a difficulty occurs if the investment in the lease by the lessor is markedly different from lease to lease. We have referred to the difference as a result of term in the examples above. Similar problems occur when the investment size is markedly different. For example, if the net present value of a $10,000 investment and the net present value of a $100,000 investment are identical, which should the company accept? This could happen, for instance, with a $10,000 investment in a lease providing for 23 payments of $500 and a discount rate of 1% per month, giving a net present value of $227.91. Similarly, $100,000 investment in a lease providing for 23 payments of $4,899.73 at an interest rate of 1% per month gives a present value of $228, which is close enough to $227.91. Which contract is preferable? One way around this problem is to use a device called the "profitability index." This takes the present value of the cash flows and divides it by the amount of the investment to give a ratio of the cash flows to the investment. In the above example, the $10,000 investment would have a profitability index of 1.02 and the $100,000 investment would have a profitability index of 1.00 (in each case to two decimal points). Again, ignoring other factors, the contract with the higher profitability index would be preferable. Note that in these two examples the term is identical. Other factors, such as administration costs, credit risk, or desire to spread contracts over smaller amounts versus larger amounts would also enter into, and might well alter, the decision, depending on the company's policy at the particular time.

AFTER-TAX RATE OF RETURN

This topic is one of the most important and difficult facing the lessor. Some of the issues to be considered are:

1. Should the after-tax rate of return be calculated as the pre-tax rate multiplied by (1 − tax rate)?
2. Should the after-tax rate be calculated by discounting the cash flows including tax shelters or tax reductions, if any, with the resulting rate divided by (1 − the tax rate) to compare to a pre-tax rate of return?
3. Should the after-tax rate recognize that income tax is imposed on net profit rather than on gross income, and the return should therefore be calculated by reference to net-tax recoveries or payments expected over the life of the contract?
4. How does one compare a pre-tax yield on a loan, a pre-tax yield on a lease, and an after-tax yield on one or the other?
5. In computing returns on large contracts with specific leverage and sufficient tax benefits that the net principal invested by the lessor is negative, is it appropriate to discount the negative investment at the same rate as the positive investment (implying that the company's borrowing and lending rates are the same)?
6. In dealing with after-tax rates of return, particularly in long-term contracts, the lessor is combining contractual cash flows from the lease and perhaps contractual cash flows from a loan agreement with estimated residual values and estimated tax savings and payments, which are a function of future taxable income, tax rates, etc., which are not as firm as the contractual cash flows.

In some cases, the after-tax cash flow is not a factor in settling the lease rates and should simply be ignored. Once the lessor has computed costs to ensure that the pricing method arrives at a yield which covers all of the costs of operation and a profit, the incidence of income tax will often be much less important. This will be the case for most small ticket leasing, and was for much of the leasing industry during the early 1980s since much of the industry was working from a non-taxable base. This has been the case for several years as a result of relatively low spreads, high interest rates, credit losses, and the ability of the industry to use capital cost allowance to shelter leasing income. In other cases, the lessor's product is being priced on a basis comparable to that of a loan (money-on-money-leasing rate). In this case, the income tax implications may well be unimportant. If the after-tax rate is important, then the method of calculation is equally relevant; therefore, the above questions will be reviewed.

After-tax Equals Pre-tax Times (1 − Tax Rate)

This rate is derived from the individual's tax position when he or she looks at the income on an after-tax basis from a bond. If an individual receives a $100 interest coupon and is in a personal marginal tax rate of 48%, giving rise to $48 of income tax, the after-tax income is $52. Therefore, the after-tax yield on bond interest could be calculated as the pre-tax yield times (1 − tax rate of .48) equals .52 times the pre-tax rate. This is not useful in leasing since it implies that there are no deductions against the income and the taxation of interest income and lease income is identical. This is not usually the case.

After-tax Rate Divided By (1 − Tax Rate)

This calculation is sometimes used to compare an investment having a post-tax yield to an equivalent bond rate, assuming that the bond income would be fully taxable by the recipient at the highest marginal rate. Accordingly, this rate is not particularly useful in lessor or lessee analysis. It may have some application in spreading income in a company's portfolio when the yield on a lease — for example, a leveraged lease transaction — has been calculated on an after-tax basis, but the income has to be spread on a pre-tax basis. This has the assumption implicit in its use that the income is differential income, which may be accurate in limited circumstances.

NET-TAX PAYMENTS OVER THE LIFE OF A CONTRACT

When business people speak of yields on investments, they are generally thinking of the available cash flow to their organization. In general, this is their net profit before or after tax on the investment. When dealing with lending and leasing, we must therefore differentiate between the gross yield on the investment, which is the interest rate payable by the customer, and the net yield to the organization. For example, if one were to consider a loan of $10,000 at 1% per month for three years, the simple annual interest rate to a customer is 12% and it is the lender's gross yield. If the lender has a spread of 2½ percentage points and administration and credit costs amount to 18% of income, then a table of pre-tax and post-tax income can be prepared, as indicated in Exhibit 9-1.

Exhibit 9-1

Example Loan #1

Principal	$10,000
Rate per month	1%
Payment	$332.14
Cost of borrowing per month	0.7857
(78.57% of income)	
Admin. and credit costs	18% of income

Year	1	2	3	Total
Interest income	$1,041.46	668.16	247.42	1,957.04
Interest expense	818.27	524.99	194.40	1,537.66
Admin. and credit	187.46	120.27	44.54	352.27
	1,005.73	645.26	238.94	1,889.93
Income before tax	35.73	22.90	8.48	67.11
Tax at 51%	18.22	11.68	4.32	34.22
Net income	$ 17.51	11.22	4.16	32.89

This indicates that the pre-tax income of $35.73 in year one is 3.43% of gross income, and it represents a return on average principal outstanding of about .41 of 1% per annum. From the lender's point of view then a return of 12% on principal loaned becomes a return of about ½ of 1% after all of the lender's costs and expenses. Income tax will further reduce this return by about ½ to about .2 of 1% of the principal amount from time to time outstanding. While the individual rates of return will vary from lender to lender, particularly because 100% financing of the loan and a relatively low interest spread have been assumed, the point to make is that the net return to a lender is much lower than the gross return, and the incidence of income tax to a lender is relatively low when compared to other costs. In most circumstances, however, a lender will be taxable each year a loan is outstanding since there are no present provisions for deferral of interest income for income tax purposes. In contrast, a lease involving the same principal amount of $10,000, the same total charge to the customer, $10,000 principal plus $1,957.04 interest, but payable in the form of rent, would yield the results shown in Exhibit 9-2.

Exhibit 9-2

Lease with 50% CCA — No Residual

Year	1	2	3	Total
Rental income	$3,985.68	3,985.68	3,985.68	11,957.04
CCA (25/50/25%)	2,500.00	5,000.00	2,500.00	10,000.00
Interest, admin. and credit	1,005.73	645.26	238.94	1,889.93
	3,505.73	5,645.26	2,738.94	11,889.93
Initial taxable income/loss	479.95	(1,659.58)	1,246.74	67.11
Loss carry-over allocation	(479.95)	(1,659.58)	(1,179.63)	—
Taxable income	—	—	67.11	67.11
Tax at 51%	—	—	34.22	34.22
Net income	$ —	—	32.89	32.89

We can make the following observations from the above calculations:

1. For simplicity, it is assumed that the entire cost of the leased asset is written off by the lessor over the three years of the lease. This was appropriate for certain machinery and equipment used in the manufacturing and processing business in Canada. These rates are, of course, subject to alteration from time to time and differ for different equipment categories.
2. The lease generates taxable income in the first year as a result of the present provision for claiming CCA, which provide for only one-half year's CCA in the years of addition of equipment. In practice, if leases are written evenly over the year, one would have the same capital cost allowance, but only half a year's income and expenses, which would again result in a loss of income tax purposes in the year in which the lease was recorded.
3. The provisions of the *Income Tax Act* provide for loss carry-forward

and carry-back. Again for simplicity, the large tax loss incurred in the second year of the lease has been applied to reduce the otherwise taxable income in the first and third year. As a result, this lease contract generates taxable income only in its final year. Since the cash flow, except for the incidence of income tax, is the same for the two contracts, the lease contract will be more profitable than the loan contract. This will provide a slightly higher internal rate of return or a slightly higher net present value on a net profit basis for the lease.

Accordingly, this comparison indicates that two contracts with the same cost of borrowing to the debtor/lessee can have a different after-tax return to the lender/lessor. The above example, where the loss for income tax purposes in one or more years is used to offset taxable income in the same lease, but where the loss is not used to "shelter" other taxable income, is referred to as a "self-shelter lease." That is, the capital cost allowance shelters the income from the lease from taxation until the later periods of the lease. However, this lease was constructed so that all of the cost of the leased asset was deductible as CCA over the term of the lease. Unfortunately, with the "pool" concept of CCA which is normal in Canada, the above situation is not the usual result. In most cases a portion of the cost of the asset is left unclaimed at the end of the lease term and will serve to reduce future taxable income of the organization. When the unclaimed CCA is large, the lessor's return is adversely affected as his or her income taxes are prepaid, as compared to a finance contract.

Up to this point, the residual value of the leased asset has been ignored for purposes of simplicity. In practice, the option price will reduce the undepreciated capital cost of the asset at the end of the lease and neutralize the potential adverse tax position whenever the option price is close to the undepreciated capital cost. In addition, the lessor can, in some circumstances, take advantage of the pool concept for CCA and arrange to have an option price which will exceed UCC. This will result in a gain for income tax purposes which will be deferred as long as there are other assets in the pool that leave the pool positive. As soon as the total pool is driven negative at the end of a taxation year, the negative balance becomes taxable income of the leasing company. Let us examine two examples, one where the CCA leaves a balance in the pool, and one where the receipt of a residual value creates a negative balance for the particular leased asset, but the gain is deferred as a result of other assets in the pool.

When dealing with examples such as these, the cash flows in the lease contracts either require more funding or permit a faster paydown of debt than is the case with the comparable loan transactions. These alterations to the loan cash flow pattern are very important to the lessor, but they have not been worked into these examples, merely for simplicity. In addition, we have not worked in a theoretical leverage, but have assumed 100% borrowing for the particular assets being acquired. With this caveat, let's look at a loan transaction similar to Exhibit 9-1 but now having an additional $3,000 advance paid off by a $3,000 final or "balloon" payment. Assuming the same ratios for interest expense, administration, and credit as in Exhibit 9-1 the tax position of such a loan is reflected in Exhibit 9-3 below. The pre-tax income of $104.16 and the after-tax income of $51.04 are spread over the life of the contract, as was the case with Exhibit 9-1.

Exhibit 9-3

Example Loan #2

Same as Loan #1 but with a "balloon" payment of $3,000 paying a $3,000 higher principal.

Year	1	2	3	Total
Interest income	$1,401.46	1,028.16	607.42	3,037.04
Interest expense	1,101.13	807.82	477.25	2,386.20
Admin. and credit	252.25	185.09	109.34	546.68
	1,353.38	992.91	586.59	2,932.88
Income before tax	48.08	35.25	20.83	104.16
Tax at 51%	24.52	17.98	10.62	53.12
Net income	$ 23.56	17.27	10.21	51.04

We would now like to contrast this with two comparable lease situations, where the cash flow paid by the lessee is identical to that received by the lender in Exhibit 9-3. However, we are presenting situations where the CCA rate is low enough that there is a significant unclaimed capital cost allowance at the end of the lease, after receipt of the residual value (indicated by Exhibit 9-4), and a second situation where the CCA is all claimed and the residual value is credited to the pool, with the result that tax thereon is deferred. The rental income and cash flows in the first example are illustrated by Exhibit 9-4.

Exhibit 9-4

Lease wih 20% CCA — 30% Residual

Year	1	2	3	Total
Rental income	$4,345.68	4,345.68	4,345.68	13,037.04
Interest, admin. and credit	1,353.38	992.91	586.59	2,932.88
Margin before CCA	2,992.30	3,352.77	3,759.09	10,104.16
CCA at 10%/20%/20%	1,300.00	2,340.00	1,872.00	5,512.00
Taxable income	1,692.30	1,012.77	1,887.09	4,592.16
Tax at 51%	863.07	516.51	962.42	2,342.00
	$ 829.23	496.26	924.67	2,250.16
Cash flow				
Rental income	$4,345.68	4,345.68	4,345.68	13,037.04
Debt repayment (P&i)	(4,128.73)	(4,128.73)	(7,128.74)	(15,386.20)
Admin. and credit	(252.25)	(185.09)	(109.34)	(546.68)
Income tax	(863.07)	(516.51)	(962.42)	(2,342.00)
Residual*			3,000.00	3,000.00
Net cash flow	$ (898.37)	(484.65)	(854.82)	(2,237.84)

* Residual is treated as received immediately after end of fiscal year. Present value of unclaimed CCA of $4,488 @ .7857/mo. is $1,533.

This type of lease is sometimes referred to as a "tax-trap lease" because the taxable income is so large that it creates a significant negative cash flow each year on the contract. In practice, if the company was in fact taxable, the true cost of the lease would be greater as a result of a need to finance the advance tax payments. The tax prepayment, compared to a loan contract, amounts to $2,288.88, or 51% of the UCC of $4,488. If this amount could be claimed immediately, at least some of the adverse cash flow would be recovered. However, the future CCA can be claimed to reduce future income tax only at the rate of 20% of the UCC per annum. If we take the present value of these future tax reductions at the borrowing rate in Exhibit 9-4, the future tax reductions have a present value of $1,533. Accordingly, this contract would have an eventual negative cash flow of $704.84

($2,237.84 − $1,533.00). There are, in fact, many leases written like this, and the adverse effects are offset only because extra CCA is claimable on other leases. In effect, one lease with a high CCA rate is subsidizing a lease with a lower CCA rate. Presumably, the lessor would be seeking compensation for the CCA differences by differences in the interest rate implicit in the lease. In contrast, Exhibit 9-5 provides for the claiming of capital cost allowance on a 50% straight-line basis (with 25% claimable in the first year), which provides the tax position as shown.

Exhibit 9-5

Lease with 50% CCA — 30% Residual

Year	1	2	3	Total
Margin before CCA, as in Lease 9–2	$2,992.30	3,352.77	3,759.09	10,104.16
CCA – 25%/50%/25%	3,250.00	6,500.00	3,250.00	13,000.00
Gain (loss) for tax purposes	$ (257.70)	(3,147.23)	509.09	(2,895.84)
Cash flow:	$ (35.30)	31.86	107.60	104.16

PV of tax payable on negative UCC of $3,000 = $1,330
(In this case the liability is offset by losses available
from the second year)

In this case, the lease reflects a loss for tax purposes through its life of $2,895.84. This contrasts to a pre-tax profit on the loan contract (Exhibit 9-3) of $104.16, with the difference being the $3,000 negative UCC on the lease. On the assumption that the negative UCC will be taxable 50% in each of the next two years, which assumes other assets of a similar pool, the present value of the future tax payable is $1,330. In practice, this type of transaction might well give rise to increased cash flow to the leasing company as a result of being able to shelter significant, otherwise taxable income in years one and two, with the result that the leasing organization would be in a more favourable cash position than a comparable lender would be.

DEALING WITH A NEGATIVE INVESTMENT BALANCE

There are a number of transactions where the net investment by the lessor becomes negative as a result of the ability to offset losses for income tax purposes against income which would otherwise be taxable. The reduction in income taxes payable can be treated as a positive cash flow associated with the lease contract. In general, the tax losses in the early years of such a lease are offset by larger taxable incomes in later years. Accordingly, the tax reduction is temporary, and one might think of it as a temporary interest-free loan from the tax department. It is, in fact, similar to the deferred income tax which arises in accounting as a result of a variety of provisions in the *Income Tax Act* in Canada providing deductions for tax purposes in one year that are not made for accounting purposes until a later period. The deferred income tax represents the income tax effect of such timing difference. In leases that give rise to this situation, one will have an investment period early in the lease, a negative investment period, and then a further period when one would ordinarily have an investment in the lease. When the internal rate of return (IRR) on these contracts is computed, the variety of cash flows can result in a variety of answers to the IRR calculation, some of which can be negative. One can get around this by doing a net present value calculation at an assumed yield, to get an approximation of the rate that one is after. Then the actual rate which is close to the expected rate is probably the one sought. The other question, however, is whether interest should be recorded at the internal rate of return when in a borrowing position, as well as recording interest at the internal rate of return when in a lending position. If individuals were to use this method for purposes of preparing financial statements and tax returns, they would in effect be charging themselves interest expense at the same rate at which they are lending money on the lease. This hardly seems realistic.

Another method is to take the income to be earned on the contract and allocate it to the periods when the contract is in an investment position, allocating neither income nor expense to periods when the contract is in a negative position. This seems to be more reasonable but probably understates the actual income of the contract during the lending periods, just as it understates the business's cost of funds in the period when the investment is negative.

A third system is to allocate interest expense in the periods when the lease investment is in the negative position on the basis that the lessor is borrowing money and the proper charge during this period is the lessor's cost of borrowing. As a variant on this latter system, some indicate that the contract should be charged "a bargain borrowing rate" rather than the full cost of normal borrowing, as there are costs normally associated with borrowing that are not required for these borrowings.

Finally, it could be suggested that what is really happening is that the contract generates funds in excess of those which the lender has invested (usually as a result of a short-term, non-interest-bearing loan created by tax write-offs), and the excess funds have really been "loaned" to other parts of the organization. As a minimum, the organization can pay down other short-term borrowings, so the surplus funds should earn interest vis-à-vis the rest of the organization at least at a savings rate.

An argument can be made for the above suggestions. There are so many imponderables in long-term lease contracts, particularly when dealing in future income tax rates, tax savings, etc., that the decision as to how to treat the negative investment should ordinarily not be a determinant as to whether to enter into a contract or not. In practice, if a company receives a sum of money as a result of tax savings and the amount has to be repaid in the relatively near future, the company would ordinarily pay down short-term borrowings. To review this, let us assume in Exhibit 9-5 that we were allowed a full write-off of the cost of the asset in the year of acquisition, for income tax purposes, and that the lessee provided a deposit equal to the residual value of $3,000. Assume further that all of our borrowings are short-term borrowings at a rate of .7857% per month and that the organization has adequate income otherwise taxable to take advantage of any tax losses generated by the lease.

In addition, let us assume that this particular lease comes with its own special leverage debt of $8,000 repayable with blended principal and interest payments of $350 per month which are deducted from the rental payments and repay the debt in 26 months. The company's net investment at the beginning of the lease is $2,000, represented by the initial cost of the leased assets of $13,000 less the deposit of $3,000 and the leverage of $8,000. The tax loss in the first year gives rise to a tax recovery of $4,962 which, after receipt of rent, service of debt, and payment of expenses, leaves the company with a negative cash investment of $2,856. In practice, the company would still have an investment in the lease and cash on hand at the end of the period. If one were to draw up a financial statement reflecting just this lease transaction, the tax position and financial position would be as indicated in Exhibit 9-6.

Exhibit 9-6

Leveraged Lease with 100% CCA — 30% Residual

Year	1	2	3	4
Rental income	$ 4,346.00	4,346.00	4,346.00	13,038.00
Interest	823.00	269.00	8.00	1,100.00
Admin. and credit	252.00	185.00	109.00	546.00
CCA	13,000.00	—	—	13,000.00
	14,075.00	454.00	117.00	14,646.00
Taxable income (loss)	(9,729.00)	3,892.00	4,229.00	(1,608.00)
Tax payable (recoverable)	(4,962.00)	1,985.00	2,157.00	(820.00)
Net after-tax income (loss)	$(4,767.00)	1,907.00	2,072.00	(788.00)

Financial Position

Year	0	1	2	3	4
Investment in lease	$13,000.00	10,056.00	6,738.00	3,000.00	
Less:					
Deposit	3,000	3,000.00	3,000.00	3,000.00	
Leverage debt	8,000.00	4,623.00	692.00	—	
	11,000.00	7,623.00	3,692.00	3,000.00	
Net	2,000.00	2,433.00	3,046.00	—	
Excess cash	—	4,856.00	2,832.00	4,212.00	2,682
Net investment	$ 2,000.00	(2,423.00)	214.00	(4,212.00)	(2,682)

Note: 1. Tax payable on negative UCC balance in year 4 is $1,530.
2. Closing net investment represents initial cash of $2,000 invested in the lease plus $682 after-tax profit.

Cash Flow

Year	1	2	3	4	Total
Rent received	$ 4,346.00	4,346.00	4,346.00		13,038.00
Paid on debt	4,200.00	4,200.00	700.00		9,100.00
	146.00	146.00	3,646.00	—	3,938.00
Admin. and credit cost	(252.00)	(185.00)	(109.00)	—	(546.00)
Tax recovery (paid)	4,962.00	(1,985.00)	(2,157.00)	(1,530.00)	(710.00)
Cash flow	$ 4,856.00	(2,024.00)	1,380.00	(1,530.00)	2,682.00

The large tax recovery in the first year results in a large cash balance at the end of that year. From the company's perspective this lease transaction has a negative net investment as far as income earning balances are concerned. The company's financial statement taken as a whole would show the tax recovery as a deferred tax liability. In year two and year three a large part of the tax recovery in the first year is repaid to the government as a result of the high tax liability in those two years. By the time the contract is complete and tax on the residual value is paid, likely in year four or five, the overall result is a profit of $1,392 before income tax, a tax liability of $710, and a net profit of $682. This is reflected in the final balance of the fourth year.

From a corporate perspective the organization still has a $10,056 investment (calculated as $7,056 investment in payments of $322.14 for 24 months

@ 1%, plus $3,000 book investment in the residual) in the lease at the end of its first period and has liabilities of $7,623 plus a deferred income tax liability. The income statement would reflect income on the $10,056 in the company's ordinary method (irrespective of whether the transaction is treated as an operating lease or a financing lease). The company would also benefit from a reduction in interest expense, since the large tax refund would permit the paydown of debt incurred on a short-term basis. However, the company would have to have the borrowing capacity to incur additional debt as the deferred income tax reversed in years two, three, and four. During this period, the company has replaced interest-bearing debt with non-interest-bearing debt as a result of the income tax treatment of the particular investment. Accordingly, it would seem appropriate to attribute the saving in interest expense to the particular investment when appraising it as compared to other investments. It would not be necessary to make any adjustment to the method of picking up income on the $10,056 of investment in the lease, as the "additional income" would be reflected in the income statement of the leasing company by a reduced interest expense in exactly the amount by which the company was actually able to reduce its interest expense. While this is clerically correct, it does not present the correct allocation of income on funds from time to time outstanding in the contract. This is the central issue in allocating income to investments. In effect, the cash flow resulting from the reduction in income tax and the cash out-flow resulting from the later repayment of this reduction are both directly associated with the contract, and therefore ought to be reflected in the series of cash flows which are used to determine the internal rate of return and the recording of income on the contract.

This is the method required by the CICA in paragraph 3065.38 of the *Handbook*. The *Handbook* does not deal, however, with the difficulty of a negative investment. Here are three suggestions:

1. Compute the internal rate of return and allocate the income in accordance with that, which allocates negative income (interest expense to periods when there is a negative investment). These periods will benefit at least from reduced interest expense, and the only cost to the period would be the difference between the internal rate of return and interest expense. If the surplus funds generated by the lease are invested at a rate at least equal to the internal rate of return, then the negative investment period will in fact break down.

2. Divide the amount of the negative investment into two or more parts and allocate to consecutive periods when the investment is positive. This results in the division of the investment into three parts: a positive part, usually at the beginning of the lease, a part when there is zero investment, and a final part which is again usually positive. While we have not experimented with this approach extensively, it would appear that

it distorts the income pick-up and the income of the period of the nil investment since that period will in fact have benefited from the higher cash flow that resulted in a negative investment in the first place.

3. Allocate interest expense to the negative investment period in proportion to the negative investment at the short-term interest cost incurred by the company. This will just offset the interest saving for that period, leaving it neutral. The interest expense allocated to those periods becomes increased income of the periods when the investment is positive. This method has the appeal that it leaves the negative investment period neutral and more or less fits the cash flows that are expected to be realized.

There is a tendency to consider that the transactions where income taxes are important parts of the calculation are rare. This has certainly been the case in leasing in Canada for the last several years. However, it is far from the case in other countries. For example, in the United Kingdom lessors once enjoyed the advantage of being able to write off the entire cost of an asset in the year of acquisition. This advantage is now phased out, but the loss is being partially offset by a lowering of the overall corporate income tax rate. Therefore, there was an unusual situation in the United Kingdom for 1984 where the lessor saved income taxes at approximately a 50% rate by being allowed virtually complete write-off of assets purchased, with the expectation that income tax will be paid at about a 35% rate over the next few years as the lease payments are included in taxable income. For these lessors there is a 15% real tax saving. As one can imagine, there was considerable activity in the leasing business in the United Kingdom, and particularly with first-rate credits and high-value transactions. It was not uncommon, for example, to have large value transactions carried out at an implicit rate of under 3% per annum.

CONTRACTUAL VERSUS ESTIMATED CASH FLOWS

The preceding sections have dealt with the before and after tax position of lessors at some length. In all of the calculations, it has been assumed that the cash flows called for by the contracts, whether they be lending or borrowing contracts, and the cash flows resulting from income tax and residual values were equally certain to occur. There are many examples where the estimate of contractual cash flows has proved optimistic. These lead to litigation and credit losses. Nevertheless, these cash flows are unquestionably more certain than the income tax estimates for several years into the future. For this reason, it is useful to put some measure of assurance on the cash flows, perhaps by the use of probabilities, to attempt to recognize their uncertain character. For example, one might wish to do cash flow calculations treating the residual value and income tax estimates as certain; that is, as certain as the remaining cash flows. Then one might wish to assign a probability to each of the uncertain cash flows. If the uncertain cash flows were multiplied by the probability, then one would arrive at a probability adjusted cash flow. For example, if it is expected that a residual value in five years will be $3,000, the range of estimates might be as follows:

1. 90% sure that it will be not less than $2,000;
2. 70% sure that it will be $3,000;
3. 40% sure that it could be $4,000;
4. 0% sure that it could be above $4,000.

In general, in dealing with residuals one does not have a situation where one is going to get some funds or no funds. Accordingly, one may be 90% sure of getting $2,000 and only 70% sure of getting $3,000; but it is the added thousand dollars that decreases the assurance from 90% to 70%. Accordingly, the person who assesses a 70% probability of receiving $3,000 would also assess a much higher percentage of receiving at least $2,000. If this is the case, the probability might be restated as: "I am 90% sure that I will receive $2,000 and 70% sure that I will receive an additional $1,000." Overall, then, one might say that one is reasonably sure of receiving 90% of $2,000, plus 70% of $1,000, equals $2,500. The $2,500 could then be inserted into the residual value calculation with some confidence that it was at least as sure to be received as are the contractual payments under the lease. In general, where pre-estimate of assurance is relatively low, say 60% or below, one would tend to ignore the cash flow as a reasonable probability.

A similar procedure can then be used with respect to the income tax cash flows, dealing with the significant variances:

1. Will the company have sufficient taxable income to be able to use proposed income tax losses or investment tax credits?
2. Will tax losses from the lease be unquestionably deductible against other income?
3. Will income and capital tax rates stay the same or go down in the period following the tax saving, so that the tax payments will be at the same or lower rates of taxation?
4. Will capital cost allowances stay the same over the life of the lease?
5. Will the tax treatment of residual values remain at least as favourable as when the lease was signed?

After considering these and any other imponderables that are peculiar to the company, it is possible to recast the cash flows by inserting those with a high probability of occurring. Then the net present value or IRR can be calculated based on these cash flows so that management can be aware of the spread of returns to be expected. In computing the spreads, one should try to differentiate between cash flows, such as residual values where there is fairly high assurance that some value would be received as opposed to those where an "all or nothing" situation would occur. For example, if there is doubt that losses from leasing can be offset against other income, the result will be that the losses will either be offset or not. There will be no middle ground. With income tax rate changes, on the other hand, it is likely that the tax rate will vary, but it will not disappear.

There are other techniques which may be used to assess the degree of risk that a particular cash flow will not be received when anticipated. Where large amounts are involved, sophisticated techniques are useful. For example, one long-term leasing contract written in the early 1970s as an operating lease included reliance on the residual value of rolling stock at the end of the lease term, perhaps seventeen years later. This lessor used "the Delphi Process" to increase its assurance as to the residual value of the equipment. This process required estimates from people in the company that made the equipment and several users of the equipment, as well as people in business who were unconnected with the particular industry in which the equipment was used. Interest rates at the time were about 6% and declining. Inflation was about 4% and declining. The present value of a million-dollar residual due in fifteen years, with interest rates at 6%, is $420,000. If the calculation had been done at 12%, the residual value would have been only $185,000. A good estimate was made of the residual value, and of its present value at the then-current interest rates, and the financial statement treatment for the intervening years was determined.

It is particularly interesting to review the fifteen years following the writing of the contract to see what major changes occurred that were not contemplated when the lease was written:

1. Inflation increased from 4% to around 12% in the early 1980s and then declined to about 4% again.
2. With the rise in inflation, interest rates rose dramatically to a prime rate of 18%, and at the time of writing the prime rate is near 8%.
3. Interest rates have generally increased in absolute terms; that is, the spreads between inflation and market rates are currently much larger than in the 1970s, and therefore the return on assets has been affected.
4. The inflation of costs other than interest has probably eroded the interest margin provided for in the original contract.
5. The high interest rates and high inflation led to two severe recessions in a period when many lenders were showing losses for income tax purposes rather than gains. It was not contemplated, when the lease was written, that the company would not have sufficient taxable income to absorb all of the capital cost allowance on the assets. On the other hand, the contract is probably generating income in excess of CCA, and it was expected that this would be taxable. The tax shelter created by other operating losses in the early 1980s would probably increase the return to the lessor marginally.
6. Capital tax rates have tripled over the period, severely eroding the expected margin.

7. The residual value estimate is holding up well.

With all of these variables, most of which cannot be predicted, reliance on estimates of tax rates and taxable income as well as interest rates in the future must be taken with "a large dose of salt." If the economic events of the future have to unfold favourably for a long period of time for the particular lease to be profitable, and if the lessee is unwilling to share the risk of adverse change, the transaction should probably not be undertaken.

Chapter 10

The Lessor and the Insolvent Lessee

INTRODUCTION

No lessor enters into a lease arrangement expecting that the lessee will experience financial difficulties and become insolvent. Nevertheless, each year thousands of lease contracts go into default and lessors must decide what action to take to protect their position. This chapter sets out some of the issues which lessors may face when their lessee becomes insolvent and a receiver or trustee in bankruptcy is appointed.

The appointment of a receiver or trustee in bankruptcy brings control of the lessee's assets to a different party — typically one who is acting in the interests of a particular secured creditor of the lessee or of all the creditors of the lessee. The receiver or trustee will review the lease and, if there is any question as to its validity, may refuse to honour it or may attack it. The lessor must, therefore, at the time the lease is signed, be sure that it has no legal defects and, if appropriate, be sure it is registered in the provincial registry system. The lessor should also ensure that any appropriate acknowledgements are obtained from other potentially adverse interests — for example, a prudent lessor might require from the landlord an acknowledgement of the ownership of an air conditioning unit being leased to a tenant in a building to ensure there is no subsequent claim that the unit is considered a leasehold improvement and therefore part of the building.

This chapter does not deal with real estate leases as they are beyond the scope of this book.

VALIDITY OF A LEASE

A lease agreement typically sets out the rights of the lessor and the lessee. Once signed by both parties, unless defective, it is a legal contract and is binding on both lessor and lessee. However, if the lease transaction is classified as a security agreement or a form of purchase transaction, it may not be binding on third parties in many provinces in Canada unless it is registered under the provincial security registration system.

CLASSIFICATION OF LEASES

Chapter 2 has already discussed how leases are classified for accounting purposes. Leases are typically classified as operating or capital for the lessee and as operating, sales type or direct financing for the lessor. These are distinctions which are made to help classify them for accounting purposes and financial statement presentation. They are only somewhat useful in considering classifications for legal purposes.

In classifying leases for legal purposes, the courts seem to have divided leases into three categories: disguised sales, disguised loans and true leases.

Disguised Sales

The courts have considered a lease to be a disguised sale when the rental is effectively partial payment of the purchase price. If there is a requirement that the lessee purchase the asset at the end of the lease period, the lease may be deemed to be a conditional sale agreement — i.e., a disguised sale. In such an instance, the lease will be considered to have created a security interest for the lessor to help ensure payment of the contract or to enable it to repossess the asset in the case of non-payment.

The issue of a purchase option also plays a part in determining the legal character of a lease. If there is a purchase option based on fair market value at the option date, the lease may not be classified as a disguised sale. If the option is at a nominal amount which bears no relationship to the fair market value at the option date, the lease may be classified as a disguised sale or even a disguised loan. An option price of 10% of the original purchase price, which may be acceptable to Revenue Canada for tax purposes, may not be accepted by the courts as fair market value. Thus, a difference may arise in structuring a lease for tax purposes and for legal purposes if it is to be considered a true lease.

The lack of an option price does not necessarily construe a lease to be a true lease. If the term of the lease is the effective life of the asset such that there is no residual value at the end of the lease period, the lease may be considered to be an effective or disguised sale.

Disguised Loans

A sale and leaseback may effectively be a disguised loan as it is making assets available which the lessee might otherwise have to borrow money to retain. A sale and leaseback reverses the normal sequence of ownership in that it turns an owner into a lessee whereas many leases, when the purchase option is exercised, transform a lessee into an owner. This reverse order of the normal ownership chain is one aspect in classifying it as a disguised loan. Similarly, as set out above, the lack of a purchase option or the ability of the lessor to claim ownership of the asset at the end of the lease period may indicate that the transaction was a disguised loan.

True Lease

Some leases can clearly be classified solely as true leases. Perhaps the most obvious example is the daily car rental where the period is short, the asset has significant value at the end of the lease period, the contract normally states that the vehicle remains the property of the lessor and there is no purchase option. Another example of a true lease may be the lease agreement for a photocopier or postage meter. Such agreements normally contain no purchase option and the asset remains the property of the lessor at all times. Many such agreements permit the exchange or upgrading of equipment during the lease period but at no time does the lessee have an opportunity to become the owner of the equipment.

Other Factors

In considering the classification of a lease, the courts will also consider the intention of the parties rather than the form used in documenting the transaction. Over a period of time, the courts have considered two other factors in classifying lease transactions: the role of the parties and the intent of the parties.

To determine the role of the parties, the business of both lessor and lessee must be examined, together with whether the lessee was in financial difficulty at the time of the transaction, and whether the lessor was in the business of providing financial assistance. If either the lessor or lessee is not acting in its normal role in a lease transaction, or if one party is effectively rendering financial assistance to the other through the lease transaction, it may be deemed to be either a disguised loan or a disguised sale rather than a true lease.

The intent of the parties is perhaps the most important consideration and overlaps the other areas. If the lessor is effectively only providing financing while the lessee enjoys the use of and responsibility for possession and maintenance of the leased equipment, the lease may be characterized as a financial lease or as a disguised sale which merely provides security to the lessor for the unpaid amount.

PERSONAL PROPERTY SECURITY ACTS

Over the past 15 years, several of the common law provinces of Canada (common law provinces being all except the province of Quebec) have passed legislation dealing with secured transactions in personal (as distinct from real) property. It is under this legislation that leases which may be characterized as security agreements or forms of purchase transaction are dealt with. Ontario first enacted such legislation in 1970 as the *Personal Property Security Act* ("PPSA") and it has served as the basis for enactment of similar legislation in several other provinces. The legislation was modelled on the

Uniform Commercial Code which has been in place in virtually all states in the United States since the 1930s. Reference in this chapter is to the Ontario Act, although the legislation in the other provinces is similar in most respects.

The Act is intended to apply to all transactions which create a security interest, regardless of the form of the transaction. The definition of security interest in the Ontario *PPSA* specifically includes leases that secure payment or performance of an obligation. A security interest is deemed to be created when an interest in personal property is given to secure the payment or performance of an obligation.

As mentioned above, a lease transaction is typically binding upon both the lessor and lessee when they have signed the documentation. To be enforceable against third parties, the security interest must have "attached" and been "perfected"; both are terms defined in the *PPSA*.

Attachment is generally considered to have occurred when the lessee (or debtor) has signed an agreement which describes the assets pertaining to the transaction, value is given and the lessee (or debtor) has rights to the asset. At this time, under the *PPSA*, the security interest is enforceable between the two contracting parties, lessor and lessee (or lender and debtor).

For perfection to occur, attachment must have occurred (as above) and, generally, the agreement must have been registered under the Act. Registration consists of completing a prescribed form which sets out the name of the lender, the name and address of the debtor, a general description of the goods securing the transaction and certain other information. This form must be entered into the *PPSA* registration system, which, in Ontario, is an online computer system based in Toronto but with terminals throughout the province. Once so perfected, the transaction is valid as against third parties, provided the process was properly followed and completed on a timely basis.

(Note: The above outline of attachment and perfection is not intended as a complete or legal explanation of those terms. There are alternative forms of perfection, and details of both processes are not included in these outlines. A lessor who wishes a lease transaction to be registered under the *PPSA* is strongly urged to seek competent legal advice.)

WHEN TO REGISTER UNDER THE *PPSA*

Despite the guidelines set out above and numerous court cases considering when leases fall under the *PPSA*, there is no simple rule to determine the applicability of the Act to such transactions. A few simple leases such as those cited above as true leases clearly are excluded from the Act because of their nature. Such leases probably do not need to be registered under the *PPSA*.

However, to be safe, the prudent lessor may wish to register the lease contract under the *PPSA* to avoid any subsequent attack that the transaction was primarily intended to provide security or was a form of purchase transaction. If such an attack were made and the transaction had not been registered, the lease would not be binding against a receiver or a trustee in bankruptcy. This would result in the receiver or trustee having legal title to the asset and the ability to dispose of it for the benefit of other creditors at the expense of the lessor.

THE INSOLVENT LESSEE

If a lessee defaults under the terms of the lease agreement, the lessor must consider its remedies, in accordance with the contract. As long as no third party has acted to take control of the lessee or its assets, the lessor can usually act without question or challenge. However, if a third party such as a receiver or trustee in bankruptcy has taken possession of the lessee's assets, the lessor may be subject to a challenge. It is at such time that registration under the *PPSA* may be critical to enable the lessor to assert its rights, unless the contract is obviously a true lease.

A receiver is typically a party acting on behalf of a secured creditor or the general body of creditors. The appointment may be by legal instrument (a private appointment) or by application to the court (a court appointment). A privately appointed receiver is responsible to its appointing creditor and acts on its behalf. Normally the appointment is as receiver and manager, in which case the receiver is also empowered to carry on the business of the debtor and not merely receive its assets. A court-appointed receiver (or receiver and manager) is responsible to the court that appointed it but will act in accordance with the various security agreements which the debtor has signed.

A trustee in bankruptcy is responsible to all the creditors of a business and may be appointed in either of two ways. A debtor may make a voluntary assignment in bankruptcy in which a trustee is named. Alternatively, a creditor may petition the court to have a debtor declared bankrupt and will name a trustee in the petition. If the court adjudges the debtor to be bankrupt, it will issue a receiving order and the trustee will take possession of the assets of the now bankrupt debtor. In both instances, all the assets of the bankrupt vest in the trustee.

OBLIGATIONS OF THE RECEIVER OR TRUSTEE

It is incumbent on either a receiver or a trustee in bankruptcy to try to maximize the realization of the debtor's assets. This may be achieved by carrying on the business of the debtor and trying to achieve a sale as a going concern, or selling the assets through a tender sale or auction. In any situation, the greater the available assets, the greater is likely to be the realization. Thus, the receiver or trustee will challenge ownership of any assets in its possession to which another party (possibly a lessor) is also laying claim.

It is at this stage that registration under the *PPSA* becomes important to the lessor. It must be remembered that the assets in question will normally have been in the possession of the debtor and thus will now be in the possession of the receiver or trustee. The lessor must be able to convince the receiver or trustee that the lessor has valid title to the assets before the receiver or trustee will give up possession of these assets. The receiver or trustee will usually seek a legal opinion as to the validity of the contract between debtor and lessor. If that opinion is that the contract is in any way deficient or should have been registered under the *PPSA* and was not, or was not registered properly, the receiver or trustee will not yield possession of the assets but will consider them part of the debtor's property to be available for sale. The lessor then has the option of commencing a legal action to regain possession of the assets or to abandon its claim and leave the assets to the receiver or trustee.

CONSIDERATIONS FOR THE PRUDENT LESSOR

To protect its position as owner of a leased asset, the lessor should be watchful at all times of its lessee. Consistently slow or missed payments may be a danger signal that the lessee is encountering financial difficulties. Credit reports on the lessee may indicate strained working capital, deteriorating sales or margins or other signs of financial weakness. Such signals may not necessarily place the lessor in a position of weakness but should alert it to watch the lessee carefully.

If the lease is a true lease, there should be no difficulty in the lessor removing its leased asset at any time, in accordance with the terms of the lease. If other than a true lease, the contract should have been registered under *PPSA* at its inception and renewed periodically if so required. If it has not yet been registered, the lessor should arrange for its immediate registration, recognizing that other parties who registered agreements between the time the lease contract was signed and the time it was registered may have a prior right to the asset.

Good recordkeeping can be essential to support a lessor's position. Date of delivery of the leased assets may be an issue in some situations; hence, a signed and dated receipt by the lessee may significantly bolster the lessor's position. If the lease is a true lease, it is often helpful to clearly identify with a sticker, sign or other mark, that the equipment is owned by the lessor.

Steps to Consider Prior to a Formal Insolvency

Once the lease is in default, the lessor will normally have rights under the contract. This default may well occur before there is a formal insolvency — i.e., before the appointment of a receiver or trustee in bankruptcy. If the lessor is satisfied that it has unquestioned rights in the leased asset, either because the lease is a true lease or has been validly registered under the *PPSA*, it may decide to press for a cure of the default (usually making up missed payments) and leave the asset with the lessee. However, if there is a question as to the legal title to the lease asset, the lessor may he well advised to exercise its rights upon default and seize possession of the leased asset before another party — receiver or trustee in bankruptcy — appears on the scene and questions its rights to the asset.

Steps to Consider After a Formal Insolvency

Once a receiver or trustee in bankruptcy is appointed, the rules change. The receiver or trustee will take possession of all assets previously in the possession of the lessee and will normally not release them unless it is satisfied that the party making claim on them has valid title. The question of valid title will be considered by the legal counsel for the receiver or trustee. If such opinion is that the lease is a true lease, the leased asset will usually be surrendered to the lessor without further delay. However, if there is a question as to the validity of the lessor's title, the receiver or trustee will not give up possession short of a court determination of the title or a financial settlement with the lessor. Thus, the earlier advice that the lessor keep a watchful eye over its lessee and repossess the leased asset upon default and before a formal insolvency appointment if there is any likelihood of a dispute over legal title to the asset.

If title to the asset is accepted as resting with the lessor, what should be the lessor's next step? This decision will probably depend upon the nature of the leased asset and the likely future of the insolvent business. Is the receiver or trustee continuing to operate the business and, if so, is the leased asset vital to the ongoing operations? Some lessors have been able to extract an agreement from the receiver to pay up all arrears under the lease and keep it current during the receivership if the leased asset is critical to maintaining the business as a going concern. A telephone system, computer hardware or software or a specialized piece of machinery may be essential to the operations of a business as a receiver would be unable to replace them on a timely basis.

If an agreement cannot be reached with the receiver or the lessor does not wish to do so, it may take possession of the asset. Taking possession normally entails removing it from the receiver; however, it may also be effected by disabling the asset (for example a major piece of machinery) by removing a vital part. This latter step may be much less costly than physical removal until the future of the insolvent business and/or the leased asset can be determined.

If the asset is removed and sold, any shortfall can be claimed against the lessee by the lessor as an unsecured creditor. However, in most insolvency situations, the return on such a claim will be small or non-existent. Thus, the lessor should consider its other options carefully before deciding upon this course of action.

If the receiver is attempting to continue the business and/or offer it for sale as a going concern, the best return for the lessor may be to leave the leased asset in place (assuming it is being properly safeguarded by the receiver and continues to be insured) to see if the business is continued and the new purchaser will assume the existing lease or enter into a new one. Many leased assets (for example customized telephone systems) may have limited residual value if removed from their original installation, but may have continuing value to a new purchaser. A receiver may find it beneficial to co-operate with the lessor because the leased asset remaining in place will enhance the value of the business and therefore increase the realization to the receiver, as well as maximizing the position of the lessor. In other circumstances the receiver may decide to exercise the purchase option under the lease and acquire the asset because its residual value exceeds the cost. Obviously under this alternative, the lessor should be satisfied as the terms of the lease have been adhered to.

Finally, if the title to the leased asset is claimed by the receiver and the lessor believes that the receiver's position is wrong, it can commence a legal action to recover possession (or possibly to force adherence to the lease). If successful, the lessor, in addition to recovering the leased asset or the stream of payment under it, may well recover its legal costs.

LESSOR BEWARE

While various alternatives and scenarios have been presented in this chapter, dealing with a insolvent lessee or its receiver or trustee in bankruptcy can be simplified and the lessor's position strengthened if legal advice is sought prior to the commencement of the lease and any appropriate action taken. Unless the lease is clearly a true lease, it should be registered under the *PPSA* if such legislation exists in the province where the transaction is taking place or in the province where the leased asset will be situated. Then, in the unfortunate circumstance where the lessee defaults and the lessor must take action, the lessor will be able to do so from a position of strength and, hopefully, minimize its loss or maximize its realization.

In anticipation of such eventualities, the default provisions and the rights of the lessor upon default should be complete and clear in the lease document. Acceleration of all future payments and right to immediate repossession are just two considerations for inclusion in the contract.

The issue of the insolvent lessee is a potential scenario where thought and action at inception of the lease transaction may save a lot of money and grief. Let the lessor beware!

Chapter 11

Odds and Ends of Business Issues

This chapter introduces a variety of subjects to alert lessors and lessees to particular risks and opportunities. The material is divided into three main areas:

- leasing outside Canada;
- a "hodgepodge" of tax caveats;
- a number of business issues designed to reduce the risk in portfolios or to improve the return.

INTERNATIONAL LEASING

When leasing transactions involving large amounts of money are contemplated, or if the acquisition of high-value, standardized capital equipment is considered, it is worthwhile looking to leasing conditions outside Canada to see if overall cost can be reduced. Over the years there have been a wide variety of advantages in examining the income tax laws of different countries to see if a disproportionate advantage could be obtained. For example, there was a period of time when it was possible to lease an asset in the United Kingdom to a U.S. lessee and have both the lessor and the lessee claim capital cost allowance. Since the income tax rates in each country were high and there were opportunities for fast write-off of the cost of the asset for tax purposes in each country, the overall cost to the lessee was reduced. This was referred to as "double-dip" depreciation and was successful until changes in the tax laws eliminated this advantage.

It was the practice in the United Kingdom in 1984 to provide for a 100% write-off of the cost of equipment acquired by the leasing company in the fiscal year of acquisition. Since the corporate tax rate was in the vicinity of 50%, this provided a considerable tax shelter for the leasing company. As a result, the leasing company was able to pass the cost of leased equipment on to a prospective lessee at a much reduced rate.

For example, an aircraft purchased in the United Kingdom for approximately $50,000,000 (Canadian) was available for lease in the U.K. for an annual payment of $7.8 million for seven years. Had this transaction been carried out in Canada at the then-current interest rates, the payment by the Canadian purchaser would have been in the order of $11.7 million (Canadian). The saving of $3.9 million a year for seven years would occur because the U.K. lessor could write off substantially all of the aircraft cost in the year of acquisition and reduce its tax at an approximate 50% rate. It would include the rents in income in future years when the corporate tax rate was to be reduced to approximately 35%. Accordingly, the lessor would reduce its 1984 tax bill by $25.9 million, reducing the cost of the aircraft to it to approximately $26 million. Against this it will receive rental income of some $54 million which will be taxable, after deduction of borrowing and other costs, although the income tax rate payable will only be 35%. In effect, the taxation authorities have reduced the cost of the aircraft on an outright basis by the 15% tax difference and have provided a "loan" through tax deferral, which loan is without interest and is repayable out of taxable income over the next seven years. This is, of course, an unusual and transitory situation resulting from a change in the U.K. taxation laws. It does show, however, that there are opportunities for those who review the taxation laws in different countries.

There are other examples of potential tax savings, including the preferential 10% income tax rate offered to certain Irish leasing companies to carry on offshore leasing, and the additional opportunities through the acquisition of partnerships that own substantial fixed assets. Since the opportunities change from time to time as income tax and corporation tax laws change, each situation has to be investigated on its merits and the tax position of a variety of countries has to be reviewed at the time a transaction is to be undertaken. Considerable lead time is therefore advantageous.

There is not a large volume of cross-border leasing in Canada as a result of the taxation and business barriers to such transactions. The dominant barrier is the withholding tax on rents payable by a Canadian lessee to a non-resident lessor. The withholding tax is payable by the lessee on each periodic payment. If you accept a rate of 15% and contrast this with the normal yield in a large contract, a 15% withholding tax would be easily 2½ times the entire contribution margin on a lease (rents less interest and recovery of capital cost). The Canadian withholding tax basic rate is 25%; however this is normally reduced by treaties and could vary from 0 (Norway) to 25%. For example, the Canada-U.S. treaty reduces the withholding tax rate to 10%, the same as the Canada-U.K. treaty. The withholding tax is payable whether or not the lessor makes a profit on the transaction, whereas income tax is a tax only on profit. Accordingly, withholding taxes are the single largest barrier to cross-border leasing with domestic lessees and foreign lessors. There are limited exceptions to this, predominantly in transportation equipment for international usage.

In addition to the withholding tax risk, a foreign lessor faces a variety of other risks. For example, there is an exchange risk on principal and interest, risk of changes in taxes, such as the GST, Provincial Capital Tax and Federal Large Corporations Tax (although the latter two apply to businesses carried out in Canada).

Canadian lessors also face the risks of foreign exchange variances even if they "match-fund" the transaction in the foreign currency. While the exchange risk may seem to have been removed by match-funding, the taxation treatment of exchange rate variances may differ between income and capital transactions. The rental income and interest expense in the transaction will be treated the same for Canadian tax purposes; however, foreign exchange variances on debt repayment are capital transactions which are only taxable or deductible on a realized basis. If a loss on the principal portion of a foreign debt is incurred and the loss is on capital account, the loss will only be deductible against other capital gains. While the cash loss on debt may be offset by the cash gain on the rent, the gain on the rent is an income gain which is currently taxable on an accrual basis. The offsetting capital loss on the debt payment may not be deductible until realized and then only against other capital gains. Of course the reverse could happen and you can suffer an exchange loss on the rent and a gain on settlement of debt. The exchange loss on rent would be immediately deductible for Canadian tax purposes. The exchange gain on the debt payments would be taxable only on a realized basis, but would be immediately taxable, when realized, as a capital gain.

There are also a number of business risks in dealing in foreign transactions which are not the same as in domestic transactions. For example one is not sure how a foreign jurisdiction will enforce a contract. Will they enforce specific performance? Will they enforce penalties built into the contract or could local practices reduce the penalty? Will foreign jurisdictions interpret a contract in the same manner as the lessor/lessee intended when they signed it? There may be increased time and cost in pursuing a legal action outside the lessor's country of origin to enforce a contract or recover the leased asset. In addition, many contracts contain casualty or stipulated loss values (SLV). On some occasions breach of the agreement results in a payment equal to the SLV. These values are usually quite high because the lessor may face tax on the SLV (similar to recapture of capital cost allowance). The SLV may also contain a penalty to recognize that the lessor may have to pay a penalty to cancel long-term borrowing contracts. This introduces an added financial risk to these contracts.

Accordingly the incidence of cross-border leases is not high in Canada and when they do occur they are generally larger value transactions wherein the lessee is a very good credit risk.

**Summary of Taxes to be Paid by Domestic Lessors and Lessees
in Cross-Border Leases**

The tax position of domestic companies acting as lessors or lessees is not straightforward. However it may be useful to look at a summary of the tax incurred by a lessor in operating from a Canadian taxable base and leasing to a foreign lessee. Similarly, it may be instructive to review the taxes to be incurred by a Canadian lessee leasing goods from a foreign lessor.

Exhibit 11-1

**Canadian Lessor — Foreign Lessee (Assuming Canadian Lessor
has no Permanent Establishment in the Foreign Jurisdiction)**

Type of Tax	Incurred	Notes
GST	No	Goods zero-rated for export.
PST	No	Goods exported, no PST (in general)
Provincial Capital Tax	Yes	On taxable capital employed at fiscal year-end.
Large Corporation Tax	Yes	On capital employed at fiscal year-end.
Withholding Tax	Yes	Except for exemptions, similar to that for transportation equipment used in international traffic, payable generally at rates of 0% (Norway) to 25% or perhaps more, depending on whether or not there is a treaty with the country, on gross rent, payable by lessee to the country in which the equipment is used. Generally payable at time of remittance of rent. But if there is no treaty, other countries' withholding tax laws may require a different rate.
Income Tax	Yes	Both federal and provincial income tax payable on taxable income; in general, rent less CCA, interest and costs incurred to earn the rent and administrative costs.
Relief for Foreign Tax Paid	Yes	Foreign tax credit, generally calculated as the lesser of Canadian tax on the rent income and the foreign tax paid. In general this would not recover the withholding tax.

Exhibit 11-2

Foreign Lessor — Canadian Lessee

Type of Tax	Incurred	Notes
GST	Yes	On rent? — No. On fair value of equipment when imported? — No, on the defined "Duty-Paid Value" in general, and in general, paid by the "importer of record". (Actually the tax is on the lessor, but is collected and paid by the lessee) Both operating and finance leases are a "supply of service" for purposes of GST.
PST	Yes	On duty-paid value.
Duty	Yes	On fair value for duty purposes, transaction is subject to Customs and Excise Tax Act.
Provincial Capital Tax and Large Corporations Tax	No	In general the capital taxes are avoided unless the lessor is carrying on business in Canada through a permanent establishment. If the lessor is carrying on business, then there is tax on net income and LCT as well.
Withholding Tax	Yes	Except for specific exemptions for transportation equipment used in international traffic. Lessee remits the tax at time of rental payment at rate which varies depending on tax treaty with foreign government (0% — Norway to 25%, with main trading partners at 10%).
Income Tax	No	Rent is deductible to lessee.

There are a number of particularly detailed tax questions to be considered which are largely beyond the scope of this book. The tax position changes at least annually and must be researched on a transaction by transaction basis. However, at the time of writing, the following special notes should be made, with the provision that rules relating to real estate are not covered.

Withholding Taxes

The subject of taxation of cross-border leasing was covered in considerable detail in "Studies on International Fiscal Law" XLIV Congress of the IFA

127

(International Fiscal Association), Volume LXXVa from the International Tax Congress — Stockholm Sweden — 1990. That material covers the taxation of leases in a number of jurisdictions around the world (31) and a general report summarizes the positions of the other reporters. This impressive 684 page study, which has been translated into several languages covers a very complex subject from a worldwide perspective and provides much insight into the complicated subject of cross-border leasing. The section on Canada covers the main areas of importance to lessors/lessees in some detail.

There are provisions in the *Income Tax Act* relating to transportation equipment, principally ships and aircraft (the international traffic section of the *ITA*, s. 81(1)(*c*)) or in separate tax treaties. The Minister of Finance also announced relief from withholding tax for payments on leases for aircraft used on domestic flights by domestic lessees to foreign lessors. This amendment was announced on December 6, 1991 and had not been enacted at time of writing. In addition s. 212(1)(*d*)(ix) of the *ITA* exempts from withholding the portion of rental payments made for the use or right to use any corporeal property outside Canada. Accordingly, transactions relating to transportation equipment used in international traffic will generally escape withholding, except for the portion of rent that relates to the period when the asset is used in Canada.

There is a secondary issue to consider with respect to withholding requirements, the so-called second-tier withholding. Part XIII of the *ITA* may deem a non-resident payor to be a resident of Canada for certain payments to non-residents and thereby subject to Canadian tax. This is referred to in the above mentioned IFA Report, at p. 295.

Carrying on Business in Canada or a Foreign Jurisdiction

While one would ordinarily expect that a domestic lessor whose only activity in a foreign country is leasing property to a foreign lessee to be used in a foreign country might not be carrying on business in the foreign country, that is not always the case. In some transactions the lessor is deemed to be carrying on business. In general, if you own real estate in the foreign jurisdiction or a foreign lessor owns real estate in Canada, then you have a permanent establishment (in Canada in any event) and if you lease that to a user you might well be considered doing business in the country where the real estate is situate.

For example, Canadian investors in a U.K. partnership which owns real estate in the United Kingdom would be considered to be carrying on business there and would individually be liable for U.K. tax on the profits earned. Since the computation of taxable income in the United Kingdom is different from that in Canada you could run into the situation where you might have no taxable income in the United Kingdom but, if you are a Canadian resident, you might have taxable income in Canada. This would give rise to Canadian tax on the income and no credit for U.K. taxes. In a different fiscal year you may have no foreign source income taxable in Canada in accordance with the Canadian income tax calculation but be taxable in the United Kingdom in accordance with the U.K. calculation. Since your foreign source income is NIL you would not receive a credit for the foreign taxes paid. In general, there is a carry-over period for foreign tax credits so you might get the benefit in a later year. However, this has to be looked on quite carefully before you enter the transaction to ensure that you have designed the transaction properly to avoid a negative cash flow from non-recoverable foreign taxes. Then you might wish to pray that there are no serious adverse changes in the tax laws of either country to ruin your planning!

In addition, a corporate lessor in Canada pays Provincial Capital Tax and Large Corporation Tax — as a form of minimum tax — on taxable capital employed in the jurisdiction. Canada and other jurisdictions also have a "thin capitalization" provision which could result in a disallowance of interest if the lessor is resident in Canada with minimum equity and high debt thereby not producing any taxable income in Canada. The thin capitalization rules are designed to disallow interest expenses over a threshold amount and thereby attempt to create taxable income in Canada.

Operating Lease, Conditional Sale or Immediate Sale?

As indicated earlier in this book Revenue Canada treats some lease transactions as sales. Accordingly, it is important for the lessor to ensure that the lease will be treated as an operating lease for income tax purposes by meeting the test of IT-233R. However, in the case of cross-border transactions, the above IFA Report identifies a particular problem. It indicates, at p. 285 that "Revenue Canada, Taxation has for many years followed an unpublished assessing practice whereby, in the case of cross-border transactions, they rely on legal form rather than the guidelines set out in IT-233R". It goes on further to state: "The authorities have also indicated that, even in the context of domestic leases, they will henceforth normally rely on the assumption that the legal form of an agreement (and not its legal or economic substance) reflects the true relationship and intentions of the parties involved and that, to the extent that it is subsequently determined that the agreement does not reflect the actual legal rights and obligations of the parties, Revenue Canada, Taxation (but not the taxpayer) may choose to disregard the legal form of the transaction and revert to what it believes the substance of the transaction to be." While it may be awkward for Revenue Canada to have to apply different views in different circumstances, this will not necessarily stop them from doing so and may create havoc for a lessor (or for a lessee if the transaction is deemed to be a purchase and not a lease). Also their determination may be several years after the lease started or indeed after it finished. Accordingly these provisions and General Anti-Avoidance Regulations ("GAAR") create a potential risk environment for both the lessor and lessee in cross-border transactions.

As a result of the withholding tax situation in Canada cross-border transactions have generally been constructed as conditional sales agreements in Canada and specifically designed to eliminate the withholding tax requirement on interest paid by a Canadian payor to a non-resident payee. If the transaction is structured such that the Canadian corporation may not under any circumstances (subject to limited exceptions) be obliged to pay more than 25% of the principal amount of the debt arising under the conditional sales agreement within five years from the date of issue, the interest element of the payments may be exempt from Part XIII withholding under the provisions of para. 212(1)(*b*)(vii) of the ITA.

Double Dip Transactions

There are a number of countries where the taxation authorities treat leases as an acquisition of an asset based on the economic substance (Canada and U.S.A. for example). Other jurisdictions look to the legal form of the transaction and treat the apparent legal owner as the owner for tax deduction purposes (for example Italy, Spain and the U.K.). Accordingly, if you can find a situation where the legal owner can claim capital cost allowance in one jurisdiction and the economic owner in the other jurisdiction you have the opportunity for two users to claim capital cost allowance in one jurisdiction and the economic owner in the other jurisdiction you have the opportunity for two users to claim capital cost allowance or equivalent. Accordingly, you might dream up a transaction where a U.S. aircraft manufacturer sells an airplane to a Canadian company under a conditional sales agreement and the Canadian company sells the aircraft under a conditional sales agreement to a U.K. company (who would claim depreciation for tax purposes) and the U.K. company would lease the aircraft into a country where economic ownership is the test for depreciation (Germany or the U.S.). Then you might have both the U.K. lessor and the foreign lessee claiming depreciation on the same asset and the Canadian company earning interest income and incurring interest expense on the conditional sale.

As one might imagine, these transactions are involved. There are implications for customs duties, GST, income tax and withholding taxes in each jurisdiction and therefore they have very high administrative and legal costs at the outset. Since they may also be subject to changes in withholding tax and income tax laws, changes in interest rate, and currency variances, they are extremely difficult and time-consuming to put together.

In fact, leasing has been more important as a source of capital formation in Europe than in Canada for several years. Exhibit 11-3, originally presented by David Porter of London Leasing at the 1985 annual meeting of the Equipment Lessors Association of Canada, illustrates the impact of leasing for the period 1978 to 1982. It is interesting that leasing has been of increasing importance in European countries over the five-year period, whereas in Canada the importance has been declining since 1979. Indeed, the growth of leasing is best shown by the accompanying graph for the period 1972 to 1983 (see Exhibit 11-4). Nor is this a passing phenomenon, as David Porter indicated at the above-mentioned meeting. The annual projected rate of increase for the European leasing market for the period 1985 to 1995 showed rates of increase for 17 European countries, with nine countries showing increases of more than 10% per annum and only one country, Austria, scheduled for a reduction over that period of time.

The situation changed in Canada by 1989 when the penetration is shown to have increased to a more representative 9.3%. This was prior to the implementation of the new tax changes in 1989 which were expected to result in an overall decline in leasing, particularly in "big-ticket" transactions. Unfortunately, the data from the annual Statistics Canada survey of leasing for 1990 has been delayed and the effect of the tax changes on leasing volume is not yet known.

Clearly, leasing is considered an important source of financing in Europe and also in the United States. This is in part due to the investment allowances and accelerated capital cost allowances (or depreciation allowances) in various countries. It is dangerous to present these kinds of allowances in a text because tax laws change so rapidly. Nevertheless, Table 11-5 gives an indication of the position of several European countries versus that of Canada. This table also indicates that Canada's accelerated allowances are less favourable (and they have been moving to less favourable rates) than those of other European countries. Undoubtedly this explains in part why leasing is a less important factor in capital formation in Canada when compared to Europe. Of equal importance to the lessor, however, is the ability to claim depreciation allowances on finance leases versus operating leases. Under these circumstances it may be possible to design a lease to obtain the so-called "double-dip" depreciation, with depreciation being claimed in the country of the lessor and perhaps also by the lessee. For example, a finance lease written in the United Kingdom would be eligible for depreciation by the lessor, as indicated by Exhibit 11-6. In this case, it would appear possible to design a lease where depreciation could be claimed for income tax purposes in both the United Kingdom and Canada. If the capital cost allowance rates were also favourable in both countries, it might well be possible to design a lease where the write-offs in the two countries could provide income tax advantages.

In some countries it is possible to offset losses from leasing operations (often caused by the high depreciation allowances and interest in the early years of the lease) against non-leasing income. Exhibit 11-7 indicates for certain countries where this is permitted and not permitted. It will be noted that it is generally not permitted in Canada except for those companies where leasing, or sale and servicing of the products plus leasing, represents the dominant business of the company (the "principal business tests" referred to earlier). In countries where the offset of losses from leasing against other income is permitted, and where depreciation is high, it is possible to construct leases that provide considerable income tax advantages to the lessor in that they provide high write-offs in the early years, thereby sheltering income which would otherwise be taxable to the corporation. Of course, if this is abused by a large number of companies with the result that large amounts of taxes otherwise payable are deferred, it will have a significant impact on the tax collections of the countries and will thereby attract the attention of income tax legislators. This happened in Canada, with the result that the ability to offset losses from leasing against other income has been restricted for individuals and non-leasing companies for several years.

Exhibit 11-3

Penetration of Leasing in Capital Formation, 1978-1982, 1989

	1978 %	1979 %	1980 %	1981 %	1982 %	1989 %
Europe						
Belgium	2.6	3.4	3.3	3.0	4.6	8.3
Denmark	1.3	1.9	2.0	2.6	8.3	11.0
France	6.8	7.9	7.9	7.3	8.5	19.7
West Germany	2.0	2.2	2.2	2.8	3.0	17.8
Ireland	0.5	0.5	0.6	1.6	2.0	28.4
Italy	4.7	5.2	5.3	6.2	6.8	14.7
Luxembourg	0.5	3.1	2.2	2.5	5.1	9.0
Netherlands	4.7	5.1	5.9	6.2	5.1	17.4
Spain	2.5	3.6	2.2	3.2	4.5	27.0
U.K.	8.0	10.0	11.6	13.3	13.0	23.5
North America						
Canada	4.4	6.3	5.6	4.7	3.3	9.3
United States	15.6	17.0	21.9	25.6	27.9	33.0
Japan	4.8	5.8	6.2	7.0	8.3	10.0
A/Nz						
Australia	26.4	30.2	25.0	22.2	23.1	30.0
New Zealand	3.6	4.9	3.0	14.2	20.4	N/A
Overall Penetration	9.2	10.5	12.3	14.1	15.0	16.9

Source: London Financial Group Ltd.

ECU
(billion)

Exhibit 11-4

Growth of Leasing in Europe, 1972-1989

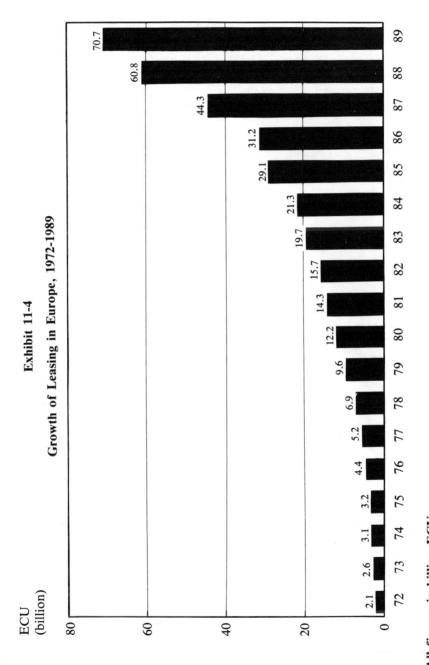

All figures in billion ECU
Source: Leaseurope

Exhibit 11-5

Equipment Investment Incentives of Selected Countries

	Investment Allowances	Cash Grants	Regional Specific Industry Aid	Accelerated Depreciation Allowances
Belgium	Yes	Yes	Yes	Double declining balance, maximum 40% for under five-year life equipment
Denmark	No	No	Yes	25% year 1, 30% thereafter declining balance
France	No	Yes	Yes	1.5 to 2.5 times straight line allowance
Germany	Yes	Yes	Yes	Lesser of 3 times straight line rate and 30%
Ireland	No	Yes	Yes	No
Italy	Yes	Yes	Yes	200% increase for tangible assets
Netherlands	Yes	No	Yes	No
Spain	Yes	No	No	No
United Kingdom	No	Yes	Yes	No
Canada	No	No	Yes	No

Exhibit 11-6

Recipient of Tax Depreciation Allowances

	Finance Leases	Operating Leases
Belgium	Lessee	Lessor
Denmark	Lessor*	Lessor
France	Lessor	Lessor
Germany	Lessor/Lessee	Lessor
Ireland	Lessor/Lessee	Lessor
Italy	Lessor	Lessor
Netherlands	Lessee	Lessor
United Kingdom	Lessor*	Lessor
Canada	Lessee	Lessor

* Under same circumstances the lessee may claim tax depreciation.

Exhibit 11-7

Offset Leasing Losses
Against Other Income in Same Company

Permitted	Not Permitted**
Argentina	Canada*
Australia	Ireland
Belgium	South Africa
Brazil	
Denmark	
France	
Germany	
Hong Kong	
Ireland	
Italy	
Japan	
Mexico	
Netherlands	
New Zealand	
Norway	
Puerto Rico	
Saudi Arabia	
Singapore	
Spain	
Sweden	
Switzerland	
United Kingdom	
United States	
Venezuela	

* Except for a "principal business corporation" where 90% of the gross revenue is from property rental or leasing.

** Tax depreciation restricted on leasing assets

A "HODGEPODGE" OF TAX CAVEATS

There have been a number of restrictions placed on the ability of leasing companies and individuals to claim operating losses from leasing to reduce taxable income from non-leasing activities. These restrictions were first introduced in the mid-1960s to cure a perceived abuse of capital cost allowance claims by individual lessors, in particular, who would acquire a portion of a large asset (typically an aircraft). The revenue would be assured by leasing to a first-rate credit, and the individual would benefit from capital cost allowance far in excess of the rental income in the early years. This would serve to reduce or eliminate otherwise taxable income. As a result, a number of tax provisions were introduced, including:

1. Restrictions on claiming of capital cost allowance to net rental income, except for "principal business corporations."
2. The elimination of leverage leasing as a financing tool by restricting CCA to amounts which the lessor had at risk (although this does not appear to be the assessing practice at present).
3. Provision for the classification of buildings as separate assets rather than the use of a pool, so the gains on disposal could not be sheltered from income tax.
4. The April 1989 tax changes to tax the interest element of rents of specified leasing property.

Of these, the restriction on CCA to net rental income was the most severe and virtually eliminated individuals from acquiring leased assets. Two techniques have been introduced to reduce the impact of this change. First, a company wishing to offer leasing can establish a leasing subsidiary which will be a "principal business corporation." There will be no restriction on its ability to claim CCA. If the leasing subsidiary is financed entirely with equity, common shares, or participating preferred shares, the parent company can then borrow funds to invest in the subsidiary and deduct the interest on its borrowed funds from other income. This permits the parent company to enjoy most of the benefits of the leasing tax shelter, and it might improve this position by offering the subsidiary a credit guarantee and credit checking facility at a relatively low cost, to guard against credit losses building up in the leasing subsidiary which would negate the benefit desired.

In addition, this subsidiary is permitted to have up to 10% of its income from non-leasing activities; the profit from this can be entirely sheltered by the leasing income.

In other cases it may be possible to turn the leasing activity into an active business so that the income is income from an active business rather than income from leasing. In this event, there would currently be no restriction on the ability to claim capital cost allowance.

If a leasing company is in a seasonal business it is desirable to arrange to have its fiscal year end immediately after the period of greatest activity. This permits a full year's capital cost allowance to be claimed in the fiscal year (albeit currently at half rates except for specified leasing property, for which the new 1989 calculation is required), although only one or two months of rental income are likely to have been received. Therefore, maximum tax losses are generated. If the taxation year begins just before the busy period, which might result in a whole year's income being included to be offset by the same amount of capital cost allowance, the difference in cash flow to the leasing company on a 48-month lease can be in the order of 5%. If the business is not seasonal it may be desirable to have four separate companies with year ends at each calendar quarter, so that leases can be written in the company with the nearest fiscal year end. In this case the lessor will have to assess whether the added administration and the necessity to generate sufficient taxable income in each of the companies is justified by the savings.

One of the difficulties a lessor faces in a competitive leasing environment is the incidence of capital tax in certain provinces in Canada and the Federal Large Corporations Tax. In Ontario, this tax has increased from 1/10th of 1% of capital employed (including loans and other funded debt) to 3/10ths of 1%. Although the rate as a percentage of year-end capital is not high, the effect on net earnings is dramatic, and if the spread was low to start with, the capital tax may well erode 30% or more of the spread, depending on the average term of the leases. It is therefore worth some attention over the course of the contracts. The following steps could be considered:

1. Delay payment for contracts written close to the end of the fiscal year so that the amount due to the supplier will be a trade account, rather than indebtedness for borrowed money. Trade accounts payable are excluded from the capital base, whereas the indebtedness will be included for purposes of the capital tax calculation. Moreover, maximum capital cost allowance can be claimed and can be used to reduce the Provincial capital base, obtaining a double benefit, from the reduction of the capital base by the capital cost allowance and a failure to include the debt to the supplier in the capital base.
2. Wherever possible pay down borrowings before the end of your fiscal period rather than immediately after. Every dollar paid down saves a combined one half of 1% if the company is taxable in Ontario.
3. It may be worth establishing the leasing company in a province either where there is no Provincial capital tax, such as Alberta, or where the tax is low. If the asset is to be used in a province where the tax is low, it may be worthwhile having an establishment in that province to avoid the capital tax being attributed to a province where it is higher.

In addition to capital tax there are differences in sales tax provisions from province to province, and it is beneficial to review those in the province where the asset is to be used.

BUSINESS ISSUES TO REDUCE RISK OR IMPROVE RETURN

Over the past 30 years leasing in Canada has gone through at least three cycles. The first cycle ended in the early 1960s and might be referred to as the "novice's cycle." Many inexperienced lessors entered the industry and paid a high price for their inexperience, which resulted in a decline in the industry for a few years around the mid-1960s. This was also the time of the fall of Atlantic Acceptance Corporation, which resulted in a sharp restriction of credit to a number of leasing and other financial corporations. The second cycle went from about the mid-1960s to the mid-1970s and might be referred to as the "expert's cycle." This included the introduction of computers and computerized calculations to leasing, the extension of leasing into the international market for Canadians, the lengthening of the term of leases from relatively few years to 10, 15, 20, and more, and finally, to the large, complex leverage lease transactions. This cycle ended when leveraged leasing and tax-shelter leasing were substantially curtailed by changes in the *Income Tax Act*, S.C. 1970-71-72, c. 63. The final cycle started towards the end of the 1970s and was battered by the high inflation and high interest rates of the early 1980s and the deep recession of 1990 and 1991. During each cycle old faces left the industry and experience was lost. Companies started, found the business unprofitable, and fell by the wayside. The third cycle might well be referred to as the "survivor's cycle".

From a business perspective, leasing has been treated by many as a clerical exercise in computing interest rate spreads and projecting future income tax positions. This has resulted in lack of adequate attention to four critical areas:

1. *Funding*
In many cases leases have been written on a fixed-rate basis and funded on a partially fixed or substantially floating-rate basis. The rapid escalation of interest rates in the early 1980s indicated the risk inherent in this practice, and much of the leasing industry found that it had written "under-water" leases.

2. *Credit Losses*
The leasing industry must pay as much attention to credit as any other lending organization. Unfortunately, in a push for volume, inexperienced lessors have paid too little attention to credit criteria and have found in later years that credit losses not only ate up their spreads, but in some cases were greater than the cost of funds. This area must be watched with vigilance, particularly in highly competitive periods.

3. *The Lease and the Law Courts*
For some reason, the court's view of a lease and the industry's view of a lease are often at variance, with the result that the position of lessors is frequently not as strong as expected, particularly if they have failed to register the lease with appropriate authorities when they should, or if their leased asset is a piece of equipment attached to real estate or attached to, and forming part of, another piece of equipment. Such lessors have often had difficulty in becoming other than an unsecured creditor in the event that their lessee was caught in financial difficulty. Would-be lessors might well have a course in the legal side of leases to follow their course in credit granting.

4. *Residual Values*

One of the greatest difficulties of the second cycle in leasing was the over-reliance on residual values, particularly for computer equipment, other specialized equipment, and ships. Unless the lessor feels content as a gambler, reliance on residual value in specialized situations increases the risk of the contract. Even the automobile industry, which has been protected by rapid inflation over several years prior to 1990, found that its reliance on high residual values resulted in "future shock" as their leases had to be terminated in 1991 and residual values had dropped dramatically.

The four areas of fixed-rate funding, good credit granting, clear understanding of legal position, and intelligent use of residuals represent areas of greatest loss to the leasing industry over the last 30 years. There are two strategies worth considering at present:

1. The decline in interest rates in the last few years provides an opportunity for lessors with fixed-rate funding to refinance at lower current rates. This would be appropriate for lessors where the funding agreements provide for an interest penalty in the event of prepayment and do not preclude refunding based on a decline in interest rate. A three-month interest penalty which is built into many lending agreements may be a small price to pay for refunding at the current low rates, as long as this can be done without damage to lending relationships.
2. In the past three years there has been considerable exposure of the financial community to greater sophistication in the handling of foreign exchange and interest rate risks. The use of futures and options, interest rate and foreign exchange swaps, and similar transactions permit lessors to protect themselves against interest rate and foreign exchange variance. This protection is well worth researching in some situations, particularly for large contracts. In addition, the use of interest rate and/or foreign exchange options should be considered when quoting on potential leases in foreign currencies or in fixed rates. The foreign exchange option contract can protect the yield by guarding against adverse foreign exchange fluctuations, and the interest rate options can protect the yield by guarding against variances in interest rate from the time that a lease is quoted to the time when funding is obtained.

CONCLUSION

This book started by indicating that leasing is a business decision. One should decide what business result is required, then determine how to achieve it from a legal, tax, and accounting perspective. These issues have been dealt with from the viewpoint of the lessor and the lessee, and the important issues in the lease agreement have been reviewed. We have then considered various techniques to assess rate of return in a lease before and after income tax, and dealt at some length with a number of the problem areas in this assessment of leasing. Finally, we have indicated the utility of considering the treatment of leases on an international scale, some particular taxation issues that can be minimized, and a number of business points that are critical to the lessor. The purpose of this book is to introduce these subjects to lessors and lessees with a view to enhancing leasing as a viable and profitable business in Canada, and to pass on some experiences that have been gained over the last 30 years.

Appendix

Lease Examples

In the following lease examples:

- the interest rates are rounded for ease of presentation;

- the payments are assumed to be made at the end of each period;

- the accounting and income tax treatment expected is outlined for both lessor and lessee, based on criteria appropriate at time of writing;

- leases are assumed to be non-cancellable;

- "initial direct costs" are assumed to be minor and therefore charged to expense as incurred.

EXAMPLE 1(a):

TAX AND ACCOUNTING CLASSIFICATION

Lessee's Perspective: Accounting			Lessor's Perspective: Accounting		
This Lease:	Yes	No	This Lease:	Yes	No
Will result in the transfer of ownership at end of term		X	Will result in the transfer of ownership at end of term		X
Has a term of at least 75% of the asset's economic life		X	Has a term of at least 75% of the asset's economic life		X
Has minimum lease payments with a NPV of 90% of the asset's fair value		X	Has minimum lease payments with a NPV of 90% of the asset's fair value		X
Risks of ownership substantially acquired		X	Risks of ownership substantially retained	X	
Benefits of ownership substantially acquired		X	Benefits of ownership substantially retained	X	
The lease is an operating lease			The lease is an operating lease		

144

Lessee's Perspective: Tax This Lease:	Yes	No	Lessor's Perspective: Tax This Lease:	Yes	No
Allows lessee to automatically acquire asset at end of lease		X	Allows lessee to automatically acquire asset at end of lease		X
Requires the lessee to buy the asset at end of lease		X	Requires the lessee to buy the asset at end of lease		X
Requires the lessee to guarantee the asset's option value		X	Requires the lessee to guarantee the asset's option value		X
Contains a bargain purchase option		X	Contains a bargain purchase option		X
The lease is an operating lease			The lease is an operating lease		

	Lessee	Lessor
Include/(Deduct) lease payments in taxable income	(X)	X
Eligible for CCA (if applicable)		X
Eligible for ITC (if applicable)		X

Example 1(a) — Cont'd

Lessee's Perspective

LEASE TERMS:

Property	computer	Contingent rental	none
Lease term	36 months	Fair value	$1,000,000
Minimum lease payments	$945,000	Residual value	$300,000 (not guaranteed)
Bargain purchase option	no	Lessee's incremental borrowing rate	12.00% (p.a., comp'd monthly)
Bargain renewal option	no	Implicit interest rate in lease	12.00% (p.a., comp'd monthly)
Economic life	5 years	Lease classification	operating
Executory costs	none	Capitalized value	N/A
		Life for depreciation	N/A

ACCOUNTING ENTRIES:

Journal entries for the first year of lease:

A.	Rent expense	$315,000	
	Cash		$315,000

to recognize annual expense of leasing computer
(made annually)

Financial statement presentation:
(for the first year)

> Balance Sheet: not recorded
> note disclosure required as to nature of lease and annual expenses

> Income Statement: recorded as part of cost of goods sold or as computer expense

Example 1(a) — Cont'd

Lessor's Perspective

LEASE TERMS:

Property	computer	Contingent rental	none
Lease term	36 months	Fair value	$1,000,000
Minimum lease payments	$945,000	Residual value	$300,000 (unguaranteed)
Bargain purchase option	no	Lessee's incremental borrowing rate	12.00% (p.a., comp'd monthly)
Bargain renewal option	no	Implicit interest rate in lease	12.00% (p.a., comp'd monthly)
Economic life	5 years	Lease classification	operating
Executory costs	none	Capitalized value	$1,000,000
		Life for depreciation (straight-line basis)	3 years, depreciated to residual value

ACCOUNTING ENTRIES:

Journal entries for the first year of lease:

A. Computer $1,000,000
     Cash $1,000,000
    to record purchase of asset

B. Cash $315,000
     Rent revenue $315,000
    to record receipt of lease payment
    (recorded annually)

C. Depreciation expense $233,333
     Accumulated depreciation on $233,333
     leased computer
    to record expense at end of year
    (recorded annually)

Example 1(a) — Cont'd

Financial statement presentation:
(for the first year)

Balance Sheet
_____

Assets

Non-current:
Computer $1,000,000
    less accumulated depreciation   ($233,333) $766,667

Income Statement
_____

Revenue from leasing $315,000
Depreciation expense on leased assets   ($233.333)

EXAMPLE 1(b):

TAX AND ACCOUNTING CLASSIFICATION

Lessee's Perspective: Accounting			Lessor's Perspective: Accounting		
This Lease:	Yes	No	This Lease:	Yes	No
Will result in the transfer of ownership at end of term		X	Will result in the transfer of ownership at end of term		X
Has a term of at least 75% of the asset's economic life		X	Has a term of at least 75% of the asset's economic life		X
Has minimum lease payments with a NPV of 90% of the asset's fair value	X		Has minimum lease payments with a NPV of 90% of the asset's fair value	X	
Risks of ownership substantially acquired	X		Risks of ownership substantially retained		X
Benefits of ownership substantially acquired		X	Benefits of ownership substantially retained		X
The lease is a capital lease[1]			The lease is a direct financing lease[1]		

---

[1] When the risks of ownership have been assumed, but the benefits not transferred to the lessee for a large portion of the useful life, it is possible to classify the lease as either capital or operating. Since computer equipment is subject to high obsolescence, capital lease accounting has been assessed as preferable.

Lessee's Perspective: Tax This Lease:	Yes	No	Lessor's Perspective: Tax This Lease:	Yes	No
Allows lessee to automatically acquire asset at end of lease		X	Allows lessee to automatically acquire asset at end of lease		X
Requires the lessee to buy the asset at end of lease		X	Requires the lessee to buy the asset at end of lease		X
Requires the lessee to guarantee the asset's option value	X		Requires the lessee to guarantee the asset's option value	X	
Contains a bargain purchase option		X	Contains a bargain purchase option		X
The lease is a purchase			The lease is direct financing lease		

	Lessee	Lessor
Include/(Deduct) lease payments in taxable income	No	No
Eligible for CCA (if applicable)	X	
Eligible for ITC (if applicable)	X	

Example 1(b) — Cont'd

Lessee's Perspective

LEASE TERMS:

Property	computer	Contingent rental	N/A
Lease term	36 months	Fair value	$1,000,000
Minimum lease payments	$1,245,000	Residual value	$300,000 (guaranteed)
Bargain purchase option	no	Lessee's incremental borrowing rate	12.00% (p.a., comp'd monthly)
Bargain renewal option	no	Implicit interest rate in lease	12.00% (p.a., comp'd monthly)
Economic life	5 years	Lease classification	capital
Executory costs	N/A	Capitalized value	$1,000,000
		Life for depreciation (straight-line basis)	3 years

ACCOUNTING ENTRIES:

Journal entries for the first year of lease:

A.	Asset – computer leasehold	$1,000,000	
	Liability – obligation under capital lease		$1,000,000
	to recognize acquisition of asset and related liability (made at date of acquisition)		
B.	Interest expense	$108,909	
	Liability – obligation under capital lease	$206,091	
	Cash		$315,000
	to recognize lease payment, interest on liability, and reduction for liability (made annually; the amounts above are for the first year)		
C.	Amortization expense on computer leasehold	$233,333	
	Accumulated amortization of computer leasehold		$233,333
	to record amortization of computer pursuant to capital lease (made annually)		

Example 1(b) — Cont'd

Financial statement presentation:
(for the first year)

Balance Sheet:

Fixed Assets
_____

Computer leasehold	$1,000,000	
less accumulated amortization	($233,333)	$766,667

Liabilities
_____

Obligation under capital lease:	
current portion	$232,228
long term	$561,681

Income Statement:

Amortization expense on computer leasehold	$233,333
Financing expense on computer leasehold	$108,909

1. Note disclosure is required as to the nature of lease and annual payments required, as well as the nature of obligations under lease agreements. The specific requirements are set forth in Section 3065 of the *CICA Handbook*, paragraphs 20 to 28 inclusive.

Example 1(b) — Cont'd

Lessor's Perspective — Direct Financing

LEASE TERMS:

Property	computer	Contingent rental	none
Lease term	36 months	Fair value	$1,000,000
Minimum lease payments	$1,245,000	Residual value	$300,000 (guaranteed)
Bargain purchase option	no	Lessee's incremental borrowing rate	12.00% (p.a., comp'd monthly)
Bargain renewal option	no	Implicit interest rate in lease	12.00% (p.a., comp'd monthly)
Economic life	5 years	Lease classification	direct financing
Executory costs	none	Capitalized value	N/A
		Life for depreciation	N/A

ACCOUNTING ENTRIES:

Journal entries for the first year of lease:
(assuming that initial direct costs have been charged to expense as being minor in amount)

A.	Computer	$1,000,000	
	Cash		$1,000,000
	to record purchase		
B.	Finance lease receivables	$945,000	
	Guaranteed residual receivable	$300,000	
	Computer		$1,000,000
	Unearned income		$245,000
	to record lease of property under a direct financing lease (made on signing lease)		
C.	Cash	$315,000	
	Finance lease receivables		$315,000
	to record receipt of lease payment (made annually)		
D.	Unearned income	$108,909	
	Finance income		$108,909
	to record earned income for first year of lease (made annually; the above figure is based on first year's interest income)		

Example 1(b) — Cont'd

Financial statement presentation:
(for the first year of lease)

     Balance Sheet
           Assets

Finance lease receivable – long term	$930,000
less unearned income	($136,091)
	$793,909
less current portion	($232,228)
	$561,681

     Income Statement

Interest from finance leases	$108,909

Comparison of Impact of Various Methods Used to Calculate Income
(based on the data used in the above example)

	ACTUARIAL	STRAIGHT LINE	SUM OF THE DIGITS
YEAR 1	$108,909	$81,667	$134,640
YEAR 2	$82,772	$81,667	$81,666
YEAR 3	$53,319	$81,666	$28,694
TOTAL	$245,000	$245,000	$245,000

EXAMPLE 1(c):

TAX AND ACCOUNTING CLASSIFICATION

Lessee's Perspective: Accounting This Lease:	Yes	No	Lessor's Perspective: Accounting This Lease:	Yes	No
Will result in the transfer of ownership at end of term		X	Will result in the transfer of ownership at end of term		X
Has a term of at least 75% of the asset's economic life		X	Has a term of at least 75% of the asset's economic life		X
Has minimum lease payments with a NPV of 90% of the asset's fair value	X		Has minimum lease payments with a NPV of 90% of the asset's fair value	X	
Risks of ownership substantially acquired	X		Risks of ownership substantially retained		X
Benefits of ownership substantially acquired		X	Benefits of ownership substantially retained	X	
The lease is a capital lease[1]			The lease is a direct financing lease[1]		

[1] When the risks of ownership have been assumed, but the benefits not transferred to the lessee for a large portion of the useful life, it is possible to classify the lease as either capital or operating. Since computer equipment is subject to high obsolescence, capital lease accounting has been assessed as preferable.

Lessee's Perspective: Tax			Lessor's Perspective: Tax		
This Lease:	Yes	No	This Lease:	Yes	No
Allows lessee to automatically acquire asset at end of lease		X	Allows lessee to automatically acquire asset at end of lease		X
Requires the lessee to buy the asset at end of lease		X	Requires the lessee to buy the asset at end of lease		X
Requires the lessee to guarantee the asset's option value	X		Requires the lessee to guarantee the asset's option value		X
Contains a bargain purchase option		X	Contains a bargain purchase option		X
The lease is a purchase			The lease is a sale		

	Lessee	Lessor
Include/(Deduct) lease payments in taxable income	No	No
Eligible for CCA (if applicable)	X	
Eligible for ITC (if applicable)	X	

Example 1(c) — Cont'd

Lessor's Perspective: Sales Type

LEASE TERMS:

Property	computer	Contingent rental	none
Lease term	36 months	Fair value	$1,000,000
Minimum lease payments	$1,245,000	Residual value	$300,000 (guaranteed)
Bargain purchase option	no	Lessee's incremental borrowing rate	12.00% (p.a., comp'd monthly)
Bargain renewal option	no	Implicit interest rate in lease	12.00% (p.a., comp'd monthly)
Economic life	5 years	Lease classification	sales-type
Executory costs	none	Capitalized value	N/A
		life for depreciation	N/A

ACCOUNTING ENTRIES:

Journal entries for the first year of lease:

A.	Cost of goods sold	$800,000	
	Inventory		$800,000
	to relieve inventory for sale		
B.	Finance lease receivables	$945,000	
	Guaranteed residual receivable	$300,000	
	Sales		$1,000,000
	Unearned income		$245,000
	to record lease of property under a sales-type lease		
C.	Cash	$315,000	
	Finance lease receivables		$315,000
	to record receipt of lease payment		
D.	Unearned income	$108,909	
	Finance income		$108,909
	to record finance income for first year of lease		

Example 1(c) — Cont'd

Financial statement presentation:
(for the first year of lease)

    Balance Sheet

        Assets

Finance lease receivable – long term	$930,000
less unearned income	($136,091)
	$793,909
less current portion	($232,228)
	$561,681

    Income Statement

Interest from finance leases	$108,909
Sales revenue	$1,000,000
Cost of goods sold	($800,000)

EXAMPLE 2(a):

TAX AND ACCOUNTING CLASSIFICATION

Lessee's Perspective: Accounting			Lessor's Perspective: Accounting		
This Lease:	Yes	No	This Lease:	Yes	No
Will result in the transfer of ownership at end of term		X	Will result in the transfer of ownership at end of term		X
Has a term of at least 75% of the asset's economic life		X	Has a term of at least 75% of the asset's economic life		X
Has minimum lease payments with a NPV of 90% of the asset's fair value		X	Has minimum lease payments with a NPV of 90% of the asset's fair value		X
Risks of ownership substantially acquired		X	Risks of ownership substantially retained	X	
Benefits of ownership substantially acquired		X	Benefits of ownership substantially retained	X	
The lease is an operating lease			The lease is an operating lease		

Lessee's Perspective: Tax			Lessor's Perspective: Tax		
This Lease:	Yes	No	This Lease:	Yes	No
Allows lessee to automatically acquire asset at end of lease		X	Allows lessee to automatically acquire asset at end of lease		X
Requires the lessee to buy the asset at end of lease		X	Requires the lessee to buy the asset at end of lease		X
Requires the lessee to guarantee the asset's option value		X	Requires the lessee to guarantee the asset's option value		X
Contains a bargain purchase option		X	Contains a bargain purchase option		X
The lease is an operating lease			The lease is an operating lease		

	Lessee	Lessor
Include/(Deduct) lease payments in taxable income	(X)	X
Eligible for CCA (if applicable)		X
Eligible for ITC (if applicable)		X

Example 2(a) — Cont'd

Lessee's Perspective

LEASE TERMS:

Property	car	Contingent rental	none
Lease term	36 months	Fair value	$13,900
Minimum lease payments	$10,800	Residual value	$6,300 (not guaranteed)
Bargain purchase option	no	Lessee's incremental borrowing rate	12.00% (p.a., comp'd monthly)
Bargain renewal option	no	Implicit interest rate in lease	10.25% (p.a., comp'd monthly)
Economic life	8 years	Lease classification	operating
Executory costs	none	Capitalized value	N/A
		Life for depreciation	N/A

ACCOUNTING ENTRIES:

Journal entries for the first year of lease:

A. Rent expense $3,600
        Cash $3,600
     to recognize annual expense of leasing car
     (made annually)

Financial statement presentation:
(for the first year)

> Balance Sheet: not recorded
> note disclosure required as to nature of lease and annual expenses
>
> Income Statement: recorded as part of automobile expense

Example 2(a) — Cont'd

Lessor's Perspective

LEASE TERMS:

Property	car	Contingent rental	none
Lease term	36 months	Fair value	$13,900
Minimum lease payments	$10,800	Residual value	$6,300 (unguaranteed)
Bargain purchase option	no	Lessee's incremental borrowing rate	12.00% (p.a., comp'd monthly)
Bargain renewal option	no	Implicit interest rate in lease	10.25% (p.a., comp'd monthly)
Economic life	8 years	Lease classification	operating
Executory costs	none	Capitalized value	$13,900
		Life for depreciation (straight-line basis)	3 years, depreciated to residual value

ACCOUNTING ENTRIES:

Journal entries for the first year of lease:

A.	Car	$13,900	
	Cash		$13,900
	to record purchase of asset		
B.	Cash	$3,600	
	Rent revenue		$3,600
	to record receipt of lease payment (recorded annually)		
C.	Depreciation expense	$2,533	
	Accumulated depreciation on leased car		$2,533
	to record expense at end of year (recorded annually)		

Example 2(a) — Cont'd

Financial statement presentation:
(for the first year)

<u>Balance Sheet</u>

Assets

Non-current:		
Automobile	$13,900	
less accumulated depreciation	($2,533)	$11,367

<u>Income Statement</u>

Revenue from leasing	$3,600
Depreciation expense on leased assets	($2,533)

EXAMPLE 2(b):

TAX AND ACCOUNTING CLASSIFICATION

Lessee's Perspective: Accounting			Lessor's Perspective: Accounting		
This Lease:	Yes	No	This Lease:	Yes	No
Will result in the transfer of ownership at end of term		X	Will result in the transfer of ownership at end of term		X
Has a term of at least 75% of the asset's economic life		X	Has a term of at least 75% of the asset's economic life		X
Has minimum lease payments with a NPV of 90% of the asset's fair value	X		Has minimum lease payments with a NPV of 90% of the asset's fair value	X	
Risks of ownership substantially acquired	X		Risks of ownership substantially retained		X
Benefits of ownership substantially acquired		X	Benefits of ownership substantially retained	X	
The lease may be a capital or an operating lease[2]			The lease may be a direct financing or an operating lease[2]		

---

[2] In many cases where the lessee assumes the risks of ownership and the lessor retains the benefits of ownership (through re-lease or sale at termination of the lease), it is appropriate to treat the transaction as an operating lease, particularly where the guarantee is in part to assure that the lessee will maintain the asset in a responsible manner.

Lessee's Perspective: Tax This Lease:	Yes	No	Lessor's Perspective: Tax This Lease:	Yes	No
Allows lessee to automatically acquire asset at end of lease		X	Allows lessee to automatically acquire asset at end of lease		X
Requires the lessee to buy the asset at end of lease		X	Requires the lessee to buy the asset at end of lease		X
Requires the lessee to guarantee the asset's option value[2]	X		Requires the lessee to guarantee the asset's option value[2]	X	
Contains a bargain purchase option		X	Contains a bargain purchase option		X
The lease is an operating lease (if the guarantee is to assure that there is no excessive wear and tear)			The lease is an operating lease (if the guarantee is to assure that there is no excessive wear and tear)		

	Lessee	Lessor
Include/(Deduct) lease payments in taxable income	(X)	X
Eligible for CCA (if applicable)		X
Eligible for ITC (if applicable)		X

Example 2(b) — Cont'd

Lessee's Perspective

LEASE TERMS:

Property	car	Contingent rental	N/A
Lease term	60 months	Fair value	$13,900
Minimum lease payments	$20,500	Residual value	$2,500 (guaranteed)
Bargain purchase option	no	Lessee's incremental borrowing rate	14.70% (p.a., comp'd monthly)
Bargain renewal option	no	Implicit interest rate in lease	14.70% (p.a., comp'd monthly)
Economic life	8 years	Lease classification	capital
Executory costs	N/A	Capitalized value	$13,900
		Life for depreciation (straight-line basis)	5 years

ACCOUNTING ENTRIES:

Journal entries for the first year of lease:

A.	Asset – automobile leasehold	$13,900	
	Liability – obligation under capital lease		$13,900
	to recognize acquisition of asset and related liability		
	(made at date of acquisition)		
B.	Interest expense	$1,933	
	Liability – obligation under capital lease	$1,667	
	Cash		$3,600
	to recognize lease payment, interest on liability, and reduction for liability		
	(made annually; the amounts above are for the first year)		
C.	Amortization expense on automobile leasehold	$2,280	
	Accumulated amortization of automobile leasehold		$2,280
	to record amortization of automobile pursuant to capital lease		
	(made annually)		

Example 2(b) — Cont'd

Financial statement presentation:
(for the first year)

Balance Sheet:

Fixed Assets
_____

Automobile leasehold	$13,900	
less accumulated amortization	($2,280)	$11,620

Liabilities
_____

Obligation under capital lease:	
current portion	$1,928
long term	$10,305

Income Statement:

Amortization expense on automobile leasehold	$2,280
Financing expense on automobile leasehold	$1,933

1. Note disclosure is required as to the nature of lease and annual payments required, as well as the nature of obligations under lease agreements.

Example 2(b) — Cont'd

Lessor's Perspective — Direct Financing

LEASE TERMS:

Property	car	Contingent rental	none
Lease term	60 months	Fair value	$13,900
Minimum lease payments	$20,500	Residual value	$2,500 (guaranteed)
Bargain purchase option	no	Lessee's incremental borrowing rate	14.70% (p.a., comp'd monthly)
Bargain renewal option	no	Implicit interest rate in lease	14.70% (p.a., comp'd monthly)
Economic life	8 years	Lease classification	direct financing
Executory costs	none	Capitalized value	N/A
		Life for depreciation	N/A

ACCOUNTING ENTRIES:

Journal entries for the first year of lease:

A.	Car	$13,900	
	Cash		$13,900
	to record purchase		
B.	Finance lease receivables	$18,000	
	Guaranteed residual receivable	$2,500	
	Car		$13,900
	Unearned income		$6,600
	to record lease of property under a direct financing lease (made on signing lease)		
C.	Cash	$3,600	
	Finance lease receivables		$3,600
	to record receipt of lease payment (made annually)		
D.	Unearned income	$1,933	
	Finance income		$1,933
	to record earned income for first year of lease (made annually; the above figure is based on first year's interest income)		

Example 2(b) — Cont'd

Financial statement presentation:
(for the first year of lease)

Balance Sheet

Assets

Finance lease receivable – long term	$16,900
less unearned income	($4,667)
	$12,233
less current portion	($1,928)
	$10,305

Income Statement

Interest from finance leases	$1,933

EXAMPLE 2(c):

TAX AND ACCOUNTING CLASSIFICATION

Lessee's Perspective: Accounting This Lease:	Yes	No	Lessor's Perspective: Accounting This Lease:	Yes	No
Will result in the transfer of ownership at end of term		X	Will result in the transfer of ownership at end of term		X
Has a term of at least 75% of the asset's economic life		X	Has a term of at least 75% of the asset's economic life		X
Has minimum lease payments with a NPV of 90% of the asset's fair value	X		Has minimum lease payments with a NPV of 90% of the asset's fair value	X	
Risks of ownership substantially acquired	X		Risks of ownership substantially retained		X
Benefits of ownership substantially acquired		X	Benefits of ownership substantially retained	X	
The lease may be a capital or an operating lease[2]			The lease may be a direct financing or an operating lease[2]		

---

[2] In many cases where the lessee assumes the risks of ownership and the lessor retains the benefits of ownership (through re-lease or sale at termination of the lease), it is appropriate to treat the transaction as an operating lease, particularly where the guarantee is in part to assure that the lessee will maintain the asset in a responsible manner.

Lessee's Perspective: Tax This Lease:	Yes	No	Lessor's Perspective: Tax This Lease:	Yes	No
Allows lessee to automatically acquire asset at end of lease		X	Allows lessee to automatically acquire asset at end of lease		X
Requires the lessee to buy the asset at end of lease		X	Requires the lessee to buy the asset at end of lease		X
Requires the lessee to guarantee the asset's option value[2]	X		Requires the lessee to guarantee the asset's option value[2]	X	
Contains a bargain purchase option		X	Contains a bargain purchase option		X
The lease is an operating lease (if the guarantee is to assure that there is no excessive wear and tear)			The lease is an operating lease (if the guarantee is to assure that there is no excessive wear and tear)		

	Lessee	Lessor
Include/(Deduct) lease payments in taxable income	(X)	X
Eligible for CCA (if applicable)		X
Eligible for ITC (if applicable)		X

Example 2(c) — Cont'd

Lessor's Perspective — Sales Type

LEASE TERMS:

Property	car	Contingent rental	none
Lease term	60 months	Fair value	$13,900
Minimum lease payments	$20,500	Residual value	$2,500 (guaranteed)
Bargain purchase option	no	Lessee's incremental borrowing rate	14.70% (p.a., comp'd monthly)
Bargain renewal option	no	Implicit interest rate in lease	14.70% (p.a., comp'd monthly)
Economic life	8 years	Lease classification	sale
Executory costs	none	Capitalized value	N/A
		Life for depreciation	N/A

ACCOUNTING ENTRIES:

Journal entries for the first year of lease:

A.	Cost of goods sold	$11,120	
	Inventory		$11,120
B.	Finance lease receivables	$18,000	
	Guaranteed residual receivable	$2,500	
	Sales		$13,900
	Unearned income		$6,600
	to record lease of property under a sales-type lease		
C.	Cash	$3,600	
	Finance lease receivables		$3,600
	to record receipt of lease payment		
D.	Unearned income	$1,933	
	Finance income		$1,933
	to record earned income for first year of lease		

Example 2(c) — Cont'd

Financial statement presentation:
(for the first year of lease)

Balance Sheet

Assets

Finance lease receivable – long term	$16,900
less unearned income	($4,667)
	$12,233
less current portion	($1,928)
	$10,305

Income Statement

Interest from finance leases	$1,933
Sales revenue	$13,900
Cost of goods sold	($11,120)

EXAMPLE 3(a):

TAX AND ACCOUNTING CLASSIFICATION

Lessee's Perspective: Accounting			Lessor's Perspective: Accounting		
This Lease:	Yes	No	This Lease:	Yes	No
Will result in the transfer of ownership at end of term		X	Will result in the transfer of ownership at end of term		X
Has a term of at least 75% of the asset's economic life		X	Has a term of at least 75% of the asset's economic life		X
Has minimum lease payments with a NPV of 90% of the asset's fair value		X	Has minimum lease payments with a NPV of 90% of the asset's fair value		X
Risks of ownership substantially acquired		X	Risks of ownership substantially retained	X	
Benefits of ownership substantially acquired		X	Benefits of ownership substantially retained	X	
The lease is an operating lease			The lease is an operating lease		

Lessee's Perspective: Tax			Lessor's Perspective: Tax		
This Lease:	Yes	No	This Lease:	Yes	No
Allows lessee to automatically acquire asset at end of lease		X	Allows lessee to automatically acquire asset at end of lease		X
Requires the lessee to buy the asset at end of lease		X	Requires the lessee to buy the asset at end of lease		X
Requires the lessee to guarantee the asset's option value		X	Requires the lessee to guarantee the asset's option value		X
Contains a bargain purchase option		X	Contains a bargain purchase option		X
The lease is an operating lease			The lease is an operating lease		

	Lessee	Lessor
Include/(Deduct) lease payments in taxable income	(X)	X
Eligible for CCA (if applicable)		X
Eligible for ITC (if applicable)		X

Example 3(a) — Cont'd

Lessee's Perspective

LEASE TERMS:

Property	machinery	Contingent rental	none
Lease term	5 years	Fair value	$3,200,000
Minimum lease payments	$3,250,000	Residual value	$2,000,000 (not guaranteed)
Bargain purchase option	no	Lessee's incremental borrowing rate	14.72%
Bargain renewal option	no	Implicit interest rate in lease	14.72%
Economic life	10 years	Lease classification	operating
Executory costs	none	Capitalized value	N/A
		Life for depreciation	N/A

ACCOUNTING ENTRIES:

Journal entries for the first year of lease:

A.   Rent expense $650,000
          Cash $650,000
          to recognize annual expense of leasing
          machinery
          (made annually)

Financial statement presentation:
(for the first year)

      Balance Sheet: not recorded
      note disclosure required as to nature of lease and annual expenses

      Income Statement: recorded as part of equipment expense

Example 3(a) — Cont'd

Lessor's Perspective

LEASE TERMS:

Property	machinery	Contingent rental	none
Lease term	5 years	Fair value	$3,200,000
Minimum lease payments	$3,250,000	Residual value	$2,000,000 (unguaranteed)
Bargain purchase option	no	Lessee's incremental borrowing rate	14.72%
Bargain renewal option	no	Implicit interest rate in lease	14.72%
Economic life	10 years	Lease classification	operating
Executory costs	none	Capitalized value	$3,200,000
		Life for depreciation (straight-line basis)	5 years, depreciated to residual value

ACCOUNTING ENTRIES:

Journal entries for the first year of lease:

A.	Machinery	$3,200,000	
	Cash		$3,200,000
	to record purchase of asset		
B.	Cash	$650,000	
	Rent revenue		$650,000
	to record receipt of lease payment (recorded annually)		
C.	Depreciation expense	$240,000	
	Accumulated depreciation on leased equipment		$240,000
	to record expense at end of year (recorded annually)		

Example 3(a) — Cont'd

Financial statement presentation:
(for the first year of lease)

<u>Balance Sheet</u>

Assets

Non-current:		
Equipment	$3,200,000	
less accumulated depreciation	($240,000)	$2,960,000

<u>Income Statement</u>

Revenue from leasing	$650,000
Depreciation expense on leased assets	($240,000)

EXAMPLE 3(b):

TAX AND ACCOUNTING CLASSIFICATION

Lessee's Perspective: Accounting This Lease:	Yes	No	Lessor's Perspective: Accounting This Lease:	Yes	No
Will result in the transfer of ownership at end of term		X	Will result in the transfer of ownership at end of term		X
Has a term of at least 75% of the asset's economic life	X		Has a term of at least 75% of the asset's economic life	X	
Has minimum lease payments with a NPV of 90% of the asset's fair value	X		Has minimum lease payments with a NPV of 90% of the asset's fair value	X	
Risks of ownership substantially acquired	X		Risks of ownership substantially retained		X
Benefits of ownership substantially acquired	X		Benefits of ownership substantially retained		X
The lease is a capital lease			The lease is a direct financing lease[3]		

---

[3] Although the benefit of ownership is retained, it is expected to be so minor that the lease should be considered a direct financing lease.

Lessee's Perspective: Tax This Lease:	Yes	No	Lessor's Perspective: Tax This Lease:	Yes	No
Allows lessee to automatically acquire asset at end of lease		X	Allows lessee to automatically acquire asset at end of lease		X
Requires the lessee to buy the asset at end of lease		X	Requires the lessee to buy the asset at end of lease		X
Requires the lessee to guarantee the asset's option value	X		Requires the lessee to guarantee the asset's option value	X	
Contains a bargain purchase option		X	Contains a bargain purchase option		X
The lease is a purchase for tax purposes			The lease is a direct financing for tax purposes		

	Lessee	Lessor
Include/(Deduct) lease payments in taxable income	No	No
Eligible for CCA (if applicable)	X	
Eligible for ITC (if applicable)	X	

Example 3(b) — Cont'd

Lessee's Perspective

LEASE TERMS:

Property	machinery	Contingent rental	N/A
Lease term	10 years	Fair value	$3,200,000
Minimum lease payments	$6,010,000	Residual value	$10,000 (guaranteed)
Bargain purchase option	no	Lessee's incremental borrowing rate	13.46%
Bargain renewal option	no	Implicit interest rate in lease	13.46%
Economic life	10 years	Lease classification	capital
Executory costs	N/A	Capitalized value	$3,200,000
		Life for depreciation (straight-line basis)	10 years

ACCOUNTING ENTRIES:

Journal entries for the first year of lease:

A. Asset – machinery leasehold $3,200,000
        Liability – obligation under capital lease $3,200,000
    to recognize acquisition of asset and related
    liability
    (made at date of acquisition)

B. Interest expense $430,616
    Liability – obligation under capital lease $169,384
        Cash $600,000
    to recognize lease payment, interest on
    liability, and reduction of liability
    (made annually; the amounts above are for
    the first year)

C. Amortization expense on machinery $319,000
    leasehold
        Accumulated amortization of machinery $319,000
        leasehold
    to record amortization of machinery
    pursuant to capital lease
    (made annually)

Example 3(b) — Cont'd

Financial statement presentation:
(for the first year)

Balance Sheet:
Fixed Assets

Machinery leasehold	$3,200,000	
less accumulated amortization	($319,000)	$2,881,000

Liabilities

Obligation under capital lease:	
current portion	$192,178
long term	$2,838,438

Income Statement:

Amortization expense on machinery leasehold	$319,000
Financing expense on machinery leasehold	$430,616

1. Note disclosure required as to the nature of lease and annual payments required, as well as the nature of obligations under lease agreements.

Example 3(b) — Cont'd

Lessor's Perspective — Direct Financing

LEASE TERMS:

Property	machinery	Contingent rental	none
Lease term	10 years	Fair value	$3,200,000
Minimum lease payments	$6,010,000	Residual value	$10,000 (guaranteed)
Bargain purchase option	no	Lessee's incremental borrowing rate	13.46%
Bargain renewal option	no	Implicit interest rate in lease	13.46%
Economic life	10 years	Lease classification	direct financing
Executory costs	none	Capitalized value	N/A
		Life for depreciation	N/A

ACCOUNTING ENTRIES:

Journal entries for the first year of lease:

A.
Machinery	$3,200,000	
Cash		$3,200,000
to record purchase		

B.
Finance lease receivables	$6,000,000	
Guaranteed residual receivable	$10,000	
Machinery		$3,200,000
Unearned income		$2,810,000
to record lease of property under a direct financing lease (made on signing lease)		

C.
Cash	$600,000	
Finance lease receivables		$600,000
to record receipt of lease payment (made annually)		

D.
Unearned income	$430,616	
Finance income		$430,616
to record earned income for first year of lease (made annually; the above figure is based on first year's interest income)		

Example 3(b) — Cont'd

Financial statement presentation:
(for first year of lease)

Balance Sheet

Assets

Finance lease receivable – long term	$5,410,000
less unearned income	($2,379,384)
	$3,030,616
less current portion	($192,178)
	$2,838,438

Income Statement

Interest from finance leases	$430,616

EXAMPLE 3(c):

TAX AND ACCOUNTING CLASSIFICATION

Lessee's Perspective: Accounting			Lessor's Perspective: Accounting		
This Lease:	Yes	No	This Lease:	Yes	No
Will result in the transfer of ownership at end of term		X	Will result in the transfer of ownership at end of term		X
Has a term of at least 75% of the asset's economic life	X		Has a term of at least 75% of the asset's economic life	X	
Has minimum lease payments with a NPV of 90% of the asset's fair value	X		Has minimum lease payments with a NPV of 90% of the asset's fair value	X	
Risks of ownership substantially acquired	X		Risks of ownership substantially retained		X
Benefits of ownership substantially acquired	X		Benefits of ownership substantially retained		X
The lease is a capital lease			The lease is a direct financing lease[3]		

[3] Although the benefit of ownership is retained, it is expected to be so minor that the lease should be considered a direct financing lease.

Lessee's Perspective: Tax			Lessor's Perspective: Tax		
This Lease:	Yes	No	This Lease:	Yes	No
Allows lessee to automatically acquire asset at end of lease		X	Allows lessee to automatically acquire asset at end of lease		X
Requires the lessee to buy the asset at end of lease		X	Requires the lessee to buy the asset at end of lease		X
Requires the lessee to guarantee the asset's option value	X		Requires the lessee to guarantee the asset's option value	X	
Contains a bargain purchase option		X	Contains a bargain purchase option		X
The lease is a purchase for tax purposes			The lease is a sale for tax purposes		

	Lessee	Lessor
Include/(Deduct) lease payments in taxable income	No	No
Eligible for CCA (if applicable)	X	
Eligible for ITC (if applicable)	X	

Example 3(c) — Cont'd

Lessor's Perspective — Sales Type

LEASE TERMS:

Property	machinery	Contingent rental	none
Lease term	10 years	Fair value	$3,200,000
Minimum lease payments	$6,010,000	Residual value	$10,000 (guaranteed)
Bargain purchase option	no	Lessee's incremental borrowing rate	13.46% (p.a., comp'd monthly)
Bargain renewal option	no	Implicit interest rate in lease	13.46% (p.a., comp'd monthly)
Economic life	10 years	Lease classification	sale
Executory costs	none	Capitalized value	N/A
		Life for depreciation	N/A

ACCOUNTING ENTRIES:

Journal entries for the first year of lease:

A.	Cost of goods sold	$2,560,000	
	Inventory		$2,560,000
	to record cost of sale		
B.	Finance lease receivables	$6,000,000	
	Guaranteed residual receivable	$10,000	
	Sale		$3,200,000
	Unearned income		$2,810,000
	to record lease of property under a sales-type lease		
C.	Cash	$600,000	
	Finance lease receivables		$600,000
	to record receipt of lease payment		
D.	Unearned income	$430,616	
	Finance income		$430,616
	to record earned income for first year of lease		

Example 3(c) — Cont'd

Financial statement presentation:
(for first year of lease)

Balance Sheet

Assets

Lease receivable – long term	$5,410,000
less unearned income	($2,379,384)
	$3,030,616
less current portion	($192,178)
	$2,838,438

Income Statement

Interest from finance leases	$430,616
Revenue from sale	$3,200,000
Cost of goods sold	($2,560,000)

EXAMPLE 4:

COMPARISON OF TAX POSITION OF
A PRINCIPAL BUSINESS CORPORATION AND AN INDIVIDUAL
SHOWING THE RESTRICTION OF CCA TO NET LEASING INCOME*

	Principal Business Corporation (no restriction on CCA)				Individual (restrictions on CCA apply)			
	Year 1	Year 2	Year 3	Total	Year 1	Year 2	Year 3	Total
Rental income	$315,000	$315,000	$315,000	$945,000	$315,000	$315,000	$315,000	$945,000
Interest expense	$81,366	$61,409	$39,579	$182,354	$81,366	$61,409	$39,579	$182,354
Income before CCA	$233,634	$253,591	$275,421	$762,646	$233,634	$253,591	$275,421	$762,646
CCA claimable	$250,000	$500,000	$250,000	$1,000,000	$233,634	$253,591	$275,421	$762,646
Taxable income (loss)	($16,366)	($246,409)	$25,421	($237,354)	$0	$0	$0	$0

Note: for a principal business corporation, the tax loss may be offset against other taxable income.

Note: for an individual, CCA on leased property may not exceed net leasing income.

Example 4—Cont'd at p. 190

Example 4 — Cont'd

Capital Cost Allowance Schedule

Principal Business Corporation

	Year 1	Year 2	Year 3	Year 4
Opening balance	$0	$750,000	$250,000	$0
Additions	$1,000,000	$0	$0	$0
CCA	$250,000	$500,000	$250,000	$0
Closing balance	$750,000	$250,000	$0	$0
Proceeds on disposal				$300,000
Recaptured CCA				$300,000

(taxable if no other assets of this class were owned by the corporation)

Individual

	Year 1	Year 2	Year 3	Year 4
Opening balance	$0	$766,366	$512,775	$237,354
Additions	$1,000,000	$0	$0	$0
CCA	$233,634	$253,591	$275,421	$0
Closing balance	$766,366	$512,775	$237,354	$237,354
Proceeds on disposal				$300,000
Recaptured CCA				$62,646

(taxable if no other assets of this class were owned by the individual)

* This comparison is based on the same set of assumptions as Example 1(a), except that, for simplicity, we have assumed the property to be machinery, subject to class 29 CCA.

Glossary

Acceleration of Income Tax
The payment of taxes earlier than they would otherwise be required due to an inability to match taxable income with tax-deductible costs (usually due to CCA restrictions).

Advanced Rentals
Rent paid at start of the lease to provide added security to the lessor.

After-tax Rate of Return
Rate of return after allowing for tax effects.

After-tax Yield
Yield after allowing for tax effects.

Ascending Payments
Payments which increase over the life of the lease.

Balloon Payments
Larger than normal payments, usually occurring at the end of the lease term (sometimes called a "bullet").

Bargain Borrowing Rate
Lower than prevailing market interest rates.

Bargain Purchase Option
Option to purchase a leased asset which, at inception of lease, appears to be at less than estimated fair value at the option date.

Bargain Renewal Option
Option to renew the lease which, at inception of the lease, appears to be at less than a reasonable lease payment at the renewal date.

Base Rent
Basic or minimum amount of rent for a given asset, to which contingent rents may be added in order to calculate total rental payments required.

Borrowing Short
The practice of borrowing for a period which is shorter than that of related investment.

Buyout
Option whereby the lessee agrees to pay compensation in order to terminate the lease before the end of the lease term.

CCA
Capital cost allowance (the annual amount which a taxpayer may deduct in computing taxable income).

CCA Recapture
The excess of the sale price of a leased asset over the asset's remaining UCC. If the sale price is less than original cost, this amount is subject to tax in full — CCA is therefore "recaptured."

CICA
Canadian Institute of Chartered Accountants.

CICA Handbook
Authoritative handbook containing the current pronouncement of the CICA on specific accounting and auditing issues.

Capital Cost Allowance
Depreciation for tax purposes, see "CCA."

Capital Expenditure
Purchase of an asset with an economic life of more than one year.

Capital Gain
The excess of the sale price of an asset over that asset's original cost.

Capital Lease
A lease which transfers substantially all the risks and benefits of ownership of the leased asset to the lessee.

Capital Tax
Tax based on a firm's taxable capital; tax rate varies among provinces.

Contingent Rent
Rent which is based on something other than the passage of time, e.g., on sales, mileage, usage.

Debt/Equity Ratio
A measure used to assess a firm's exposure to debt risk: calculated as total liabilities/total equities or as indebtedness for borrowed money/total equity.

Declining Payments
Payments which decrease over the life of the lease.

Deductions — Expiry of
Non-capital losses and certain tax incentives are restricted as to the period in which they may be applied to reduce taxable income.

Deemed Interest
An amount which the tax authorities relate to interest payments for tax purposes, although the contract may not specify such an amount.

Deemed Value
An amount which the tax authorities relate to a specific item.

Delphi Process
A process of negotiation of values in which individuals submit written opinions to a central arbitrator in order to achieve a consensus.

Depreciation — Declining Balance
A system where depreciation is taken as a constant percentage of the original cost of the asset less accumulated depreciation taken to date.

Depreciation — Straight-Line
A system where depreciation is taken as a constant percentage of the original cost of the asset less estimated residual value; the formula used is (cost minus residual)/estimated economic life equals annual depreciation.

Direct Financing Leases
Capital leases which provide the lessor with financing income; the lessor is essentially a financial intermediary.

Discount Rate
The rate at which future cash flows are adjusted to reflect the time value of money; $1 today is worth more than $1 next year because the $1 in hand could earn interest — the discount rate is the rate of interest that the $1 could earn.

Discounted Value
Future cash flows that have been adjusted to reflect their current value by applying a discount rate.

Double-dip Depreciation
Tax planning technique where, due to differing definitions of capital and operating leases, both the lessee in country A and the lessor in country B can claim CCA or its equivalent and thereby achieve tax reductions.

Economic Life
The period during which an asset is expected to have economic value.

Equity
An ownership right in property; the interest in a property in excess of the liens or claims against it.

Glossary

Executory Costs
Costs related to the operation of the leased property (e.g., insurance, maintenance costs, and property taxes).

Exempt Property
These are assets exempt from the April 1989 tax changes and include much office furniture and equipment, computers costing less than $1 million, furniture and equipment for residential use, automobiles, vans or trucks, most buildings and railway cars.

Fair Market Value
The amount that a "reasonable person" would pay in a competitive market.

Financial Accounting Standards Board
Board established by American accountants to set accounting standards, similar to the CICA in Canada.

Fixed-rate Basis
Method of determining interest, as where the rate is explicitly stated in the contract as, for example, 13.5% per annum.

Floating-rate Basis
A rate which is allowed to vary over time in response to general or specific economic factors, generally varying with a central bank rate.

Full-payout Lease
Lease which provides for recovery of the full cost of an asset to the lessor over the lease term plus a return to the lessor, by way of rent plus guaranteed residual.

Full-term Lease
Non-cancellable lease.

Generally Accepted Accounting Principles
Accounting practices which have been codified in the *CICA Handbook* or which are in common usage.

Gross Yield
Yield before taxes and incidental costs; the yield which discounts rental payments plus guaranteed residual value to the lessor's cost.

IRR
See "Internal Rate of Return."

Implicit Interest Rate
Interest rate implied by the terms of the lease; this may differ from that which the contract explicitly states as the interest rate, and is found by discovering the lease's IRR.

Inception of the Lease
The earlier of the date of the lease agreement and the date of commitment which is signed by the parties to the lease transaction and includes the principal terms of the lease (this is the effective date used for classification of the lease).

Income Tax Act
S.C. 1970-71-72, c. 63 and amendments.

Income Tax Deferral
To postpone taxes payable by using tax credits, high CCA, etc.

Incremental Borrowing Rate
The cost of borrowing an additional dollar; this rate increases as the amount of debt outstanding increases.

Initial Direct Costs
Costs incurred by the lessor that are directly associated with negotiating and executing a specific leasing transaction; such costs include commissions, legal fees, and costs of preparing and processing documents for new leases.

Interest Spread
The difference between the cost of borrowing money and the rate at which it can be lent out.

Internal Rate of Return
The rate of return on an investment, calculated by finding the discount rate which equates the present value of future cash flows to the initial cost of the investment.

Interpretation Bulletins
Statements issued by the tax department (Revenue Canada) stating the position it assumes with respect to specific issues; they do not have the force of law.

Investment Tax Credit
Credit granted to the purchaser of specified new equipment; this credit varies with geographic region and type of equipment.

Lending Long
The practice of lending for a longer period than an investment life, at fixed rates, in the belief that interest rates will decline in the short or intermediate term.

Lessee
The party who obtains the use of an asset through a lease agreement.

Lessor
The party who owns the leased asset.

Leverage
The degree to which debt is employed in a firm's capital structure.

Minimum Lease Payments
From the viewpoint of the lessee, minimum lease payments comprise:
(a) the minimum rental payments required by the lease over the lease term;
(b) any guarantee, by the lessee or related party, of the residual value. Where the lessee agrees to make up any shortfall in the lessor's realization of a residual value below a stated amount, the guarantee included in the minimum lease payments should be the stated amount rather than an estimate of the shortfall; and
(c) any penalties required to be paid by the lessee for failure to renew or extend the lease at the end of the lease term;
if the lease contains a bargain purchase option, only the total rental payments over the lease term up to the option date and the bargain purchase price would be included.

For the lessor, minimum lease payments comprise:
(a) all of the above; and
(b) any residual value or rental payments beyond the lease term which a party unrelated to either the lessor or lessee has guaranteed, provided the guarantor is financially capable of discharging the obligations under the guarantee.

NPV
See "Net Present Value."

Net Present Value
The sum of a series of future cash flows, discounted at an appropriate rate to a current value.

One-dollar Options
A purchase option price used in some leases, usually a "bargain purchase option", allowing the lessee to purchase an asset for one dollar.

Open-ended Lease
Lease where the lessee guarantees the asset's residual value, common in the car leasing industry.

Operating Lease
Lease where the benefits and risks of ownership related to the leased property are substantially retained by the lessor.

Pay-back Period
The period required for the net revenues of an investment to equal the original investment.

Percentage Rent
A rent which is based on a percentage of the lessee's revenue.

Prepayment Penalties
A monetary penalty required for cancelling a financial obligation early and thus reducing the interest income of the lessor.

Prepayment Rights
The contractual right to prepay a financial obligation; this right may not preclude one from prepayment penalties.

Prescribed Property
Refers to exempt property and assets with an FMV of $25,000 or less per lease. It is used for purposes of the section 16.1 lessor/lessee election introduced in April 1989.

Prescribed Rate
This is the interest rate applicable to determine the portion of lease payments that are treated as notional repayments of principal under the April 1989 income tax revisions. The rate is set monthly and is one point greater than the long term Government of Canada bond rate of the month before the immediately preceding month.

Primary Lease Term
The original lease term, not including any renewal or extension options.

Prime Interest Rate
The rate at which Canadian chartered banks lend to their most credit-worthy clients.

Principal Business Corporation
For income tax purposes, a taxpayer which was, throughout the year: a corporation whose principal business was the leasing or rental of property, or the leasing and rental of property combined with the selling and servicing of property similar to that which it leases, provided that the gross revenue for the year from such business was not less than 90% of the gross revenue for the year from all sources.

Profitability Index
Present value of future returns divided by the present value of the investment.

Residual Value
The value of the leased property at the end of the lease term.

Revenue Canada
The department of the government of Canada with responsibility for income tax legislation enforcement.

Revenue Recognition — Actuarial
Method of recognizing income as a constant percentage of the outstanding investment.

Revenue Recognition — Straight-Line
Method of recognizing income in equal annual amounts.

Revenue Recognition — Sum-of-the-Digits
Once a popular method of recognizing income, this system works as follows:
(a) number the periods over which revenue is to be recognized (i.e., period 1, 2, . . . n);
(b) sum the periods;
(c) in the first period, divide the number assigned to the last period by the sum of the periods, and multiply this by the finance charge;
(d) in the next period, divide the number assigned to the last-1 period, etc.
(e.g., for a 12-month period the digits 1 to 12 sum to 78, in the first month you record 12/78's of the income, in the next 11/78's, and so on to 1/78th in the last period; hence this is called "Rule of 78's").

Sale and Leaseback
The sale of property where the purchaser leases it back to the seller.

Sales-type Leases
Lease normally arising when a manufacturer or dealer uses leasing to effect a sale of its products; such lease transactions give rise to two types of income: the initial profit or loss on the sale of the product at the inception of the lease, and finance income over the lease term.

Seasonal Payments
Payments which are tailored to fit the lessee's cash flow cycle, and where the lessee is in a seasonal business, such as tourism.

Self-shelter Lease
A lease in which the CCA is claimed in an amount which just shelters the income from the lease from tax.

Skip Payments
Payments which are not required to be made during a specified interval (e.g., the first payment may be due in 90 days, which would be a "three-month skip").

Small Ticket Leases
Leases of equipment with a relatively low dollar value, perhaps less than $25,000.

Special Use Property
Property designed for a specific purpose and which cannot be readily converted to another use.

Specified Leasing Property
Essentially, depreciable property leased by a lessor to a lessee for a term of more than one year. Leases having a FMV of $25,000 or less per lease are excluded and it does not include intangible property, including systems software or certified feature films or certified productions.

Stretch Leases
An agreement whereby the lessee has the option, at the end of the primary lease term, to either extend the term of the lease or purchase the asset; should lessees choose to extend the term, they have no purchase option later; the present value of the extended rent usually equals the value of the option price.

Tax-sheltered Income
Income against which sufficient deductible expenses are available so that no taxable income results.

Tax-trap Lease
A lease which accelerates the payment of income tax as compared to alternate leasing on purchase arrangements, and leaves unclaimed CCA at termination of the lease.

Terminal Loss
For tax purposes, the excess of UCC over selling price of an asset. Since Canada tends to use a pooling of like assets to calculate CCA, terminal losses occur only when the taxpayer has no other assets of the particular class.

UCC
See "Undepreciated Capital Cost."

Undepreciated Capital Cost
The remaining value of an asset for tax purposes; used as the basis for calculating annual CCA.

Under-water Leases
Unprofitable leases from the lessor's view, generally because the cost of financing the lease exceeds the revenue generated due to increased interest rates.

Undiscounted Cash Flows
Cash flows which are not adjusted for the time value of money.

Unearned Income (Interest)
Income which is not recognized in the current period for accounting purposes as it relates to future periods.

Upgrading
The replacement of an asset with a similar but more serviceable asset, generally in an attempt to forestall or correct obsolescence.

Variable Rate
Interest rate or implicit interest rate which varies usually with the bank prime or other quoted rate.

Variable Rate Basis
Method of determining interest where the rate is based on some "peg" which can be expected to vary over time, such as the prime interest rate.

Weighted Cost of Capital
A weighted average of the after-tax cost of debt, preferred stock, and common equity.

Index

A

Accounting for leases, 5-11
  Canadian and United States
    compared, 33
  direct financing leases, 45-47
    actuarial method, 45-46
    straight-line recording of
      income, 45-46
    sum-of-the-digits, 45-46
  inducements by lessee, 28-30
  lease classification, 5-8
  leased property, sale of, 48-49
  lessor, 43-51
    capital leases, 45-48
    operating lease, 44-45
  long-term, desired treatment of, 23
  problems, 27
  sale-leaseback transactions, 11,
    30-32
  sale-type lease, 47-48
  technical terms, 8-10
Actuarial method of recording
  income, 45-46
After-tax rate of return, 98-99
Anchor tenant, 37, 39
Ascending payments, 46
Assignment of lease, 72
Atlantic Acceptance Corporation,
  138
Automobile leases, 9, 46
  advance rental, 70

B

Balloon payments, 46
Bankruptcy. *See* Insolvent lessee
Bargain borrowing rate, 106
Bargain purchase option, 8-9, 25, 37,
  56
Bargain renewal option, 8
Base rent, 37, 70
Borrowing short, 89
Business cycles, 138
Buyout, 71

C

Canada
  leasing market, 131
Capital cost allowance, 3
  claimed by lessee, 13
  lessor, applicable to, 54-56
  long-term lease, 21
  new system compared to old, 62
  restriction on, 55-56, 137
    specified leasing property, 60-65
  rights, 71
  pool concept, 102
  tax restrictions on, 137
  tax-oriented leasing, 50
  tax-shelters, 55
  terminal loss, 62
Capital formation, 130
  penetration of leasing, 132

201

Capital lease
  categories of for lessor, 43
  compared to operating lease *re*
    GST, 66
  criteria for, 20
  defined, 1
  examples, 7-8, 148-153, 163-168
  investment recovery test, 38
  long-term agreement, 19-20
  residual value, 25
Capital tax, 129
  methods of reducing, 138
Cash flow
  contractual vs. estimated, 110-113
  factors affecting, 89
  risks for lessor, 87-90
CICA research report on leasing
  issues, 26-27
  major problems in lease
    accounting, 27
Classification of leases
  accounting purposes, 5-8
  factors considered by courts, 117
  legal purposes, 116-117
Common area costs, 9
Conjectural cash flow, 69
Conservatism, doctrine of, 47
Contingent rentals, 24, 27
Cost recovery test, 35-36
Credit losses, 139
Cross-border leasing, 124, 125
  International Fiscal Association
    report, 127-128
  Revenue Canada, treatment of,
    129
  taxes payable
    Canadian lessor/foreign lessee,
      126
    foreign lessor/Canadian lessee,
      127

Depreciation, 44
Direct financing leases, 45-47,
  148-153
Discounted pay-back method, 95
Double dip transactions, 130-132

E

Equipment investment incentives, 134
Equipment Lessors' Association of
  Canada
  view of revised leasing regulations,
    58
Europe
  leasing
    market growth, 131, 133
    source of capital information,
      130
  tax depreciation allowances, 135
Executory costs, 9, 10
  direct financing leases, 45
Exempt property, 63
  defined, 63-64

F

Fair market value, 53-54
Financial institutions
  effect on leases of by GST, 33
  GST *de-minimis* test, 66-67
Foreign exchange
  protection from, 140
  risks, 125
Franchise, 49
Funding
  inadequate attention to, 139
  risk factors, 90

D

Debt/equity ratio, 91
Declining payments, 46
Deemed costs, 58
Delphi process, 112

G

General Anti-Avoidance Regulations
  (GAAR), 129
Generally accepted accounting
  principles, 21, 26

Goods and Services Tax (GST)
  affecting classification between
    lessor and lessee, 33
  compliance requirements, 65-66
  de-minimis test for financial
    institution, 66-67
  input tax credit, 65
  operating vs. capital lease, 66
  real property leases, effect on, 66
  transitional rules, 67
Grant Co., W.T., 39
Guaranteed residual value payments,
  46

I

Income recording, 45-47
  actuarial method, 45-46
  straight-line method, 45-46
  sum-of-the-digits method, 45-46
Income tax. *See* Taxation
Income Tax Act
  capital cost allowance. *See* Capital
    cost allowance
  Part XIII, 128
  s. 13(5.2), 14, 58
  s. 16.1, 15-17
  s. 20, 57
  s. 81(1)(c), 128
  s. 212(1)(b)(vii), 130
  s. 212(1)(d)(ix), 128
  withholding tax. *See* Withholding
    tax
Initial direct costs, 44
  direct financing leases, 45
  sales-type lease, 47
Insolvent lessee, 119
  assets of, residual value, 122
  considerations of lessor after
    insolvency, 121
  considerations of lessor prior to
    insolvency, 120
  lessor's remedies, 119
Insurance, payable by lessee, 70
Interest
  expense, 48
  rate, 10, 48, 140

Internal rate of return, 96-98, 106
International Fiscal Association
  report on cross-border leasing,
    127-128
International leasing, 123-125
  cross-border, 124, 125
    taxes payable, 126-127
  double dip transactions, 130-132
  European leasing market growth,
    131, 133
  foreign exchange risk, 125
  foreign lessor, risks faced by,
    124-125
  Irish preferential tax rate, 124
  stipulated loss value clause, 125
  tax treaties, 124
  United Kingdom tax shelter, 123
  withholding tax, 124, 127-128
Investment
  measuring return to lessor, 87-113
  negative balance, 105-110
    suggestions *re* how to treat,
      109-110
  net incremental, calculation of, 93
  rate of return
    after-tax, 98-99
    internal, 96-98
    net present value, 95-96
    pay-back period, 94-95
Investment recovery test, 38
Investment tax credits, 13
  lessor, applicable to, 54
  tax-oriented leases, 51
IT-233R. *See* Revenue Canada

J

Joint venture accounting, 37

L

Large Corporation Tax, 92-93, 129
  methods of reducing, 138
Lease(s)
  accounting for. *See* Accounting for
    leases

Leases (*Cont'd.*)
  assignment of, 72
  automobile, 9, 46
    advance rental, 70
  buyout, 71
  capital. *See* Capital lease
  capital vs. operating, 8, 23-24
  capital cost allowance rights, 71
  classification
    accounting purposes, 5-8
    factors considered by courts, 117
    legal purposes, 116-117
  conflicting view of between
    industry and courts, 139
  costs payable by lessee, 70
  direct financing, 45-47
  disguised loan, 116
  disguised sale, 116
  equipment, examples of, 73-85
  examples, 73-85, 143-189
  inducements by lessee, accounting
    for, 28-30
  leveraged, 50
    rate of return on, 91-92
  long-term. *See* Long-term leases
  open-end, 1
  operating. *See* Operating lease
  ownership clause, 71
  payment frequency, 69-70
  penalties and changes in provisions
    of, 27
  pricing algorithm, 3
  purchase option, 70
  rates, determining, 3-4
  real property. *See* Real property
    leases
  renewal, 69
  residual value, 4, 70
  sale, as, 57-58
  self-shelter, 102
  short-term, 13
  stretch, 56-58
  tax-trap, 104
  term, 69
  termination, early, 71
  true, 117, 120
  types, basic tests, 8
  under-water, 89
  upgrade privilege, 71
  vaidity of, 115
Lease capitalization, 39
Lease classification
  accounting purposes, 5-8
  factors considered by courts, 117
  legal purposes, 116-117
Lease term, 8
  effects on cash-flow, 90
Lease transactions
  income tax treatment, 13-17
Lease/option agreement
  taxation of lessee, 14
Leased property
  assignment to third party, 48-49
  investment in, 27
  sale of, 48-49
  title to, 121
  transfer of ownership, 32-33
Leasing
  as source of European capital
    formation, 130
  credit losses, 139
  cross-border. *See* Cross-border
    leasing
  funding, 139
  growth in Europe, 133
  international. *See* International
    leasing
  losses, ability to offset, 136
  markets, 131
  objectives, 1-3
Lending long, 89
Lessee
  after-tax cost of asset, 94
  capital cost allowance example,
    15-16
  costs payable by, 70
  inducements by, accounting for,
    28-30
  insolvent, 115-122
  taxation of, 13-17
    Revenue Canada's position,
      14-15
Lessor
  accounting for, 43-51

Lessor *(Cont'd.)*
　accounting for *(Cont'd.)*
　　direct financing lease, 45-47
　　operating lease, 44-45
　　sale of lease property/assignment
　　　to third party, 48-49
　　sale-type lease, 47-48
　　tax-oriented leasing, 49-51
　carrying on business, 128-129
　　liability for Canadian tax, 128
　　liability for foreign tax, 128
　contractual vs. estimated cash
　　flow, 110-113
　direct financing leases, 45-47
　foreign, risks faced by, 124-125
　initial direct costs incurred by, 44
　insolvency of lessee, 115-122
　　measures to protect position as
　　　owner of leased asset, 120-122
　investment amount before and
　　after debt, 90-92
　leasing through subsidiary, 55-56
　measuring return to, 87-113
　　after-tax rate of return, 98-99
　　before or after debt, 90-92
　　cash flow, contractual vs.
　　　estimated, 110-113
　　cash-flow-related risks, 87-90
　　internal rate of return, 96-98
　　negative investment balance,
　　　105-110
　　net present value method, 95-96
　　net-tax payments over life of
　　　contract, 99-104
　　pay-back period, 94-95
　　tax benefits, 92-94
　tax implications for, 53-67
　　capital cost allowance, 54-56
　　GST, effects of, 56-67
　　investment tax credit, 54
　　lease as sale, 57-58
　　leasing regulations, revised, 58-65
　　rental credits, 58
　　sale of options, 58
　　stretch leases, 56-58
　tax shelters, 55
　terminal loss, 55

Leveraged leases, 50
　rate of return on, 91-92
　restricted CCA *re*, 137
　sample financial statements for,
　　107-108
Loan, disguised, 116
Long-term leases
　asset ownership, 19
　capital lease, criteria for, 20, 23-24
　　application of, 21
　controlling financial impact of,
　　19-33
　controlling impact of agreement,
　　22-24
　desired treatment of, 23
　operating lease, criteria for, 23
　problem areas, 24
　real property, 35-40
　structuring agreement, 21-22

M

Minimum lease payments, 8, 24, 27
MUSH-group
　effect on leases of by GST, 33

N

Negative investment balance, 105-110
Net present value method, 95-96
Net-tax payments over life of
　contract, 99-105
　loan examples, 100, 103
　tax-trap lease, 104
　variable CCA/residual percentages,
　　101, 104, 105
Non-cancellable term, 24

O

One dollar options, 49
Open-end lease, defined, 1
Operating lease
　compared to capital lease *re* GST,
　　66

Operating lease (*Cont'd.*)
  defined, 1
  example of, 7, 143-147, 158-162
  lessor, accounting for, 44-45
  tests, 43-44
  treated as sale, 129
Opportunity cost, 91
Options, sale of, 58

P

Pay-back period, 94-95
Percentage rent, 70
Personal Property Security Act
  (PPSA), 117-122
  attachment under, 118
  perfection under, 118
  registration under
    signifance of *re* receiver, 119-120
    timing of, 118-119
Principal business corporation, 63
Principal business tests, 132
Profitability index, 98
Purchase option, 70

R

Rate of return
  after-tax, 98-99
  internal, 96-98
  net present value, 95-96
  pay-back period, 94-95
Real property leases
  anchor tenant, 37
  cost recovery test, 35-36
  franchise, 49
  GST, affect on, 66
  long-term leases of, 35-40
  retail chains lease data, 41
  shopping centres, 8-9, 35-41
Receiver
  co-operation with lessor, 122
  obligations of, 119-120
Renewal of lease, 69
Rent
  contingent, 9, 70

minimum, 9
  payment frequency, 69-80
Rental credits, 58
Reserve, 57
Residual value, 25, 102, 111-112
  assets of insolvent lessee, 122
  direct financing leases, 45
  inadequate attention to, 140
  leases, 70
  sales-type lease, 48
  stretch leases, 57
Retail chains lease data, 41
Revenue Canada
  IT-233R, 14-15, 19-20, 129
  lease transactions treated as sales
    by, 129
  stretch leases, view of, 56-58
  taxation of lessee, 14-17
Risk
  business issues to reduce, 138-140

S

Sale, disguised, 116
Sale-leaseback transactions, 11, 27
  accounting for, 30-32
Sale-type lease, 47-48
  compared to direct financing lease,
    47
Seasonal payments, 46
Security agreement, 115. *See also*
  Personal Property Security Act
  (PPSA)
Self-shelter lease, 102
Shopping centres. *See* Real property
  leases
Short-term leases, tax treatment, 13
Skip payments, 46
Specified leasing property, 59, 137
  capital cost allowance calculation,
    60-63
  exclusions, 63
  tests, 63
Stipulated loss value, 125
Straight-line recording of income,
  45-46
Stretch leases, 56-58

Sum-of-the-digits method of
recording income, 45-46
Symmetry of accounting, 38

T

Tax shelter, 55
present value of, formula for
calculation, 93
Tax treaties, 124
Taxation
acceleration, 51
benefits to lessor, 92
comparison to United States
treatment, 33
criteria for capital lease, 20
cross-border leasing, 126-127
deferred, 106
depreciation allowances, European,
135
Goods and Services Tax. *See*
Goods and Services Tax (GST)
lease operating loss restrictions,
136-137
leasing losses, ability to offset, 136
lessee, of, 13-17
Revenue Canada's position,
14-15
lessor, of, 53-67
lessor's tax benefits, calculation of,
92-94
long-term leases
desired treatment of, 23
results of deferrals in, 50-51

short-term leases, 13
withholding. *See* Withholding tax
write-off methods for ownership
of assets, 13-14
Tax-oriented leasing, 49-51
cash-flow risks for lessor, 88
Tax-trade sale/leaseback, 25
Tax-trap lease, 104
Terminal loss, 55
Termination of lease, early, 71
Third party participation, 27
True lease, 117, 120
Trustee in bankruptcy, 119. *See also*
Receiver

U

Unclaimed capital cost, 13, 54-55
Under-water lease, 89
United Kingdom
leasing tax shelter, 123-124
lessors' tax advantages, 110
United States of America
accounting treatments compared to
Canadian, 33
Upgrade privilege, 71
Useful life test, 36, 37-38

W

Withholding tax, 124, 127-128
exemptions, 128
second-tier, 128